The Contempor Supervisor

The Contemporary Relational Supervisor, 2nd edition, is an empirically based, academically sophisticated, and learner-friendly text on the cutting edge of couple and family therapy supervision.

This extensively revised second edition provides emerging supervisors with the conceptual and pragmatic tools to engage a new wave of therapists, helping them move forward together into a world of highly systemic, empirically derived, relational, developmental, and integrative supervision and clinical practice. The authors discuss major supervision models and approaches, evaluation, ethical and legal issues, and therapist development. They present methods that help tailor and extend supervision practices to meet the clinical, institutional, economic, and cultural realities that CFT therapists navigate. Filled with discussions and exercises to engage readers throughout, as well as updates surrounding telehealth and social justice, this practical text helps emerging therapists feel more grounded in their knowledge and develop their own personal voice.

The book is intended for developing and experienced clinicians and supervisors intent on acquiring up-to-date and forward-looking, systemic, CFT supervisory mastery.

Robert E. Lee is a senior family science researcher and couple and family clinician who has shaped major academic CFT training programs and served on organizational and governmental panels and boards.

Thorana S. Nelson is a couple and family therapist, supervisor, and educator. She developed and has taught in the AAMFT Foundations of Family Therapy Supervision online course.

The Contemporary Relational Supervisor

Second Edition

Robert E. Lee and Thorana S. Nelson

Routledge
Taylor & Francis Group
NEW YORK AND LONDON

Second edition published 2022
by Routledge
605 Third Avenue, New York, NY 10158

and by Routledge
2 Park Square, Milton Park, Abingdon, Oxon OX14 4RN

Routledge is an imprint of the Taylor & Francis Group, an informa business

First edition published 2014 by Routledge

Library of Congress Cataloging-in-Publication Data
A catalog record has been requested for this book

ISBN: 978-0-367-56898-6 (hbk)
ISBN: 978-0-367-56896-2 (pbk)
ISBN: 978-1-003-09983-3 (ebk)

DOI: 10.4324/9781003099833

Typeset in Baskerville
by Taylor & Francis Books

Contents

About the Authors

Robert E. Lee brings diverse experience to this text. He began his career in a general medical and surgical hospital, moved to private practice and legal consultation and, at age 50, became a full-time academic. He became the Clinical Director of the MFT program at Michigan State University and, over the next 10 years, became a researcher in family science (CFT training; psychometric family assessment tools; state and federally funded family therapy foster care interventions) and a full professor. He then moved to Florida State University as director of its doctoral program in Marriage and Family Therapy. He is now Professor Emeritus. In the course of this career, Lee was a Division President of AAMFT and a member of its Ethics Committee. He also chaired his State Licensing Board. During that period, he helped construct and disseminate the National Examination Program in Marital and Family Therapy. He has written many articles about CFT supervision and reviewed others. His first text on supervision, *The Eclectic Trainer*, was co-edited with Shirley Emerson in 1999. This was followed by *The Integrative Family Therapy Supervisor: A Primer*, co-authored with Craig Everett, 2004, and translated into Japanese, 2012.

Thorana S. Nelson also brings diverse experience to this text. Trained primarily from a systemic perspective, she did not have to "unlearn" linear therapy or supervision practices. While finishing her master's program in counselor education with an emphasis in family therapy, she was encouraged by mentors to continue her education through a PhD so that she could teach and mentor new therapists. After graduating, she taught in Purdue University's COAMFTE-accredited doctoral program and then moved with her husband and cat to Utah, where she co-developed and then directed the COAMFTE-accredited master's program at Utah State University for 13 years. She continued as a member of the faculty for another six years. Nelson has taught supervision courses for AAMFT and the Utah division of AAMFT, and she developed and taught in the online 30-hour didactic and interactive supervision course for AAMFT. She was a member of the steering committee for the development of the AAMFT Core Competencies and chaired the Task Force for a revision of the AAMFT guidelines for the Approved Supervisor designation. She received the AAMFT Training Award in 2009 for her accomplishments in training and supervising relational therapists. She served on the AAMFT membership committee, the Board of Directors, and in various other capacities at both the central and divisional levels, including president of the Utah division. She has authored, edited, co-authored, and co-edited articles, chapters, and books on a variety of topics, although those related to training in Couple and Family Therapy, Solution-Focused Brief Therapy, and supervision are most dear to her heart. She is now retired in Santa Fe, New Mexico, Professor Emerita of Family Therapy at Utah State University.

Foreword

I trust Robert Lee and Thorana Nelson, two of the premiere experts in relational supervision. They have long been my go-to sources for all things associated with relational supervision. In their second edition of *The Contemporary Relational Supervisor* (Lee and Nelson, 2014), they improve on their already fine first edition. Before I mention the "something more" their second edition has, let me first identify some of what it builds upon. The first edition included major issues in relational supervision—supervision theory and practice, common factors in good supervision, core competencies, supervision ethics, manual-based (evidence-based) methods, and self-of-the-therapist issues in supervision.

In the first edition, I was particularly impressed with their chapter on developing one's own personal supervision philosophy. When I taught family therapy supervision at Virginia Tech, the first edition of their book was required reading and, consequently, my students were exceptionally well prepared to complete the Approved Supervision application of the American Association for Marriage and Family Therapy (AAMFT). They easily developed and expressed their theory and practice of relational supervision because the sections of the book were so applicable to doing this. Also, I used the questions at the end of each chapter to structure class discussions. These questions engage students to think through issues vis-à-vis their own beliefs and evolving theories (e.g., "What do you think is the most important component of the supervisory relationship and how do you promote that?"). The questions also personalized the content of each of the chapters by asking the students to connect their own experiences with the content (e.g., "What have been your best and worst supervision experiences? What do they suggest to you about how you want to be as a supervisor?")

And recently, when I introduced relational supervision to a range of international clinicians through a multi-year project of the United Nations Office on Drugs and Crime, it was the original book that I turned to; the second edition did not yet exist. Lee and Nelson's book helped me describe to novice relational supervisors the theory and practice of a range of relational supervision models. It was invaluable.

So, why write a second edition seven years after the first? As the authors explain, it is in part because of the wave of new empirical and theoretical literature in the field, much of which has come from the ever-evolving profession of family therapy. (Their terms "relational supervision" and "relational therapy" are more inclusive and perhaps more appropriate for our times.)

Also, at this writing, the world is in the midst of the COVID-19 pandemic. On top of the illness, death, economic collapse and unemployment in the wake of the virus, it also has changed the practice of relational supervision. In this edition, the authors provide much more about the ethics and practice of telehealth and virtual (on-the-computer-or-phone) supervision. The field is scrambling right now to develop appropriate standards and practices around virtual supervision, and this book addresses this issue head-on in both a practical and theoretically sensitive manner.

At its heart, this version maintains and amplifies the values of the original edition. Their book is still guided by values that I admire: systemic thinking, a focus on strengths, collaboration and safety, the importance of the supervisor-supervisee therapeutic alliance, an appreciation for the developmental aspects of supervision training, the importance of gender, race, and other contextual issues, an integrative, multi-theoretical lens, and a commitment to not "dumbing down" their ideas. Because they write so well and know so much about every aspect of relational supervision, their style and level of content is consistent from chapter to chapter, topic to topic, unlike many edited books in our field. Their writing is clear, engaging. and comprehensive.

In this new edition, the authors expand the relational, systemic parameters to include the entire training system—supervisor mentor, supervisor candidate, therapist-in-training, client, and the external environment. They contend, for example, that a good relational supervisor must first be a good relational therapist. This is not a small thing because today, more than in 2014, there are more opportunities to find good relational therapy training, and to embrace family/couple/relationship therapy as a primary professional identity.

Most impressive to me is Lee and Nelson's expanded treatment of social justice and systemic racism by examining culture, gender, race, disability, context, social location, and intersectionality in the context of supervision. The authors contend that potential bias may be found at every systemic level and can include systems that are both internal (e.g., family-of- origin, previous training) and external (e.g., professional standards and institutional racism). The authors also suggest supervision methods that more overtly address social justice issues through self-of-supervisor and therapist reflections, self-care, and methods of increasing empathy and addressing microaggressions. These additions are so important because they reflect our society's efforts to raise and address issues of race, injustice, inequality, and human dignity that are foremost issues in our world today.

There are many pragmatic practice features in this new edition, as well. For example, the authors update the current supervision literature, and provide excellent ideas for developing a supervision contract that includes the expectations of both the supervisor and supervisee. They also help the reader develop standardized feedback approaches, supervisory and therapeutic goals, and navigate clinical, ethical, and legal challenges. And for those seeking the Approved Supervisor designation of AAMFT, the suggestions the authors provide continue to be priceless and easy to follow.

In sum, this updated edition of *The Contemporary Relational Supervisor* is a gem. It is must reading for relational supervisors and supervisees, new or seasoned, and continues to be my favorite book on relational supervision. Well done!

Fred P. Piercy, PhD
Professor Emeritus of Family Therapy and
Former Editor, Journal of Marital and Family Therapy

References

Lee, R. E., & Nelson, T. S. (2014). *The contemporary relational supervisor.* New York, NY: Routledge.

Lee, R. E., & Nelson, T. S. (in press). *The contemporary relational supervisor* (2nd edition). New York, NY: Routledge.

Preface

Why a new edition? Well, our publishers' agent requested it, informed by the very credible recommendations of astute reviewers. And even though it has only been seven years since the publication of *The Contemporary Relational Supervisor* (Lee & Nelson, 2014), the world of CFT has undergone a sea change. A trickle of literature about therapy and supervision—most of it conceptual — has now become a steady stream of empirically based content. Much of that content is now coming from the discipline of marital and family therapy and family science as opposed to family psychology. Couple and family therapy has become something that diverse clinicians practice as part of what they do as well as for those using a systemic paradigm. Singular conceptual models are being added to by integrative diagnostic and therapeutic models, and interventions now are being described as "relational" and/or "systemic." These systemic interventions are being performed by increasingly diverse clinicians in increasingly diverse settings with increasing diverse clients. Accelerated in growth by the COVID-19 pandemic, formerly somewhat rare and innovative practices (for example, remote assessment, consultation, therapy, and supervision) have become dominant platforms for service—so much so that professional organizations, accreditation bodies, and state regulators are scrambling to catch up. (In this regard, see pragmatic discussion by Sahebi, 2020.)

> Relational/systemic philosophy is a framework for how MFTs view the world. This perspective focuses on relationships, including patterns of interaction between individuals that organize relationship dynamics with an emphasis on what is happening rather than why it is happening.
> (Taken from the Glossary of the Commission on Accreditation for Marriage and Family Therapy Education [COAMFTE], *Accreditation Standards,* Version 12, 2017, p. 49.)

You will see that this sea change has informed every chapter in this text. Our transcendental conceptual model goes well beyond the narrowest confines of relational and systemic: We include *the entire training system—supervisor mentor, supervisor, therapist, client, and the environments in which they are situated*—in our conceptualizations instead of mainly the supervisor and trainee. Clinical practice is increasingly being considered an applied branch of the social sciences, and it is reflecting the evolution of the latter. As such, it is embracing the notion that all human behavior is not just transactional, but the nature of that dynamic is continuously shaped by ecosystem content—including social systems (e.g., Bronfenbrenner & Morris, 2006), available resources (see McGregor, 2011), and a developmental dynamic that involves every systemic piece (Lerner, 2018; Overton & Molenaar, 2015). We talk about you, the reader, as being only one part of a training system containing supervisors, trainees, and clients, the training setting, and all stakeholders, including the profession of Couple and Family Therapy (CFT). Conceptually, we include all the unique contexts in which the participants are simultaneously embedded at any moment in time, as well as the system's history. And each system is seen as continually adjusting and adapting to each other and to life. If this strikes you as a "booming, buzzing, and confusing" experience, you will recognize that we all are on the same page. Any tableau of a clinical moment is an illusion. It is not a snapshot. Instead, it is but a stop-motion image of an ever-ongoing interaction of myriad developmental trajectories.

Our mission, in this text, is systematically and sensitively to help you make use of this evolving level of professional enlightenment while empowering the warmest aspects of your humanity. Our mission includes this latter feature because we all recognize that, beyond conceptual insight and mastery of family science lore, *quality supervision entails strong alliances in the supervisory and training systems: namely, open and safe relationships; discussion of personal and other world views, power, privilege, and bias; questioning our own cultural awareness and sensitivity; embracing personal, non-stereotypical knowledge of self and others; and openness to others.* First author Lee is wedded to and is promoting the conceptual enlightenment track. Second author Nelson, while recognizing the importance of that piece, wants to give equal—if not more—weight to the interpersonal track, to wit, the healing power of relationships regardless of perspective *(Lee totally agrees with Nelson; Nelson agrees with Lee).*

We also agree that quality supervision begins with social justice. It entails strong alliances in the supervisory and training systems characterized by open and safe relationships; discussion of personal and other world views, power, privilege, and bias; questioning our own cultural awareness and sensitivity; embracing personal, non-stereotypical knowledge of self and others; and openness to others and their unique, contextualized experiences.

Our product is, ahem, systemic and integrative. We privilege relational thinking and feminist-informed, postmodern interventions. We focus on the entire training system as it is embedded within and transacts with its larger environment. In doing so, in each chapter we celebrate the diversity of training system members; that is, the coming together of multiple realities resulting from individual experiences and interpretations of life, informed by lenses and experiences—gender, age, family form, sexual orientation and expression—and their interactions with regional beliefs about gender, age, complexion, religion, professional membership, service settings, and ethnic group legacies (to name a few). Readers are consistently kept aware of legal and ethical demands for "best CFT practice" in this new, diverse, and technological practice space. At the same time, readers' experiences and the lessons they take from them are held in high value.

Discussion of these in light of the topic at hand is consistently fostered through questions, exercises, and challenges.

Our method is informed by comprehensive, current, empirically based information and insights. We offer recommendations and encourage discussions throughout. We attempt to be attuned to the unique nature of how and where both clinical training and clinical services are being provided, and to whom.

Our goal is to provide adequate preparation for the next wave of cutting-edge CFT supervisors: knowledgeable, skilled, realistically confident, tentative about what they "know," culturally sensitive, and open to lifelong education. To that end, we have attempted to arrange a text that will serve experienced clinicians who wish to learn about doing supervision, as well as one that doctoral students will find useful as a jumping-off place for the study as well as the practice of relational and integrative supervision.

We begin, of course, with a Table of Contents. The problem with that linear presentation is that the reality of supervision requires its aspirants to have all of the information—mindsets, facts, concepts, practices, and concerns—available right from the start. Therefore, that's how we crafted each chapter from the beginning. In Chapter 1, we consider the whole kit and caboodle—because the big picture needs to be recognized. We keep "the biggest picture" present in each succeeding chapter, but with more elaboration within a theme each time. Eventually, the various topics have comprehensive chapters more or less to themselves. This is where important breadth and depth of information is contained with ample reference to other sections of the text as well as to seminal, current, and cutting-edge literature. Throughout, we invite readers to engage in discussions and experiential exercises so that they will perhaps feel more grounded in a topic, their own voices will be heard, and they will gain insight through experiencing multiple realities.

Part 1

Understanding the Supervisory Process

An Overview

DOI: 10.4324/9781003099833-1

Part I

Understanding the Supervisory Process

An Overview

1. [illegible]
2. [illegible]
3. [illegible]
4. [illegible]

1 Basic Ingredients in the Supervisory Process

> Supervision is an intervention provided by a more senior member of a profession to a more junior member or colleagues who typically (but not always) are members of that same profession. This relationship is evaluative and hierarchical, extends over time, and has the simultaneous purposes of enhancing the professional functioning of the more junior person(s); monitoring the quality of professional services offered to the clients that she, he, or they see; and serving as a gatekeeper for the particular profession the supervisee seeks to enter.
>
> (Bernard & Goodyear, 2019, p. 9)

> Relational/Systemic Supervision is the practice of developing the clinical competencies and professional growth of the student as a supervisee, consistent with the relational/systemic philosophy, ethics, and practices of the marriage and family therapy profession. Supervision is distinguishable from psychotherapy or teaching. Relational/Systemic Supervision may be provided though virtual supervision.
>
> (Commission on Accreditation for Marriage and Family Therapy Education (COAMFTE, 2017, pp. 2 & 3)

This chapter is meant to be foundational to all that follows. It intends to result in a clear understanding of those things that characterize effective couple and family therapy (CFT) or relational supervision. It is based on the distinction between *education* and *training* (Bernard & Goodyear, 2019; Lee & Nichols, 2010). *Education* in CFT is about acquiring a knowledge base. *Training* in CFT is about acquiring skill in the application of this knowledge base to therapeutic situations. Couple and family therapy supervision is a training endeavor. It follows some amount of CFT education and is dependent on a working alliance between the trainee and the supervisor in pursuit of the trainee's professional goals. In contrast, education can occur without such an alliance. Of course, supervision includes overseeing quality of care of clients as well as the development of the trainee as a therapist. Therefore, competent therapists seek collegial input when necessary or desired. This activity, however, is not considered supervision; rather, it is consultation. Supervision has an element of responsibility and liability for the conduct of a trainee.

Training of supervisors is similar. It includes education (acquiring knowledge) and skill-building. Professionals in CFT believe that supervision is a different activity from doing therapy and thus requires specialized training. This text is intended to be a

DOI: 10.4324/9781003099833-2

part of that training—the educational part. In it, we emphasize the recursivity of the training system: clients, therapists, supervisors, supervision mentors (supervisors of supervision), administrators, and so forth. We also emphasize that training and supervision are about the growth of the trainee as a therapist rather than merely consultation about cases. But unlike our peers who also are advocating for integrative, systems-based supervision (see chapters in Todd & Storm, 2014), our conceptualization of the training system explicitly denotes an overarching time or developmental factor (see below). We view training in CFT supervision as different from both training in therapy and training in supervision in other mental health approaches, although more like the latter than the former. There are important differences, however, as described by Storm (2007). First, supervisors in CFT are more likely to attend to the values and beliefs that trainees hold about couples, and couples in therapy, including same-sex couples. Second, the therapeutic alliance in couple and family therapy is systemic and complex, requiring supervision that discourages alliances that can be detrimental to the couple relationship. Finally, therapists and supervisors of CFT must be comfortable with complex emotional expressions that emerge in CFT.

In this text, we consider therapists who are learning systemic therapy as trainees regardless of their backgrounds, developmental levels, or the unique ecosystems in which they exist. This includes students in graduate programs, postgraduate trainees, and anyone else who is in a learning position with a systemic, relational, or CFT supervisor. We also recognize that training occurs in diverse settings, to wit, university or other training clinics for graduate students, behavioral science institutes, public and private agencies, and individual and group private practices, among others. These contexts are multifaceted, and we have attempted to provide ideas that apply to all as well as some ideas that apply to specific contexts. We also refer to client systems as including individuals, couples, families, and other groupings that seek services from a couple and family therapist. Training systems, in turn, include clients, therapists, supervisors, supervision mentors (supervisors of supervisors), administrative individuals, and so on, as well as the unique ecosystem in which each exists, and the developmental level of each unit. A relational supervisor ideally considers all of these systemic features while supervising therapists.

This text is based on a systemic conceptual model that includes a developmental component throughout (see Lerner, Agans, DeSouza, & Hershberg, 2014). Supervision focuses on the acquisition of skills more than education. The full training system includes many entities and subsystems: clients and their systems, therapists, therapists in training, supervisors, supervisor candidates, supervisor mentors, clinics and other agencies that provide mental health services, educational institutions, and other entities that may interact with other parts of the training system. These other entities may include courts and academic departments as well as textbook authors. From a systemic perspective, training settings also include relationships among various parts and subsystems. Not all training systems include the same parts (supervisor mentors, for example) and not all parts are housed in the same place and at the same level of developmental sophistication.

Why this developmental component? Contemporary supervision experts no longer focus primarily on the dyadic relationship that exists between trainer and trainee. Instead, they contemplate the entire training system, and this includes the contexts in which all the participants are situated. However, the most prominent of these do not include the dimension of *time*, that is, *the developmental maturity of each part of the training system.* We recommend that you consider this view because we think it is reasonable to assume that the adaptive performance of any system—in this instance, a training system—cannot rise above the capacities (level/predispositions) of its least sophisticated/mature/capable member/unit/participants. This idea has been manifest over time in interpersonal constructs such as "differentiation of self" as well as the directives by some that CFTs meet jointly with all members of a client family.

In today's parlance, one member of a system may be aware and sensitive to other parts but this awareness may not produce compatible responses from members who are not.

We suggest that a best-case scenario would have you attempt to bring discordant parties on board with your epistemology or at least help them understand it. At the very least, however, it is advisable to take the developmental capacities of the participants and their unique contexts into account when planning interventions and setting goals.

We would like the reader to perceive a training system to be a complex environment of subsystems wherein interactional dynamics occur within, between, and among those subsystems and in which these dynamics frequently are related to each other. For example, there may be multiple lines of interaction and the potential for many dysfunctional triangles (Alderfer, 2007), and the processes and patterns in one part of a system may be isomorphs of those in other parts (see Koltz, Odegard, Feit, Provost, & Smith, 2012; Chapters 2 and 3 of this text). For us that suggests that interactional patterns in the overall training system and across subsystems are replicated, each reflecting the others. That is, dynamics in the trainee/client system may be replicated in the trainee/supervisor subsystem and vice versa. We emphasize this because isomorphism is a central concept when troubleshooting difficulties in the training context.

We believe the foregoing conceptualizations are vital to supervisor training and supervision of supervision (mentoring). If supervisors are able to step back and observe themselves as living parts of the training system, they may gain important insights into and leverage within these training systems (see Lee, 1999). Indeed, looking at the training system from "the top down," it becomes clear that the manner in which supervisors construct "supervision" and "therapy" in terms of their processes and goals greatly influences trainees, clients, and supervisors, and the process of both therapy and supervision. Supervisors' constructions greatly influence "everyone's ideas about what therapy is and how it is done, how people in relationships should be, what constitutes a 'problem,' and how important it should be considered relative to other matters" (Lee & Everett, 2004, p. 12). Similarly, training therapists' ideas about these things influence processes in supervision. That is why we, the authors of this text, suggest beginning the supervisory process with discussions with trainees that alert both parties to the fit among their respective ideas about the content and process of therapy and supervision (see below). This discussion, which we might call "an appreciative interview," entails listening carefully and co-constructing understandings about each other, the supervision process, and the work together.

An essential construction in this text is the paradigm of system thinking (von Bertalanffy, 1968). As system thinkers, we see the world as a complex network of individuals and their relationships with each other that become visible through interactions. Within a system, which may be a subsystem of a larger system, change that occurs in one part reciprocally affects all other parts and is, in turn, affected by those other parts. A system is made up of ever-changing dynamics, roles, interactions, and meanings. We will discuss system ideas in more detail later in the text.

System thinking in therapy and supervision includes awareness of differences of values, attitudes, and ways of understanding the world, and the influence these have in professional work. Increasing awareness of differences should inform assessment and other interventions and result in personal commitment to enhancing services to diverse client families in diverse settings. This is a matter that goes beyond "cultural competency" (see Chapter 10). Couple and Family Therapy education and training must be infused with this matter and be attended to on a continual basis. Using common parlance, these *individual differences* should be a "dashboard" item. CFTs and relational supervisors should always be alert to multiple realities and their professional thinking and conduct guided by it.

The training system is situated within a systemic understanding of the supervisory process. Training occurs in a large, multilayered context that involves simultaneous responsibilities not only to trainees and client systems, but also to institutions and communities in which the training is being provided. Thus, one supervisory role is to facilitate the growth of trainees as professionals. However, there are other supervisory roles, namely, teachers, coaches, mentors, and administrators (Morgan & Sprenkle, 2007), gatekeepers (Baldwin, 2018; Lee & Everett, 2004), and supporter, supervisor, consultant, colleague, and socio-emotional regulator (Jethwa, Glorney, Adhyaru, & Lawson, 2019).

Therefore, supervisors oversee the treatment process so that client families are well served and trainees learn the craft of therapy. They also monitor the administrative needs of institutions such as communities, accreditation and other regulatory bodies, and the professional fields of mental health therapy to ensure that the community, if not ensured of best practices, at least is protected from harm.

Getting the Training Process Started

This text is meant to be solidly based in empirical and conceptual literature and readers will note that approach. However, this is first a pragmatic text and second, a beginning for students of CFT supervision. Doctoral students and others who are studying supervision as a discipline may note some deficits and will want to further engage with the literature.

Pragmatically, supervisor candidates' first steps should be to recognize their own philosophies of supervision, that is, their ideas about what they, as supervisors, believe about supervision, what they intend to do, its purpose, and their responsibilities and actions. These visions in turn must be attuned to those to whom they have obligations: their trainees, of course, but also to the units of the larger training system and communities in which they and their trainees are situated.

Rober (2010) suggested a process whereby new trainees attend to their "polyphony of inner voices" (pp. 158–159). Through an exercise of self-awareness, trainees become more conversant with themselves, particularly in four areas of concern: their ideas about clients' processes (listening), processing what they hear (making sense of the client's story), focusing on their own experiences related to the clients' stories, and then managing the therapeutic process. We suggest that a similar process for supervisors is quite beneficial in terms of their relationships with their trainees.

Only at this point are supervisor candidates ready to engage trainees in a supervisory process. After reflecting upon one's ideas about the purpose and goals of supervision as well as what one thinks is important in a supervisory process (the supervisor's basic philosophy), a good next step is to begin to interview trainees, being careful to privilege that which trainees "know" about therapy, supervision, and themselves as therapists. New trainees may protest that they have no clinical experience and therefore "know" nothing about therapy. However, they have ideas about the purpose of therapy, and they have had experience with work supervisors and professors. Therefore, they have a sense of what can be helpful or detrimental in a supervisory process, and they have some ideas about who they might become as therapists. Some of these matters involve attitudes and style, and others, the mechanisms of the work as well as expectations for both supervisors and trainees. Some training settings identify with a specific theoretical model of CFT. Consequently, supervision mostly is about helping trainees learn the approach specific to that theoretical model. In other settings, a supervisor helps a trainee develop his or her own approach, regardless of the supervisor's own orientation to therapy.

Experienced trainees have been consumers of supervision and have clear ideas about what they have experienced as very helpful or less so (see Anderson, Schlossberg, & Rigazio-DiGilio, 2000; Drake Wallace, Wilcoxon, & Satcher, 2010; Hildebrandt, 2009; Johnson, 2017), depending on their current level training and clinical experience (e.g., Stoltenberg & McNeill, 2010). Moreover, the authors have learned that all trainees have expectations of the training context, some good and some not so good, based on previous experiences with supervisors, teachers, coaches, parents, and other authority figures. Therefore, we recommend that a course of supervision begin with:

An Appreciative Interview

The goal of an appreciative interview is to make explicit trainees' lessons learned from their lives to date, especially in learning situations. In this way, supervisors can safely elicit and address the anxiety most trainees feel at the inception of the first or a new episode of supervision. Such an approach invokes common sense. One's transcendental goal is *to increase the probability of desirable things happening and decrease the probability of undesirable things happening.* This approach, co-constructed by the supervisor and trainee, is intended to cultivate a sense of safety in the face of vulnerability, openness of the supervisor to the person of the trainee and self, and reciprocal respect between the trainee and supervisor, and to emphasize the importance of the working relationship.

An Investigation of Both Supervisors' and Trainees' Expectations of Each Other

Where supervisors and trainees are not in agreement, the differences can be explored as stylistic or expectation differences, or for "baggage" that is relevant to the current setting. These may be barriers to positive growth and need to be considered. (Barriers to effective supervision are addressed more in Chapter 14, Troubleshooting and Pragmatics in the Relational Training System, and also in Chapter 4, wherein feedback-centered supervision is discussed.) At issue is the extent to which the supervisors' and the trainees' expectations of each other in the training setting are explicit and compatible. That is, are the supervisors' expectations of themselves compatible with those the trainees expect of the supervisors? Are the supervisors' expectations of their trainees harmonious with what the trainees expect of themselves? Differences between these expectations need to be recognized and appreciatively explored. Otherwise, members of the training team are likely to believe that they are fulfilling that which is called for in their implicit supervisory contract, but not getting the payoff they expect. The emotions attendant upon that experience constitute a serious barrier to learning.

An exercise appropriated from Cliff Sager's (1994) classic work on marital contracts can be very illuminating for trainees and supervisors alike and can be used in both individual and group supervision. Supervisors and trainees each take pieces of paper and fold them vertically in half. In the first column the supervisors list "all the things I expect from myself as a supervisor." In the second column, supervisors list "all the things I expect from trainees." Trainees concurrently make two lists: "all the things I expect of myself as a trainee" and "all the things I expect from a supervisor." The trainees' and supervisors' lists are then compared. Sager observed that what one sees is a set of implicit contracts: "If I do this, I ought to get that." An individual supervisor may feel that "if I do this as a supervisor (column 1), I ought to get that (column 2) from my trainees." Trainees will expect that if they do what they have written in their own column 1, they should receive what they have written in their own column 2. Frustration and alienation are possible when this does not occur, because both parties may be giving what they believe are their best efforts, only to experience the other party as not satisfied.

The national survey of trainees' best and worst supervisory experiences by Anderson and associates (2000) suggested that most trainees are reasonable in their expectations and their concerns quite valid, although we presume that some trainees might cite negative experiences to defend against anxiety-evoking growth experiences, or to triangulate others. According to Anderson and colleagues, beneficial experiences reported by trainees involved an open supervisory environment characterized by positive communication and encouragement in which supervisors both attended to the personal growth of trainees and provided conceptual and technical guidance. Negative experiences with supervisors included continual interruptions and distractions, emphasis on weaknesses and shortcomings accompanied by negative evaluative comments, indirect and avoidant personal styles, and intolerance of divergent viewpoints. Explicitly coming to a recognition and an understanding of trainees' past experiences through the appreciative interview facilitates beneficial opening conversations. The participants cut to the chase while reminding both parties of the importance of interpersonal skills. The desirable end result is that both training system participants understand and co-create a necessary level of safety in the current supervisory relationship.

To be sure, the constructive coming together of supervisors and trainees is a process that is not always easy. It depends on a number of factors including how much choice is involved in the relationship. Supervisor–trainee relatedness can be expected to range from immediate bonding to substantial reticence and even discord. Both extremes may prove challenging to the training relationship (again, see Chapter 14). Chronic idealization on the part of the supervisor or the trainee, and a trainee's dependency on the supervisor or excessive control by the supervisor may inhibit the trainee's professional growth and autonomy. Trainees who do not trust the supervisor or supervisory process may not seek and/or accept direction, and therefore take chances in therapy. Supervisors who do not trust the trainee or the supervisory context will likely create unhappy encounters that undermine the trainee's self-confidence. However, after goals and expectations have been discussed and agreed on in a good-enough way, the supervisor's next goal is to integrate the supervisor's own ways of working with the desired goals expressed by the trainees. Subsequently, we encourage both supervisors and their trainees to revisit these goals and expectations during the course of supervision, and to make adjustments and corrections as needed.

Paradoxically, in the midst of this process, a blending occurs even when the process is not collaborative, and supervisors unilaterally indicate that the success of the training system is a product of non-negotiable, supervisor-established ground rules. However, some ground rules provide the contextual structure necessary for the trainee's learning and growth. This is both safe and task oriented. The fundamental rationale undergirding ground rules is that effective supervision requires both structure and a working alliance (Bordin, 1979; illustrated by Enlow, McWhorter, Genuario, & Davis, 2019), that is, shared goals and enough of a relationship to support work on these goals. Even in situations where supervisors' philosophies place them in higher hierarchical positions relative to their trainees, supervision succeeds when a mutual "fit" (Holloway, 2016) between supervisor and trainee evolves. For example, one of the ground rules might be that one's trainees are obligated to bring up difficulties in supervision as necessary. When the trainee complies, goals and processes are co-constructed. And, if the trainee does not comply, a new process ensues whereby the rule is explicitly or implicitly adjusted or the supervision relationship ends. Either way, a new system has been co-created. Similarly, there is the possibility that some of the trainee's expectations are not negotiable and may be incompatible with the supervisor's and vice versa. If such incompatibility exists, the relationship is dictated by the context (e.g., setting limitations or requirements). If the parties cannot agree on good enough goals and rules, there is no fit, and effective training cannot ensue without some intervention. Again, some ideas for approaching this difficulty are presented later in this text.

Interdependent Fundamentals of Supervision of Relational Therapies

The context required for positive learning is comprised of a consistent and reasonable structure of which all members of the training system are fully aware and to which they freely commit, even when mandated. Although hierarchical to one degree or another, we believe that, as much as possible, clinical training is best accomplished through an overt collaborative process, even when there are times the supervisor must be directive. However steep or flat the hierarchy, there is agreement throughout the extant supervisory literature that an environment for the supervision of relational therapies is the product of a fundamental, interdependent commitment to quality training by all the constituent parts of the training context. In an ideal training system, supervisors continually monitor the system to see that certain fundamental structures are in place and address them effectively when they momentarily are not in place. These fundamental structures have been espoused and personally validated by generations of supervisors and trainees and, in fact, they call for both hierarchical and collaborative stances (Holloway, 2016; Selicoff, 2006). They are as follows:

A Safe Place to Be and to Learn

Family sciences often differ from clinical sciences by focusing on normative or positive aspects of human functioning. Family science interventions typically use a health model as opposed to "deficit detecting" (with regard to family assessment, see Nelson, 2019; Walsh, 2012). This is a non-pathologizing orientation that focuses on strengths.

What then happens when this potentially "positive" orientation—non-pathologizing and focusing on strengths—is brought into the supervisory relationship? Is it compatible with the administrative, limit-setting, and evaluative roles of supervisors? That is, to what extent is supervision based on an assumption that trainees are doing well and need "shepherding" (e.g., solution-focused supervision; Thomas, 2013) as opposed to an assumption that trainees do not know much about conducting effective therapy and therefore the supervisor's job is to look for, find, and ameliorate the gaps? As readers will discover, there is a continuum of thought on this topic. However, it is our belief that interdependent, effective supervision must occur in a context where trainees do not feel under a microscope that sees only their faults and yet holds them carefully so they do not harm their clients.

Supervision must be a safe place for learning. This means that supervisory relationships must be respectful, competency-based, and task-oriented. (An excellent illustration is provided by Schanche, Hjeltnes, Nielsen, Stige, & Stiegler, 2019.) Mistakes and misunderstandings happen. They provide opportunities for exploring the content and processes of clinical work and training on the one hand, and the selves of trainees on the other. That is, trainees must feel safe to bring up and discuss perceived mistakes without fear of retribution or ridicule. They also must feel safe to experiment with techniques and styles, confident that they and their supervisors will manage mistakes sensitively, with an assumption that trainees do not deliberately set out to do things badly or in a manner that might harm their clients. Supervisors must discuss mistakes respectfully and as a natural and opportune part of clinical training. Similarly, both trainees and supervisors must feel comfortable bringing up topics that may touch on tender parts of the self of either the trainee or the supervisor. Ignoring mistakes and larger issues (e.g., difficulty talking with abusive parents) not only impedes the current therapy but also the growth of both the trainee and the supervisor.

Quinn (1996) debriefed couples after a course of treatment to discover what the client families had found most valuable. They cited a "climate of discovery" and "joy in learning" and the "interpersonal relationship." They also said that their therapists were good listeners, but that they also would step in and provide direction when it was needed. These qualitative findings match the characteristics of "best" and "worst" supervision experiences uncovered by Anderson and associates (2000). Therefore, we believe that the interpersonal relationship between the trainee and the supervisor also must be one of trust, openness, vulnerability, and commitment to quality training. We believe that trainees are in supervision because they want to be the best therapists possible and, therefore, difficulties in therapy or in supervision must be open for discussion. If that assumption is false, there likely is a fatally flawed supervision relationship.

At the same time, supervisors are advised that concerns about trainees' feelings of safety cannot be allowed to tie supervisors' hands. The authors have each experienced trainees who appeared defensive, insecure, and thin-skinned in order to fend off new adventures and criticism. Trainees themselves have told the authors about supervisors who did not seem to give as much as they could because they were trying to be too gentle with and nice to their trainees. Some even described the non-productive mutuality of supervisors who wanted to be liked and trainees who were afraid of criticism.

Although needing encouragement and help as they gain reality-based confidence in their ability to provide effective therapy, trainees have often said to us, "Focusing on strengths is good; but I still need to know when I'm doing things wrong." Some trainees are more prone to this attitude than others and discussing such stylistic matters at the beginning of a new course of supervision can be valuable. For example, supervisors can inform trainees at the beginning of supervision that each will make mistakes, which, when discussed, will lead to better therapy and better supervision. One of the authors usually informs new trainees that supervision will be mostly relaxed, informative, and sometimes experimental, but that there may be times when the supervisor must be directive. Mistakes on the part of either the supervisor or trainee will be discussed. Later, when necessary, the trainee can be reminded of this statement and informed, "this is one of those times." Predicting such situations from the very beginning of the supervisory relationship eases the discomfort of the trainee in times of mistakes or when there is a need for the supervisor to be directive. It has been expected. Ensuing conversation is not meant to be criticism of the trainee as a person, or even as a therapist, but as a normal part of the learning process.

The evaluative component of what supervisors do often elicits fear in trainees. Therefore, it is prudent to explore the discrepancy between trainees' expectations and supervisors' styles and professional duties. Certainly, there are times when supervisors or trainees respond with "100 pounds of dynamite where one pound might be more appropriate" or, when listening, do not appear to *hear* or do not translate what they have heard into appropriate and effective action. At such times, the authors have found that kindness—in terms of pointing out skills but also in tone, recognizing that there are many reasons for mistakes—is more effective than any kind of negative reaction or neutrality.

At these times, baggage may be in the way; that is, distortions that are based on trainees' and/ or supervisors' current or past relationships and experiences. These need to be addressed immediately else the supervisory context is not safe for either party. Conversation can be very helpful at resolving the current issue, exploring trainee and supervisor issues, and deepening the trainee–supervisor relationship. This helps set or further a tone of working together rather than fear and distrust (see discussion of "corrective emotional experiences" by Sharpless & Barber, 2012).

Beginning supervisors themselves often are uneasy with their evaluative roles (e.g., Lee & Nelson, 2014). Trainees need to be formally evaluated, of course, but supervisors also must recognize that their trainees seek approval throughout the course of training. The formal and informal evaluative roles possessed by supervisors, as well as their administrative roles, automatically create disparities in power (see Green & Dekkers, 2010). There are times when supervisory power elicits trainee discomfort or pain, yet the supervisor must be willing to do tough things on occasion. We are not talking about abuses of power here. We are talking about appropriate roles of a supervisor such as giving grades, reporting progress or problems to necessary others, setting limits, or making unpleasant demands (e.g., getting adequate progress notes written in a timely manner, being prepared for supervision, staying late in a clinic to provide support for another trainee with a client, and so on). Sometimes, supervisors may feel a need to limit a trainee's activities until basic competency tests are satisfied, to refer a trainee to therapy, counsel a trainee out of the profession, or even "fire" a trainee to protect clients or others from harm. A supervisor may have to inflict pain in order to do good. According to trainees interviewed (Green & Dekkers, 2010; Murphy & Wright (2005), positive uses of supervisory power promote atmospheres of safety and collaboration with trainees, and cultivate a sense of direction for training. When there is such an atmosphere, it holds the trainee in safety when difficult times occur. Without it, even small problems or mistakes can be extremely difficult to manage.

When one asks trainees what ground rules of supervision are needed for them to feel safe, in the authors' experience trainees come up with several, all of which fall under a category of respect: respect for self (as a therapist in training who has skills, as a person), respect for place (including rules of a training agency, such as completing paperwork and other acts of professionalism), and respect for others (including clients, coworkers, administration, and the supervisor). Four specific rules for both trainees and supervisors include:

- Confidentiality: Confidence that what is said in the supervision session (individual or group) stays there except as agreed upon in a supervisory contract.
- Attentive and respectful listening: Honoring the sharing of others by paying close attention to their words, emotions, and body language; cultivating awareness of individual diversity, that is, appreciation of differences in lived experience and individual decision making as well as cultural and theoretical differences.
- Alertness for microaggression (Sue, 2010/2020): Put-downs and scolding, whether by colleague therapists or supervisors, erode working alliances. Supervisors and group supervision members would do well to remember their therapeutic training and focus on communication skills rather than aspersions: "You don't seem totally happy with that—What are your doubts?" "Did that get the therapy where you hoped to go?" "What would you like to have done differently?" "What might you do instead?"
- Allowing trainees the "right to pass," to not participate or respond to a question. By being free not to respond or participate, trainees are given the space and time they may need to think about what is happening and respond in a way that facilitates their learning. Forcing responses may back trainees into corners, a place few people feel safe.

As Emerson (1999) observed: "One of the most frequent problems needing amelioration in families is a lack of personal boundaries between members, yet students' boundaries are sometimes ignored in supervision. They are expected to reveal all, to be open to any criticism, to implement every suggestion without the right to say no. This does not make thinking or acting for oneself feel safe—the paradox is that being free to choose not to engage also makes one free to choose to engage. The Right to Pass creates a safe place in which one is empowered to take more risks rather than fewer" (pp. 6–7).

Experienced supervisors have stated that if trainees are to feel safe and supported (and learn), their supervisors must give balanced attention to the administrative, case management, and self-of-the-therapist parts of the clinical picture (White & Russell, 1995), which sometimes requires taking time with trainees to help them process what is or has happened. Of course, if it becomes a pattern, supervisors should deal with it directly as a potential breach in the supervisory relationship.

Clearly, many of these concerns would be relieved if CFT supervisors clearly followed the ethical principles of conduct and practice of their profession. The Code of Ethics of the American Association for Marriage and Family Therapy (AAMFT, 2015a) addresses teaching and supervision as well as clinical practice. Supervisors are advised to respect the requirements of confidentiality, privacy, and trainee capacities. They are warned against exploitation of students and trainees. They must be sensitive to conflicts of interest with the potential to exploit trainees and thus inhibit openness and behavioral flexibility within the training system. It is important to review these supervisory ethical guidelines with trainees at the beginning of a course of supervision. Supervisors' explicit openness to challenges of potential malfeasance may help their trainees feel more trust in the situation and encourage them to be open about their concerns sooner, thereby preventing disastrous results later in training, which could be harmful to clients as well as trainees and supervisors.

Having stated all of this, the truth remains that trainees have power, too (Murphy & Wright, 2005), and it can be misused. This should be brought to their attention and appreciated by all parties. Trainees and their peers constitute a formidable power base that can be helpful or harmful to clients, supervision, supervisors, and to their own learning. In many settings, trainees evaluate their supervisors by describing their own satisfaction and their perception of the supervisors' competencies to administrators. These evaluations may be used to improve supervision, to report inappropriate behavior or relationships, or to hurt supervisors. Moreover, trainees are not the only ones in the training system with a desire for approval. To the extent that supervisors have a need for approval—personal attractiveness or professional competency—they transfer power to their trainees who, in such situations, are in charge of their supervisors' senses of wellbeing. Trainees also have the power to withhold information, which can be harmful to clients, their settings, their own learning, and supervision as well as supervisors. Supervision must be a safe place for everyone.

Effective Supervision Is Based on Shared Goals and a Relationship to Sustain those Goals

At the core of research on the effectiveness of psychotherapy is the observation that psychotherapy is most effective when client families are motivated for change (e.g., Baucom & Crenshaw, 2019; Tremblay, Wright, Mamodhoussen, McDuff, & Sabourin, 2008) and their relationships with their therapists are compatible. In fact, individuals involved in any form of consultation—human services, business, or manufacturing—know that the primary requirement for success is the establishment of mutual goals, rapport (bonds), and acceptable tasks. Perhaps the most contemporary statement of this in family therapy is found in Morgan and Sprenkle's (2007) common factors supervision model. In this model the effectiveness of therapeutic interventions is thought to be directly related to conceptualizations and processes that enhance the working therapeutic relationship. The therapist–client relationship, distilled, is the synergism provided by shared goals and enough of a relationship to support work on those goals as well as agreement on tasks for reaching those goals. With apologies to the eloquent writers of today, this homily is not new. Edward Bordin (1979) stated it explicitly many years ago: A working alliance requires client-families to agree in five areas: They must be able to relate to the person of the therapist, the theory, the technique, the proposed outcomes, and the therapeutic bond itself. In a nutshell, the above indicates that a complete therapeutic alliance is a contract directing supervisors, therapists, and clients (and their significant others) to attend to mutually agreed-upon bonds, goals, and tasks. At the subsystem level, the same can be said for CFT training contexts: It is important for trainees and supervisors to have satisfactory relationships that include agreement on goals and ways to reach the goals. In addition, the reader probably will appreciate the need to attend to the values and goals of their training institutions, service delivery agencies, communities, and client families. (See Contextual Differences below.)

If the working alliance is basically a matter of shared goals and enough of a relationship to support work on them, an essential focus of supervision must be on the relationship between the supervisor and trainees. Sterner (2009) surveyed mental health counselors and revealed connections among supervisory working alliances, satisfaction with work, and work-related stress. Sterner's results suggested that better working alliances were related to greater satisfaction with work and lower work-related stress. Clearly, the working relationship must be continuously monitored and cultivated. Ideally, the phenomenon of isomorphism (see Chapters 2 and 3), will lead the trainees to do the same with their client-families. Supervisors need to be explicit about this. In supervision as in therapy, whenever supervisors sense a budding problem in working relationships, they should focus immediately on that. Without working relationships, supervisors have nothing. *The working relationship always comes first.* This statement should not be taken, however, to suggest that only the relationship is important. Learning therapy skills also is important!

Supervision Must Cultivate Awareness of Individual and Contextual Differences

This text assumes that readers have participated in cultural diversity, sensitivity, competency, and/or consciousness-raising exercises. Readers probably have found some approaches very valuable and others, less so. They also are aware of the empirical literature that suggests that there may be as much, or more, diversity within cultural groupings as between them (e.g., Willie & Reddick, 2010). The authors do not propose to take the readers through this exercise one more time. However, we do intend to highlight facts of contemporary CFT practice that underscore the timeliness and urgency of expecting and appreciating differences in lived experience and meaning making.

Falicov (1995) cautioned CFTs to remain aware of two errors in their attempts to simplify social situations: arguing that (a) fundamentally, "everyone is the same," and (b) reducing others to cultural stereotypes. Contemporary trainees should recognize by now that individuals are unique combinations of influences, experiences, and orientations (intersectionality) that affect the way they view the world and act within it, as well as their values and their senses of place in the world, often called identity. Moreover, identity is dynamic and fluid through time and in different contexts, including the CFT training system. It changes according to where individuals are on the developmental trajectories of their lives and the environments in which these lives are embedded (see Bronfenbrenner & Morris, 2006; Lerner, 2018).

We fear that therapists and their supervisors may too easily get caught up in all sorts of assumptions and stereotypes without attending to nuances of clients' contexts that would provide resources for and barriers to meeting their goals. In supervision, power differentials that often result from these differences, yet are ignored, contribute to poor clinical work and inadequate professional development. In addition to ethical and/or legal factors associated with cultural, ethnic, sexual orientation, and other differences, the practice of therapy is, at its heart, a human activity and basic respect demands attention to systemic understanding of as many factors in the clients' and trainees' lives that impact their work as is possible.

Differences between trainees and supervisors within the training context, and between the training context and larger communities, are also important to consider. Conscientious supervisors are aware of their own needs and understanding their own selves in context so that they can both help their trainees with this important aspect of clinical work as well as have a vantage point for viewing the training context and their parts in it. As a consequence, therapy and supervision education, and professional, lifelong learning goals, should include attention to, acceptance of, and respect for individual differences throughout treatment and training systems.

Relational interventions increasingly take place in diverse professional contexts. They may take place in private practice offices, in graduate school clinics, in diverse public and private agencies, or in homes. They may occur in medical, legal, or educational settings. They may be part of graduate education or post-graduate training toward a clinical credential. They may be voluntary or court-mandated (for licensure remediation). They may take non-traditional forms such as family therapy during supervised parent visitation, in school hallways, or while helping a family unload groceries or paint a room. They may occur once or more a week, once or more a month, or even once a year, in formal settings, or in cars and other less formal places (confidential places, of course). Supervisors do best when they understand the opportunities and constraints of various clinical and supervisory settings so as to optimize trainees' learning.

Theory and Transparency Form the Core of Responsible Training and Therapy

Some masterful family therapists (e.g., Minuchin & Fishman, 1981) have described mature relational psychotherapy as an "art," namely, beneficial interventions that flow unconsciously from the educated and experienced being of the therapist. Using such a metaphor, the supervisor begins as a kind of director or choreographer, teaching fundamentals and requiring practice in interviewing. The supervisor then moves to the role of an enthusiastic and appreciative mentor, which eventually culminates in a relationship as colleagues.

In our experience, this kind of presentation, although very welcomed by the anxious trainee and some new supervisors, is too simplistic and even potentially dangerous if carried on too long. Supervision may parallel the master family therapist who has read and experienced much, and who has come to appreciate common conceptual factors existing in the many approaches to relational therapy (e.g., see culling of such common elements by Midori Hanna, 2019). This may result in therapists who unselfconsciously go with the flow of what is happening in front of or between themselves and their clients and do what comes naturally to facilitate therapy without being able to easily articulate what they are doing or why. When supervisors incorporate this kind of perspective into their supervision, their trainees may learn to similarly do therapy without being mindful of what they are doing or why. Unhappily, it may be that a master clinician has been through so much and knows so much that he or she makes large intuitive jumps in therapy and does not consciously and explicitly connect the dots. Although often amazed by the interventions and insights of master therapists, trainees don't know how to emulate them. To them, masterful therapy seems more art than carefully calculated methodology. In supervision, this may result in hodgepodge directiveness or supervision that is so focused on moment-to-moment therapy that the bigger picture of systemic philosophy—extended family, larger context including the training system—and relational approaches to therapy are lost. Indeed, as one psychodynamically oriented colleague observed (personal communication), "Anything that is not mindful is an opportunity for the unconscious to shape what is going on."

We recommend a supervisory state of mind that is diametrically opposed to the above. Supervisors need to self-consciously and explicitly give fundamental education and training that provides both the dots and understanding of how they are connected. As Nichols (1975) recommended so long ago, supervisors should stop session recordings (literally or figuratively) again and again to ask therapists what they were doing and why. This procedure is necessary to develop self-awareness skills that are tied to a personal philosophy of change and approach to therapy. Trainees should be expected to be ready and able to articulate reasonable, theory-based rationale for their ideas and actions. All interventions should be thoughtful and proactive in terms of contextual nuances and short- and long-term goals—"the architecture of psychotherapy" (Sperber, 2015; Wetchler & McCollum, 1999). This may be arduous, repetitive, and time-consuming. It means that trainees must learn contemporary systemic and relational therapy constructs, be able to see them in their own lives and in the dynamics of therapy and in supervision, and to think about the implications of these in terms of both therapeutic goals and their own development as therapists (see, for example, Niñño, Kissil, & Apolinar Claudio, 2015; Niño, Kissil, & Cooke, 2016). This dynamic process is isomorphic for supervisors and is elaborated upon and illustrated in following chapters.

Prescriptive supervision, consistently faithful to a theoretical model or well-conceived pedagogic philosophy, is the best way to achieve this imperative outcome. Initially, supervisors of relational therapy may provide one pragmatically determined approach or model. It usually will be tied in some way to their own therapy model, easily applied to relationships, and highlights essential features of family systems and CFT. For this reason, when one of the authors (REL) has trainees who are not familiar with systemic thinking, he likes to begin supervision with a 25-year-old model—Colapinto's (1988) updated Structural Family Therapy (Minuchin, 1974). He refers to this model as the "PB&J" (peanut butter and jelly) of family therapy and training. Once a trainee has learned this approach and has come to perceive the family (and not an individual) as The Client, other models can be added or substituted according to the desires of the trainee and supervisor.

Of course, supervisors in various training contexts will have their own choices. Many may perhaps base their approaches on postmodern, common factors, or evidence-based therapies. Regardless, whatever models or approaches are selected, these choices will not remain static. Supervision's theoretical underpinnings are developmental and dynamic. Depending on the clinical experience of the trainees, clinical models can be expected to evolve as they gain experience, read new material, and attend workshops and trainings. In addition, they are likely to become more integrative over time (see Lebow, 1997a, b; Lee & Everett, 2004; Morgan & Sprenkle, 2007). The fortunate supervisor works with graduate students who identify clear approaches with which they want to start, or with postgraduate trainees who have identified and clarified an integrative approach to start their intermediate and advanced training. If less fortunate, working with trainees who are less able to identify the philosophies and approaches that guide their work, supervisors begin with an overview of systemic philosophy and the conceptual base of one or two CFT approaches. Supervisors can expect that their own approaches to supervision similarly start with one or two ideas and become more integrative over time. Regardless, the point we are trying to make is, supervisors, like therapists, should be able to articulate a thoughtful personal philosophy and approach to supervision.

Whatever the theoretical model or approaches informing the training system, relational supervisors know that transparent therapy—telling client families what the therapist is doing and why—provides longer-lasting outcomes than therapy that does not (Blow & Karam, 2016). Similarly, relational supervisors recognize that transparency in supervision is useful with trainees. Therefore, supervisors not only explain and discuss what is happening overall with trainees and the steps to reaching supervisory and therapeutic goals, but they demonstrate these actions in their supervision. For example, a supervisor who is helping a trainee learn structural techniques with a chaotic family will demonstrate active boundary-setting practices in supervision. This increases the probability of trainees' doing the same in their therapy. Moreover, transparency also can be expected to strengthen working alliances (Blow & Sprenkle, 2001; Blow, Sprenkle, & Davis, 2007; Friedlander, Escudero, & Heatherington, 2006; Hargrave & Pfitzer, 2011; Johnson, Wright, & Ketring, 2002; Sprenkle & Blow, 2004, 2007) by fostering shared goals and good-enough relationships to support work on both therapy and supervision goals. The training is kept reasonable, explicit, and open to negotiation if necessary or desirable, and is much more efficient when all parties are clear and open with each other.

Supervision Must Be Focused and Relational

At its core, supervision for the profession of CFT pursues three integrated developmental outcomes (Lee & Nichols, 2010): sophistication of family systems scholarship, socialization into the profession of CFT, and cultivation of professional maturity. We, the authors of this text, have clear preferences for systemic and relational therapies that are learned well by students and postgraduate trainees and our bias should be evident in this text. Some evidence-based therapy approaches may not be systemic at their core or may use more "traditional" linear bases that can be applied systemically or within a systemic paradigm. Similarly, relational supervision may be quite appropriate for non-systemic therapeutic approaches. Such supervision focuses on the relationship between the trainee and supervisor and between the trainee and clients with the goal of therapist development. Thus, although the supervision uses clinical cases as content, it focuses more on the process of therapy, the process of supervision, the trainee–client relationship, the trainee–supervisor relationship, and the development of the trainee as a therapist.

Effective family therapy requires specialized systemic knowledge and skills inherent in treating relationships and individuals in relationships. Unlike individual psychotherapy, the "client" may be an individual, a couple, family, or other relational group. We often say that the client actually is the relationship in which the so-called client is embedded. Interventions and ethical judgments are informed—even determined—by this fact. Moreover, although many mental health professions offer family therapy, the authors expect that the readers of this text identify with the epistemology of CFT and use system thinking in their work with individuals as well as dyads and larger systems. Clinical Fellow membership in the American Association for Marriage and Family Therapy (AAMFT) involves identification with that way of thinking as opposed to another or seeing oneself as a generic "psychotherapist."

An important focus of CFT supervision is the acquisition of systemic, relational skills in therapy. There are many effective therapies *du jour* that are not necessarily systemic or relational. CFT graduate programs housed within academic departments recruit faculty and students because of their alleged commitment to the profession of CFT and systemic thinking as well as their scholarly work. Therefore, although students in CFT academic programs focus on systemic concepts, they may reach outside of this conceptual envelope into evidence-based therapies that may not be systemic. It does not seem prudent to make the latter the main focus of CFT education and training and, when non-systemic interventions are explored (for example, cognitive-behavioral interventions), they should be introduced and integrated within a systemic context. Moreover, our personal experience has been that when individual and relational therapies are offered within the same program, students become confused with regard to merit, process, outcomes, and ethical decision making, and sometimes have difficulty maintaining a systemic focus unless specifically expected to do so. Furthermore, some graduate programs focus exclusively on evidence-based approaches. The authors of this text each prefers clearly systemic approaches in graduate training such as Structural (Minuchin, 1974), Strategic (e.g., Watzlawick, Weakland, & Fisch, 1974), or Bowen (1978). When this is not the case, we believe that framing such approaches within system thinking is important.

Couple and family therapy postgraduate training and supervision, whether housed in agencies, institutes, or private practice, differs from that which is focused on individual interventions and, perhaps, even highly directive manual-based family interventions. However, that does not mean that relational and systemic training and supervision should be shunted aside in such a setting. A systemic epistemology is a very valuable and powerful lens through which to view any human behavior. It provides very special enlightenment.

We emphasize this because many agencies that employ CFT trainees frequently are not systemically oriented. In these settings, it is even more important in our opinion that supervisors strive to remain systemic and yet attuned to the pragmatic needs of contemporary mental health practice, for example, necessary factors such as DSM diagnosis and doing individual therapy with clients when conjoint therapy with couples and systems would make more sense from a systemic perspective. Clearly, we hope that this text will help supervisors with this important CFT task.

A CFT mission requires supervisors to be CFTs themselves, and to set and enforce limits on that which is taught and supervised within their purview. When we have conducted postgraduate supervision courses, participants have spoken of limiting their roles as experts and, instead, being facilitative, asking how their trainees want to use them, and so on. This egalitarian and collaborative approach frees prospective supervisors from concerns about their misuse of power in setting direction, outcome goals, process, and evaluation for supervision. Nevertheless, new trainees have been explicit about their need for direction (Anderson et al., 2000) and supervisors must learn to balance directives with collaborative discussion. Moreover, supervisors have implicit contracts with their communities: If their trainees are to be given considerable power and privilege (e.g., confidentiality, a closed door, and, in some places, the capacity to suspend citizens' civil rights), the community must insist that trainees have certain skills, knowledge, and professional judgment. Therefore, an important focus in CFT supervision is competent and ethical relational practice.

In short, CFT supervisors need to have an explicit mission captured in a written contract that states that the focus of the supervisory process will occur in a systemic context, and will be on relational therapies and comprised of certain processes (including role modeling). This will have a high probability of advancing the triad of family systems scholarship, socialization into the profession of CFT, and professional maturity.

There are well-established mental health professions. Each incorporates at least some of the lore and practices of the others. Nevertheless, professional identity is a multidimensional product of a specific discipline's dominant core of facts, beliefs, and interventions (Nichols & Everett, 1986). Role modeling by educators and supervisors is multifaceted. It is the sum total of how one thinks and behaves when one is a CFT. Consequently, supervision of relational CFTs who practice from a systemic paradigm should ideally be provided by members of the CFT profession even when trainees must receive supervision from non-CFTs as well. The key is helping trainees see their clinical and professional work systemically in order to formulate and apply interventions that are contextually based. Moreover, the concept of isomorphism suggests that the extent to which supervisors think and behave as CFTs with trainees, trainees are likely to mirror that identity with client-families.

The Supervisor Does Not Treat the Client

One proper focus as a supervisor is on the therapist–client subsystem and the development of the trainee as a therapist. It is the trainee's role to provide direct clinical services to client systems, and the supervisor's role to guide trainees in such a way that they become able to do that. This is unlikely to happen if supervisors do the therapy through their trainees. Lee and Everett (2004) observed, some supervisors may be unnecessarily directive or do therapy through their trainees. This may be a way of helping a trainee experience a particular intervention and its consequences. It also may be that they fear shifting various amounts of responsibility for client families (supervisors, after all, are ultimately liable for undesirable outcomes), are tempted to show off their own knowledge and clinical skills, feel a need to rescue trainees, or do not use a developmental perspective of supervision with a focus on trainees developing their skills and requiring less supervisor intervention as training moves on. Moreover, anxious therapists may wish to transfer therapeutic responsibility to their supervisors or to be rescued. Nevertheless, to the extent that any of these scenarios occurs, trainees may not experience struggles that are important for professional and personal growth and, in so doing, do not facilitate good enough outcomes for clients and themselves. Supervisors cultivate this growth to the extent that they prepare and facilitate trainees, but allow the trainees to treat the client families, even if all participants in the training system are struggling with ambiguity and uncertainty. The second author tells trainees that unless there are issues of client welfare, family safety, or potential harm for which supervisors may need to intervene, the trainee is the therapist, not the supervisor. Early training may require more coaching or training than later, and some modes of supervision may include co-therapy (although trainees should, whenever possible, do the therapy themselves). Regardless, as soon as and as much as possible, trainee learning seems to move along when supervisors stay in the background, allowing trainees to stretch their skills and make mistakes, and discussing what happens later.

Learning to Be a Therapist Is a Developmental Process

Education and training for aspiring professional CFTs are outcome-based. At a minimum, beginners must learn central relational concepts, come to recognize them in clinical situations and in their own lives, and be able to plan, implement, and evaluate interventions (Lee & Everett, 2004). However, as observed earlier in this chapter, this narrow curriculum takes place within a larger pedagogical mission organized around the three transcendental aspects of CFT training: family systems scholarship, socialization into the profession of CFT, and cultivation of professional maturity. Although this agenda begins in master's training and education, it is expected to deepen through postgraduate training and continuing education, and to continue throughout the professional lifetime of the professional (Lee & Nichols, 2010).

Supervision develops through predictable stages. Couple and family therapy trainees range from beginners to veterans. Experienced trainees have differing exposures to and successes with specific presenting problems, clinical populations, therapeutic models, intervention techniques, and therapy settings. They differ in what they need to know, want to know, and can learn. Therefore, supervisory approaches differ according to supervisor, trainee, clinical setting, larger context, and client factors such as interests, experienced needs, therapy goals, and competencies. Supervision philosophies do best when they account for this complexity.

The AAMFT supported the development of an extensive set of core competencies (CC) for the practice of marriage and family therapy (MFT; AAMFT, 2004; Nelson et al., 2007; Northey & Gehart, 2019; Appendix B). Although the list is a daunting number of competencies, it is organized by domains such as "admission to treatment," and subdomains such as "conceptual," "perceptual," and "executive" skills. Northey and Gehart (2019) have condensed the MFT Core Competencies into a more manageable list while preserving their essence and intent. The competencies serve as a guide for graduate training and for postgraduate supervision with the aim of mastery of each competency by the time a trainee is ready to be licensed for independent practice. Trainees and supervisors can use the competency list to assess current skill levels and to develop plans for achieving both short- and long-term goals. Thus, competencies are introduced and learned to varying degrees according to the developmental phase and contextual needs of trainees.

Celano, Smith, and Kaslow (2010) suggested several areas for competency goals: (a) developing a systemic formulation for client difficulties, (b) ensuring a systemic therapeutic relationship, (c) understanding family of origin issues, (d) reframing, (e) managing negative interactions, (f) building cohesion and communication, (g) restructuring, and (h) understanding and applying evidence-based CFT approaches. These competencies differ from the AAMFT Core Competencies (AAMFT, 2004; Nelson et al., 2007) in that they all solely have to do with competency in interventions. Although many supervisors may not agree with or utilize this way of thinking, it provides another way of approaching therapist competence and may give readers ideas about structuring their own supervisory goals and ideas. Of course, this list of therapy competency categories also could dictate supervisory competencies.

The initial stages of CFT training begin with a high level of didactic education, usually in graduate programs. Supervisors of beginning trainees prescribe reading and give substantial therapeutic direction, even if the latter is implemented in an indirect fashion. For example, a supervisor might ask, "As you think about getting started with this family, what do you think would be a good place to start and what do you hope to learn?" This focuses trainees on both what they are *doing* and what they are *learning*. However, as trainees become more realistically confident in the basic conduct of interventive sessions, "space for the self of the therapist to grow" may be created by less supervisory direction (Nichols & Lee, 1999). Near the end of the supervisory period, supervisors may focus less on specific skills and competencies and, instead, engage more in mentoring roles as colleagues, and helping trainees develop plans for future professional development and continuing education and training.

A developmental approach to training is discussed more fully in Chapters 3 and 6. However, along with relational or systemic ideas, developmental aspects of training pervade this text. Relational supervisors need to have *developmental* on their dashboards to alert them to continually monitor the appropriateness of what they are thinking and doing with regard to capacities and needs of specific trainees, with specific client-families, within specific settings.

Exercises

1. What have been your best and worst supervision experiences? What do they suggest to you about how you want to be as a supervisor?
2. What are your expectations of yourself as a supervisor? What are your expectations of your trainees? What trainee expectations do you think would be appropriate and which might be inappropriate? How do you think you would (or already do) handle situations where your expectations and those of your trainees clash? What contextual factors might affect those ideas?
3. How do you think you might assess for and help trainees learn system concepts?
4. What steps can you take to ensure that supervision is a safe place for trainees to bring up and discuss mistakes, vulnerabilities, and concerns with clinical and supervisory contexts? What limits might you put on that?
5. What are some ground rules you might develop for supervision?
6. We hope that you will develop a coherent philosophy of supervision as you read this text. At this moment, how might you encapsulate your philosophy in one short paragraph? What do you think is the purpose of supervision and your main role as a supervisor? What would you put on your dashboard?
7. For those seeking the AS designation: As an exercise for getting ready to write your personal philosophy of supervision paper, copy the areas from the handbook that are required for evaluation. Copy these areas (except the last one) into a document as headings to structure your paper. Then, as you work through this text and your course, you can fill in details, editing as you go and at the end when you are ready to submit your paper to your course instructor or mentor.

2 Systemic Supervisory Relationships, Roles, and Goals

Supervisory Relationships in a Training System

Some time ago, a psychoanalyst (Bordin, 1979) stressed the importance of a "working alliance" between therapists and their clients, that is, a mutual agreement with regard to their goals, tasks, and bonds. This opinion evolved into what is now called the common therapeutic factors approach to therapy (e.g., Norcross & Wampold, 2011; Wampold, 2010). Although empirical validation of their importance—indeed, centrality—to the therapeutic process has not yet been scientifically assessed, therapeutic factors common to all popular therapies (see Midori Hanna, 2019) are thought by many to have more influence over treatment outcomes than the unique interventions advocated by the various major treatment models (Norcross & Wampold, 2011).

Although scientific delineation and validation of common factors topography awaits, it seems prudent for all therapy educators to seriously consider the notion that the relationship between therapists and clients constitutes a significant portion of therapy success. Moreover, in the field of CFT, the relationship is additionally complex because it must take into account the therapist's relationship with others in the client system, including those not present in therapy (Lee & Nelson, 2014; Sprenkle, Davis, & Lebow, 2009).

More recently, the focus has been extended to considering the role of these same common factors in the relationship between supervisors and trainees. The presumption is that supervision will be more effective when trainees and their supervisors have a good working alliance with common goals (see Karam, Blow, Sprenkle, & Davis, 2015). Suggestions for infusing common factors thinking throughout the entire training system have been offered (Karam et al., 2015), introduced in some CFT training programs (D'Aniello & Fife, 2017), and earned the approval of the trainees involved: "Participants' responses to the training were overwhelmingly positive and highlighted the ways in which studying common factors enhanced their confidence, understanding of MFT models, conceptual abilities, and clinical practice" (Fife, D'Anniello, Scott, & Sullivan, 2018, p. 191).

For supervisory training purposes, the therapist–client relationship (bonds), distilled, is the synergism provided by shared goals and enough of a relationship to support work toward those goals (tasks). Extended to your training systems, efficacious training will be enhanced to the extent that supervisors, trainees, and client

DOI: 10.4324/9781003099833-3

families agree in five areas: acceptance of each other, the theory, the technique, the proposed outcomes, and the therapeutic bond itself. This is not to imply that everything in this mix should be perfect, but that all participants can gain by being alert to these ingredients. From that corporate concern will develop a working relationship that is good enough to facilitate negotiation of clinical and supervisory elements.

This proposition is totally in keeping with empirical findings from supervision and treatment rooms (e.g., Anderson, Schlossberg, & Rigazio-DiGilio, 2000), and their larger settings (Lee, 2009). Anecdotal evidence also is plentiful: Where supervisors gather, stories abound about often-futile attempts to urge potentially useful theoretical approaches upon unwilling trainees and how some colleagues, apparently lacking in social skills, have alienated trainees. The second author (Nelson) was asked one time by a non-CFT supervisor "how to get trainees to do what [we] tell them to do." Such a statement flies in the face of a good working relationship between trainees and supervisors, the absence of which clearly hampers successful training—if the goal is to help trainees become independent therapists rather than having supervisors do therapy through their trainees.

Components of the Supervisory Training System

In light of the foregoing, supervisors, trainees, and clients, as well as the social systems in which they are embedded, need to be harmonious in their interdependency and in agreement about the theoretical approaches that the trainee is learning, common goals for both the therapy and supervision, and some consensus for how best to reach those goals. In addition, if expert opinion about what else constitutes a "good" supervisory relationship (e.g., those suggested in Kaiser 1992, 1997) are extended to the entire training system, supervisors and their trainees, as well as all of the other participants must be accountable to each other; that is, be willing to follow through on explicitly contracted agreements. Of course, trainees must be able to depend upon their supervisors to steer them away from trouble and clients must be similarly able to depend on their therapists. In addition, the welfare of the training and service settings as well as client families is dependent upon the flow of accountability throughout the system. In most situations this begins with the supervisor and this presumption has historically been accepted in civil litigation (see Chapter 11).

Self of the Therapist/Self of the Supervisor

We encourage couple and family therapists to be aware of their own legacies, family of origin factors, biases, unresolved issues, and values that impact therapy and supervision in positive and negative ways. These dynamics are often called "self of the therapist" or "countertransference" (e.g., Aponte & Ingram, 2018; Aponte et al., 2009). Because of the systemic, reciprocal, and isomorphic nature of couple and family therapy and CFT training, it is logical that supervisors also must be aware of their own blind spots, values, and beliefs. These, too, impact supervision as well as therapy.

Good supervisors must also be aware of their positions in the training system and the dynamics of which they are a part. They need to eschew notions of bestowing wisdom upon neophyte trainees and turning them into "mini-me's." While flattering, watching trainees attempt to mimic their supervisors can be embarrassing as well as ineffective. Trainees have unique personalities and contribute to unique relationships. We all appreciate these trainee assets to the extent that we better understand that therapeutic approaches are integrations of perspectives rather than imitations of master therapists or supervisors. This is so even with the integrated evidence-based models of therapy. No two therapists "deliver" an approach in exactly the same way and supervisors are more helpful when they support trainees in the trainees' styles and desired approaches to therapy (see discussion of micro skills in Chapter 14.)

Trust

Supervisory relationships must include trust. Trainees must be able to trust their supervisors to act in their best interests. Supervisors must trust that trainees will be honest and forthcoming in supervision, and will carry through with directives or discuss their concerns about directives. As a relatively new supervisor, author Nelson once had a trainee ask for advice about a couple that was re-experiencing intimate violence. Try as she might, Nelson could not recall details of the case. The trainee told her that she had not brought this case to her for supervision because she did not want supervision to "mess it up." Ultimately, this meant that the trainee and Nelson did not have a trusting relationship and that it was Nelson's responsibility to work on that with her. Trust can be enhanced through explicit supervisory contracts that have built-in flexibility for change as needed. Therefore, we reiterate that the relationship between supervisor and trainee is the number one priority for successful supervision.

Power and Hierarchy

Systemically oriented supervisors (e.g., Green & Dekkers, 2010; Lee & Nelson, 2014) have pointed out that power and hierarchy must be made explicit. Many supervisors have multiple relationships with their trainees (e.g., administrative, clinical, educational, and political) and must take care that the power that comes with such situations is not misused. Again, making these roles and relationships clear, and negotiating boundaries and appropriate behaviors from the beginning of supervision can help avoid confusion and potential exploitation either of trainees or supervisors.

Next, we need to consider hierarchy. Along with the various roles and relationships involved in supervision, hierarchy is an integral part of the relationships specified by desired theoretical models and/or approaches of supervisors and trainees. Supervision, like therapy, cannot help but be hierarchical. Supervisors are responsible for the acts of their trainees. Therefore, the wellbeing of clients as well as supervisors' licenses are at risk. Although sanctions by licensing boards or malpractice suits against supervisors are rare, supervisors are nonetheless ethically responsible for the therapy outcomes and actions of their trainees. It has been our experience as trainers that supervisor candidates, usually with postmodern philosophies, often are uncomfortable about recognizing hierarchy in training systems and go to great lengths to flatten it. Depending upon personal philosophies of supervision and developmental factors, training systems may range between extremely hierarchical and purely collaborative. Nevertheless, because of their ethical and legal responsibilities, supervisors must admit to at least some measure of hierarchy. Selicoff (2006) observed that postmodern supervisors can balance collaboration and hierarchy, depending upon the situation at hand. We believe that hierarchy and collaboration are not mutually exclusive and can complement each other as situations and philosophies require.

Common Factors in Supervision

Supervisors have multiple roles and diverse obligations mandated by these roles. A common-factors orientation may provide a beneficial character to supervision that allows comfort and integration within all of its complexities. For example, Morgan and Sprenkle (2007) have developed a schema of common factors in supervision. Three themes include (a) the emphasis of supervision on clinical versus professional competence, (b) focus on specific clinical issues versus general topics, and (c) a directive versus collaborative relationship. When the dimensions of emphasis (clinical vs. professional competence) and focus (specific vs. general topics) are combined, Morgan and Sprenkle identified four overlapping roles of supervisors: coach (clinical/particular), teacher (clinical/general), administrator (professional/particular), and mentor (professional/general). These four roles then can be combined within a preferred supervisory directive/collaborative style and the developmental phase of the trainee. This model provides a jumping-off place for discussing aspects of different supervisory roles. Readers may prefer to conceptualize their roles in other ways. For example, Ungar (2006) writes about other roles such as "supporter (to the supervisee), supervisor, case consultant, trainer/teacher, colleague, and advocate (for both the client and/or supervisee)" (p. 61).

It seems to us that some combinations suggest a less hierarchical dynamic than others. We also believe that although supervisors may have generally preferred styles of supervising, that these four factors merge in fluid ways, often within a developmental and case-specific context. Collaborative supervisors may find it necessary to be directive at times (e.g., reporting suspected abuse of a child or ameliorating a trainee's critical mistake). And directive supervisors may find themselves mentoring their trainees toward collegial relationships with themselves at times. Many supervisors, working from modernist perspectives, prefer expert roles in which they help their trainees learn explicit concepts and interventions through instruction from a directive position as an experienced clinician. Other supervisors, preferring a more postmodern or poststructural approach, use more collaborative and trainee-directed approaches (e.g., Bobele, Biever, Hassan Solorzano, & Bluntzer, 2014). All such positions should flow from personal philosophies of supervision and are defensible. What is important is that supervisors and therapists be aware of their beliefs about effective supervision so that the supervisory relationship is supported and not disjointed. That is, interventions flow from goals within the context of the supervisory relationship and the training system, informed by the supervisor's and trainee's contexts. Although contemporary focus has largely been on the roles delineated in the Morgan & Sprenkle (2007) research, readers also may want to consider one or more of the additional roles (see for example, Barker & Chang,

2013; Ungar, 2006) that come to the fore at different times in the developmental trajectories of trainees.

Coach

Supervisors engage in coaching their trainees when helping them learn specific competencies or skills, especially executive competencies, which have to do with what happens in the therapy room. Good coaches provide encouragement and direction based on trustworthy assessments of performance. They instruct trainees on skills, collaborate on strategies, and protect them from doing harm.

Teacher

When acting as a teacher, a supervisor helps the trainee learn system concepts, concepts of various therapy approaches, appropriate integration of interventions, and appropriate execution of interventions and case management. A teacher also evaluates trainees periodically and at the end of the training period, provides useful feedback for further work.

Administrator

At times, CFT supervisors act as administrators. This might be in their roles as agents of accreditation and licensure, employers in agencies, or simply as supervisors helping trainees manage professional and personal time, write adequate case notes and reports, and keep track of clinical and supervision hours. (See Killmer & Cook, 2014, for detailed discussion of the intersection of "clinical" and "administrative" supervisory roles.)

Mentor

Mentoring is an informal relationship dynamic based on mutual trust and respect. For the most part, mentoring is more likely to take place later than earlier in a trainee's development as a therapist. Mentoring often includes role modeling, especially with regard to professional guidance and development, the nuances involved in a professional journey as a member of various subcultures, encouraging attendance and participation at continuing education opportunities, and participation in organizational affairs.

Isomorphism

With a positive working relationship as a primary focus, as a matter of isomorphism (see Chapter 3), trainees will do the same with their client families. Supervisors can be explicit about this. In supervision as in therapy, whenever supervisors sense an inchoate problem in working relationships with their trainees, they should focus immediately on that, otherwise the therapist–client relationship will suffer also. Without constructive working relationships between trainees and supervisors, trainees are less likely to be responsive and trustworthy. In turn this hampers their clinical growth and may be harmful to clients. Again, the working relationship always comes first in supervision and in therapy.

If the working alliance is basically a matter of a relationship that supports work toward shared goals, the primary focus of supervisors must be on their relationships with trainees, just as therapists must continuously focus on their relationships with clients (Knobloch-Fedders, Pinsof, & Mann, 2004; Pinsof, 1994, 1995). The relationship between supervisor and trainee is the number one priority at all times (except in emergency situations). Neglect of this aspect of supervision renders other aspects of supervision, such as theoretical approach or specific interventions, ineffective. For example, focusing on self-of-the-therapist matters is not likely to be fruitful if the relationship between the supervisor and trainee does not include trust. Just as clinical relationships must be continuously monitored and cultivated, so must supervisory relationships.

Other Important Supervisory Roles

In addition to supervisory roles that evolve through relationships with trainees, other supervisory roles evolve from relationships that supervisors have with the community and the field of CFT. For example, first and foremost is the role of ensuring adequate client care. In addition, supervisors may find themselves serving as advocates for trainees when training settings refuse to accept their trainees' legal requirements or limitations. Similarly, supervisors serve as gatekeepers to the profession by carefully evaluating the competence of trainees. This may require helping the trainee who cannot seem to develop adequate skill find another supervisor or another career. It may even mean terminating the supervisory relationship or informing educational programs and/or licensing boards about unethical or illegal actions (see Russell, DuPree, Beggs, Peterson, & Anderson, 2007, for more discussion).

Working with an Impaired Therapist

Supervisors must also act when their trainees are not doing well because of personal issues. The July/August 2010, issue (Volume 9, No. 4) of AAMFT's *Family Therapy Magazine* was devoted to issues of impaired therapists. Supervisors should be keenly aware of the wellbeing of their trainees and their ability to provide services to clients. At the same time, supervisors should help trainees understand the importance of self-care and of developing a sense of themselves as capable of working with clients, and having plans in place for managing client cases when they find themselves impaired or compromised (F. N. Thomas, 2010).

Supervisor Mentors

This text would not be complete without at least a short discussion about supervisor mentors. The requirements of the AAMFT (2014) for training as a supervisor candidate call for another process layer for becoming designated as an Approved Supervisor (AS):

supervisor mentoring, formerly called supervision of supervision. There is no specialized training for Approved Supervisor Mentors, *per se.* However, they must be experienced AAMFT Approved Supervisors. Supervisor candidates must receive mentoring from such ASs as part of their supervision training process. This mentoring serves to provide the supervisor candidate with broad-range assistance during the supervision training period, to help guide the supervisor candidates through a developmental process, coaching in much the same way as candidates do in supervising trainees. This includes working over the entire development of trainees (screening, contracting, teaching, evaluating, professionalism, etc.), interventions, troubleshooting, ethics and legal matters, diversity, and so forth, focusing on the candidate's development as a supervisor. Just as supervisors do not do therapy through their trainees, supervisor mentors do not do supervision (or therapy) through supervisor candidates.

Supervisor mentors provide the same context for supervisor candidates that supervisors and supervisor candidates provide for therapist trainees. The relationship should include a contract with agreed-upon details, be confidential, focus on supervision (as much as possible through the raw data of live observation and/or recordings) rather than therapy, and assist the supervisor candidate through the process of applying for the AAMFT Approved Supervisor designation, including approving a revised (and always to be revised) version of supervisor candidates' personal Philosophy of Supervision papers (see Chapter 15 in this text).

Pragmatics of Navigating Supervision Roles

In our roles as supervisors, we encourage, teach, coach, mentor, advocate, and hold our trainees accountable. We also develop understandings of the various tasks that go along with these different roles, always differentiating between helping our trainees learn and doing the work for them. We establish clear boundaries with our trainees through contracts, conversation, and rules that may be implicit or explicit (or implicit that may become explicit). We maintain professional and appropriate personal boundaries, evaluate their work and them as therapists, and intervene when we believe their clients, the community, the field, or they are at risk of harm.

We have just discussed supervisory roles. Within those roles, as well as combining some of them, are various supervisory goals. We are confident that ideas about supervisory roles will be clearer to readers as they think about the goals of supervision. See Chapter 8 for more on working as supervisors with impaired therapists.

Supervision Goals

Within a working alliance that suits the styles of both supervisor and trainee, each has ideas of appropriate and important goals for the direction of supervision, including expansion of skills such as those found in the Core Competencies (AAMFT, 2004; Nelson et al., 2007; Appendix B). Depending upon relationship preferences and agreements, goals will ideally be negotiated between supervisors and trainees, and perhaps dictated to some extent by training contexts. Goals are likely guided or influenced by the requirements of governmental and organizational accrediting bodies, a supervisor's theoretical orientation, supervision philosophy, and developmental level, and the theoretical approach the trainee is learning. Goals also depend upon the developmental competence of the trainee. Therefore, they typically are fluid, often more specific and oriented toward basic skills for newer trainees, and more general and oriented toward the trainee as a professional as clinical training progresses. Of course, within evidence-based training contexts, goals may be quite specific.

Long-Term Goals

It may seem obvious, but we want to state clearly that the chief goal of supervision should be the development of competent, confident, lawful, and ethical therapists. Even approaches that emphasize the person of the therapist over specific techniques or models of therapy require ethical, professional, and competent therapists. These goals also should be construed in a larger context of the self of the therapist (see Chapter 13), his or her philosophy or worldview in general (e.g., modernist, realist, poststructuralist), and the values that the therapist-trainee holds dear. These ideas about reality and the trainee's developing orientation toward therapy must be in harmony for optimal professional development (Fear & Woolfe, 1999). Other aspects of trainees' development are discussed in this text, for example, how their values and worldviews affect positions on ethics and ethical decision making (Chapter 12) and culture (Chapter 10).

First, we would say that contextual goals are important. These include safe supervisory contexts so that trainees and supervisors can trust each other with important and sometimes delicate information. The supervisory context also must be clear, which can be facilitated through contracts, but also flexible, so that supervisors are available when necessary and so that changes can occur as the trainee develops and situations arise (F. N. Thomas, 2010). We believe that it is important for supervisors to help training contexts appreciate systemic, relational therapy and take into account contextual factors for individuals, couples, and families.

In addition to clinical competence, professional and personal growth, and increasing confidence levels of the trainee, goals often focus on process rather than content. For example, trainees must learn to "see" and privilege process over content. That is, within systemic training, supervisors pay attention to patterns of interaction (see Watzlawick, Weakland & Fisch, 1974): within clinical cases and between trainees and clients, between trainees and other professionals, within the trainee–supervisor relationship, and within the entire training context. It is easy for supervisors to get overly focused on content, especially when they are relatively inexperienced, when they have expertise with a particular clinical issue (e.g., eating disorders), or when they become overly interested in either the client's situation or what they perceive as problematic for the trainee (perhaps as a trainee's self-of-the-therapist factor).

Supervisors may tend to pay more attention to process when they are helping therapists develop skill within a particular theoretical approach or when their own overall paradigm is relational and systemic rather than individual and causal. An individual, linear context of supervision may pull trainees and supervisors into case or supervisory content. In these situations, supervisors help trainees become informed and flexible observers of themselves within the clinical and training settings and of themselves in general (for an illustration, see Lee, 1997).

Of course, it is appropriate for supervisors to address content at certain times. Examples are when the therapist could benefit by learning about a certain clinical situation (e.g., families and eating disorders), when the supervisor's expertise is clearly required for client wellbeing (e.g., need for detoxification of substances before commencing therapy), or when the trainee's actions suggest something is interfering with either the clinical or supervisory process (e.g., getting into power struggles with clients). However, we believe that it is just as important from an isomorphic perspective for supervisors to focus on the process and patterns of dynamic interactions in supervision as it is for therapists to focus on process rather than content in the clinical system. Regardless, the ebb and flow of a gestalt-like focus between process and content is an important dynamic for supervisors to attend to, making deliberate decisions that will best help the trainee's development as well as the client system's wellbeing. Focusing on process, we believe, and encouraging trainees to think at process levels, produces a more effective, efficient, and well-rounded therapist who can work with clients with a myriad of difficulties, even when he or she may not have specific expertise in an issue.

Developing Competence

An important long-term goal of supervision is the development of a competent therapist. Short-term goals can easily focus on different aspects of competence in MFT. For example, the AAMFT Core Competencies (AAMFT, 2004; Nelson et al., 2007; see Appendix B) provide an excellent list of competencies established for CFTs. Although daunting to look at, systemic therapists and supervisors quickly see patterns among the domains and subdomains, as well as the areas they have already mastered or are doing well in. These competencies range from microskills used during interviews with clients to professional skills such as participating in continuing education and the development of the profession.

Developing Theory-Driven Therapy

We believe that a critical goal for supervision of CFTs is the trainee's development of an articulated, integrated approach to therapy. Many CFT programs require so-called theory of change projects that help graduate students begin to identify and articulate their preferred approaches to therapy (Nelson & Prior, 2003). Supervisors of postgraduate trainees can use some of those ideas for trainees who have or have not had such opportunities. We believe that having such an articulated approach enhances supervision by giving the trainee and supervisor ideas about how to make clinical decisions, how to evaluate therapy, and how or when to enlarge a trainee's repertoire of theory and/or technique.

Any one approach may or may not prove more effective than another (see discussion in Sprenkle, Davis, & Lebow, 2009; Wedge, 1996). In fact, client families' perspectives as well as therapists' may even integrate disparate approaches. For example,

Hargrave and Pfitzer (2011) described a successful cotherapy situation in which the former offered family-of-origin work and the latter, Solution-Focused. However, "the therapy, while successful, felt like a mishmash of techniques to us as therapists as we struggled to work together and incorporate each other's ideas" (p. 5). These master therapists and supervisors went on to observe that, although "the elements of the therapeutic relationship, the therapist's confidence and clarity in the process, and the dealing with specific therapeutic opportunities" (p. 6) are crucial, these central therapeutic common factors begin with the capacity of the therapist to organize and make sense of the clinical picture, to consider various short- and long-term outcomes, and to flexibly offer appropriate interventions. Accordingly, therapists must be equipped with a suitable and clear conceptual map for therapy to be most effective.

Supervision and Therapy

One of the controversial aspects of supervisory goals is how far into the personal life of the trainee the supervisor should go. We believe that it is acceptable and, depending upon the supervisor's philosophy as the overriding guide to his or her supervision, appropriate to explore aspects of the trainee's personal life as they impact the clinical or supervisory work. However, we also believe that unresolved personal issues that trainees cannot limit in terms of negative clinical impact might also benefit from therapy in order to help trainees progress in both their personal and professional lives. Some supervisors or supervisory contexts may require that trainees have personal therapy. Within a competency-based context, however, we believe that it is important to focus on the behaviors that are desired and work with trainees to identify avenues for developing those competencies. If they and their supervisors identify barriers together, they may identify strategies that may or may not include personal or family therapy.

Supervisors with family of origin and self-of-the-therapist philosophies may believe that more extensive work—that some might identify as therapy rather than supervision—is appropriate within the supervisory context. The AAMFT (2015a) Code of Ethics specifies the following:

> *4.2 Marriage and family therapists do not provide therapy to current students or supervisees.*

Clearly, however, "provide therapy" can and has been defined in various ways. Bowen therapy (1978) requires extensive and intensive work on differentiation of self of the therapist. Therefore, Bowen coaching is appropriate as part of therapy training. We do not want to quibble about whether Bowen coaching is or is not therapy. That is a discussion for a different venue. However, the Code of Ethics does provide some guidance:

> *4.1 Marriage and family therapists who are in a supervisory role are aware of their influential positions with respect to students and supervisees, and they avoid exploiting the trust and dependency of such persons. Therapists, therefore, make every effort to avoid conditions and multiple relationships that could impair professional objectivity or increase the*

risk of exploitation. When the risk of impairment or exploitation exists due to conditions or multiple roles, therapists take appropriate precautions.

We argue that simultaneous Bowen coaching and supervision of therapy with the same trainee constitutes multiple relationships and, therefore, due care must be taken to protect trainees from exploitation. Further, we strongly believe that supervisory contracts should be explicit about the goals and limits of supervision relative to the personal life of the therapist.

Evaluation

MFT supervisors have an important responsibility to their trainees, trainees' clients, and trainees' training contexts, whether graduate programs, practicum sites/agencies, or postgraduate settings, to periodically evaluate the trainees' competence and development as clinical professionals. Later chapters of this text outline a few of the formats and processes that supervisors may use for both formative (along the way) and summative (at the end) evaluation of trainee competence and readiness to practice therapy independently.

Gatekeeping

An important goal of supervision and role of the supervisor is protection of the public (clients as well as others) and the profession. Therefore, we believe that assessing growing competence and gatekeeping is an important supervisory role toward this goal, sometimes requiring more extensive exploration of what is happening with a trainee as his or her behaviors impact therapy. Gatekeeping is a process that may result in helping the trainee find a different profession, but is better suited to appropriately helping trainees grow into the profession of CFT—keeping in rather than only keeping out. Russell and her associates (2007) surveyed faculty in Commission on Accreditation for Marriage and Family Therapy Education (COAMFTE)-accredited CFT programs to learn what the programs observed in terms of problematic trainee behaviors and ways that the programs dealt with such problems. The results of their investigation are interesting and, depending upon circumstances, include recommendations for closer supervision, more careful assigning of cases, assigned reading, required breaks from therapy, and even counseling students out of the program. We believe that the policies and procedures used in CFT programs can easily be adapted to a variety of supervisory graduate and postgraduate contexts and encourage supervisors to include such ideas in their supervisory contracts and procedures.

Short-Term Goals

Depending upon the philosophy of the supervisor, longer term goals may range from mastery of a specific therapy approach to growth of the therapist. Shorter term goals may range from negotiating goals and contracts for supervision to specific clinical skills. We suggest that supervisors and trainees clarify both short- and long-term goals as well as strategies for evaluating progress toward those goals.

The first, most pragmatic goals of supervision include establishing a relationship between the trainee and the supervisor, clarifying the theoretical approach or approaches that the trainee will learn and practice, explaining the approach of the supervisor so that compatibility or fit can be assessed, exploring specific long- and short-term goals in the minds of both the supervisor and the trainee, and clarifying roles and establishing ground rules and the supervisory contract. When these goals are met, supervision has a greater chance of succeeding both as a pleasant and educative context for both the trainee and the supervisor. Other goals can then more easily be determined in a collaborative process.

Supervision as a Safe Place

One of the most important early goals is to establish supervision as a safe place for the training to take place. According to the AAMFT (2015a) Code of Ethics, the supervisory relationship is a confidential one except as defined by the supervisor and trainee and agreed to by both. Systemic therapy acknowledges factors of the therapist that both positively and negatively impact therapy and clients. Therefore, it is necessary at times for the trainee to discuss personal matters with the supervisor and must feel safe that this information and process is respected by the supervisor. This is an almost sacred trust, akin to the one established in therapy. Yet, in some ways, it is more sacred. That is, trainees not only trust their personal selves and clinical development to the supervisor, but also their clients' wellbeing and their careers.

The second author once had a second-year student sigh with great relief during practicum when we discussed therapists' mental health and self-care. I had been talking about life changes and challenges that therapists go through as human beings, sometimes well and sometimes badly. He said, "You mean our marriages don't have to be perfect for us to be OK as therapists?" I assured him that if that were the case, and if no divorced therapists could do marital therapy, we'd have few or no therapists. His telling me that was, on one level, simply a part of the practicum class. On another level, however, he trusted me not to laugh at or judge his doubts or his personal situation. His competence as a therapist is not dependent upon his personal situations but on how he handles them and how he learned to do that through trusted supervision. If supervision had not been a safe place to talk about those things, he might never have learned how to manage his own feelings, especially during intense or stressful times in therapy or in his personal life.

Supervision must also be a safe place for trainees to explore ideas, to question what they are doing, to take risks, and to report mistakes, trusting that the supervisor will continue to help them grow as competent therapists and to protect the wellbeing of their clients. Good therapy is not a robotic activity that could be performed by a computer. Systemic and relational therapies, especially, require an ability to understand concepts, see patterns and evidence of those concepts in therapy, and to intervene in ways that include contextual information about the clients' systems. This is a complex and sometimes complicated endeavor and learning it must allow for exploration of ideas, actions, and consequences of those actions. Trainees must believe that it is acceptable and sometimes even required.

Establishing a Working Alliance

To a great extent, working alliances between supervisors and trainees develop and change over time, depending on many factors. Supervision is an intimate process and a trusting relationship facilitates all of the other goals established by trainees and supervisors. There are many ways to do this, just as there are many ways in therapy. However, we believe that spelling out ground rules and expectations as early as possible is important. Beyond that, a wise supervisor maintains a trustworthy relationship with trainees by listening carefully, validating concerns, teaching competencies as needed, coaching new techniques, often through difficult cases, and serving as an experienced mentor.

Goals while Supervising

All of the above is very important in terms of contextual long- and short-term goals of supervision. Goals *within* supervisory situations also are important. As supervisors assess situations, they must ask themselves about what to do next. Is this a safety issue that must be addressed clearly and immediately? Is it a situation where the trainee might deliver an intervention in a different way or a different intervention (in accordance with his/her philosophy of therapy)? What outcome does the supervisor wish for from the intervention? Answers to these questions help supervisors determine which role or roles to take and therefore, which interventions to use. Discussing concepts might call for a *teaching* role; helping the trainee think through delivery of boundary-making is more for a *coaching* intervention; and so on.

Ongoing Feedback

Feedback for both trainees and supervisors helps to establish atmospheres of trust and knowledge of safety nets. Feedback for trainees helps them understand what they are doing that is likely helpful to their clients and their own supervision. Feedback for supervisors helps them understand what is and is not working for their trainees in supervision. When feedback is ongoing, it is easier for everyone to bring up delicate or challenging issues before they become problematic or potentially harmful to clients.

Exercises

1 What do you think is the most important component of the supervisory relationship and how do you promote that?

2 How directive versus collaborative do you think you are or will be as a supervisor (scale of 1–5: 1 = directive, 5 = collaborative)? How hierarchical do you think you are or will be?
3 What kinds of sanctions do you think are appropriate for different kinds of trainee deficiencies (see Russell et al., 2007)?
4 What do you believe are long- and short-term goals for supervision and how might you prioritize those?

3 Getting Started

Readiness and Procedures

This chapter covers an overview of supervisory roles while sorting out education, training, and experience, all informed by participant diversity. We also discuss developmental aspects of supervision, general education and training requirements, training issues, and the fundamental processes of supervision. We end with a minimalist way for trainees to begin a case as a grounding for supervision.

Education, Training, and Experience

It is useful to distinguish between education, training, and experience. Education is the transfer of knowledge. Training teaches how to apply that knowledge to perform interventions. The authors believe that CFT is applied family science and requires clinicians to stay abreast of the data and theories of contemporary family life and the empirical support underlying applications of these to diverse clinical populations. Experience is a tricky thing. Some individuals may have 10 years of varied experience. Others may have had the experience of one year, 10 years over. Useful experience involves growth (see classic discussions by Nichols & Everett, 1986).

Many observations about diversity—context, professional history, epistemology, attitudes about authority, personal context, and experience—also describe supervisors and the institutions in which supervision takes place. Supervisors have personalities, and so do their educational, training, and practice settings, sometimes called culture. Both supervisors and their settings can be arrogant or open about the nature of knowledge and that which is transmitted, audited, and enforced. Typically, each reflects and reinforces the other.

Participant Diversity

Trainees are quite diverse. Some are eager for education and training. Others may be ambivalent about the venture. Some come from psychology and other undergraduate programs and this is their first experience with education and training in psychotherapy or systemic thinking. Others may be experienced and even credentialed providers of diverse psychotherapeutic fields such as social work, counseling, or psychology. Some may be fully trained in contemporary CFT or system

DOI: 10.4324/9781003099833-4

concepts; others in more historic approaches such as major CFT models including psychodynamic, structural, strategic, Bowen, and so forth. Certainly, lenses through which clients are viewed may be flexible (appreciating multiple realities) or more focused; scientifically critical (evidence-based theories) or more conceptual/theoretical; singularly theoretical or integrative; and so on. Finally, all parties have been shaped by their unique life experiences with power and authorities as well as their training programs.

Developmental Aspects of Supervision

Data indicate that trainees want and expect different things depending on their respective levels of training (see Lee & Nelson, 2014). Beginners look for a big picture of what therapy is and they want and expect a high degree of direction. After they have moved beyond the entry level, more advanced trainees seek less direction and more support for professional development and skill building. Finally, veteran therapists seek more consultative relationships. (Supervision of advanced trainees will be discussed in Chapter 10.)

Many beginning trainees—usually graduate students, but not solely—need an orientation to psychotherapy and, especially, to relational therapy. They need to come to some personal understanding of the difference between "therapy" and "counseling." For example, the former connotes substantive change; the latter connotes "advising." This distinction in roles and goals between therapy and counseling is often confusing to new therapists. Many are informed by the presentations of media mental health and relationship "experts." Advice-giving and quick fix scenarios may be reinforced by the allowed number of treatment sessions and the processes (reality-oriented, problem-centered) dictated by agencies, third-party payers' rules, and lengthy waiting lists. Although such interventions are meant to help therapists and clients to "move things along," inexperienced therapists may shift the responsibility for change to themselves rather than clients.

Therapy participants were debriefed some time after a course of couple therapy in a study by Quinn, Nagirreddy, Lawless, and Bagley (2000). They cited three factors that they found most helpful: a climate of discovery, the social relationship with their therapists, and the ability of a therapist to listen but also to step in and give direction when the process bogged down. *Not one participant in this study spoke of being given advice.* This study was more than two decades ago, but similar results are reported by Lloyd-Hazlett and Foster (2014).

As we pointed out in Chapter 2, clinicians and social scientists for decades have emphasized the importance of a therapeutic alliance, developed over time. That is, there is mutual agreement of therapists, clients, and their significant others with the goals, methods, and relationships of the enterprise. Also in Chapter 2, we emphasized the systemic viewpoint, namely, that this same alliance—common goals and a relationship good enough to support work on these goals—must also characterize the supervisor–trainee relationship.

Education and Training Requirements

After the orientation period, trainees first need to be taught the basic tools of therapy (education) and rehearse them thoroughly (training).

Active Listening

The foremost of foundational therapy skills is active listening (for an explication, see Rothwell, 2010). Trainees may find Carl Rogers' (2003) seminal work very helpful in this regard, in that his classic presentation of nondirective therapy puts the responsibility for change on the clients and argues the value of good therapeutic listening.

Supervisors and trainees also need to know and teach sensitivity to relationship issues, affect management, and problem-solving strategies. Couples and family members find these useful and use them in their daily lives (e.g., Fincham, Stanley, & Rhoades, 2011). As the rehearsals of the above are going on, and throughout therapeutic interventions, trainees must become aware of the importance of good interviewing skills. When clients say that they are "depressed," an alert interviewer can mine good information by asking what their clients mean when they describe themselves that way. What is happening that tells them they are "depressed." What does "depression" look like? Feel like? What are the clients saying to themselves? What are they doing? What are others doing? What are they doing when they are less depressed? What will they be doing when they are not depressed? What do patterns of interaction with others that include or don't include "depression" look like? Interviewing skills are formed within a context of theory-informed care. That is, interviewing questions flow from the therapy approach that the trainee is learning and how the client responds to questions.

Beginning therapists also need to appreciate the respect and power of good reflection back to clients. For example, when clients may be listing advice given by others, and perhaps are seeking yet another opinion, the trainee can reply, "You seem to be having a hard time making up your mind about what is best. Tell us about that."

Constructive Goal Setting

Beginning therapists, like their supervisors, need to become expert at constructive goal setting. That is, not only must their professional endeavors be mindful, but they must allow effective action. Said goals will be realistic and consist of positive behaviors that are both observable and easily measurable (see Nelson, 2019).

System Thinking

Many trainees and some relational supervisors do not think systemically and, more specifically, in terms of ecosystemic contexts (e.g., Bronfenbrenner & Morris, 2006; Bubolz & Sontag, 1993; Lerner, 2018). Their educational and training backgrounds, and often the settings within which they practice, are dominated by medical and psychological models. In both of these models, dysfunction resides within the individual, perhaps exacerbated by social factors. The medical model requires diagnoses and treats symptoms presumed to be created by physical conditions within the body or brain. The psychological model focuses on personality traits.

In contrast, the relational model does not see problems as residing within the individual. Instead, different social settings and relationships increase the probability of desirable and undesirable ideas, feelings, behaviors, and interactional dynamics as the amelioration of problematic ideas, feelings, behaviors, and interactions. Since most trainees have on one occasion or another been given a label (e.g., "she's hostile"; "he's ambitious"; "he has AD/HD"), exploration of the relational model of causality and applying its ideas to one's self can be both fun and liberating. Trainees learn to "pursue the exception," that is, to ask in what settings an individual shows more or less of the desirable or undesirable behavior and to whom. By seeing so-called traits as actually situation-specific rather than characterological or pathological within an individual, they learn about the importance of context and reciprocity, and how to use these insights for prevention of undesirable situations and enhancement of those more desirable.

Once trainees discover that relational therapy has something unique and valuable to offer, namely, the system perspective, most embrace it. They find it sensible and empowering. Therefore, it is easy to persuade them that, in their first contacts with clients, they need to convey a system perspective and consistently cultivate it. For example, they can advise clients to bring their partners or even entire family to the first session. They might ask questions about how other people in the client's system think about the presenting concern or how they respond to it. They might ask about the situation or the person conveying the label. This orientation places those others "in the room" with the therapist and client. They may ask about other factors in the client system's life: work, school, education, ethnicity, religion, and so forth, and how those factors play out in the client's life or impact the presenting difficulty.

We think that it is good pedagogy to ask trainees to conduct their initial and early interviews with a blank piece of paper in front of them (or the covers of the clients' file folders) on which they sketch and annotate family relationships in systemic fashion as their clients make that information available, perhaps as a genogram. This is not meant to be accomplished in a particular session. Instead, it is meant to be a simple and graphic way of taking session notes that convey a contextual view. Diagrams that sketch family relationships in their larger ecosystemic setting is a way to encourage both trainees and those being interviewed to comprehend things through a systemic lens. Accordingly, trainees might also be expected to diagram case presentations.

Finally, consideration needs to be given to what the most useful constructs are in relational assessments and interventions. Trainees need conceptual tools to guide their perceptions of and to capture the nature and dynamics of social groups. After initial learning goals are reached, supervisors can have the students read the classic presentation of circular questioning by Tomm (1984), and explore an illustrative teaching model by Fleuridas, Nelson, and Rosenthal (1986). Circular questions, which elicit information about systemic relationships, need to be appreciated and rehearsed thoroughly. They may help the family see themselves systemically rather than solely in terms of the identified patient and, as a result, even spontaneously change (Penn, 1982; Selvini Palazzoli, Boscolo, Cecchin, & Prata, 1980; Tomm, 1984).

System (or systemic) thinking does not come naturally. Aspiring CFTs need to move their focus of perception and meaning making away from individuals to the system patterns in which they are located. Lee and Everett (2004) lay out a useful developmental roadmap for accomplishing this.

System thinking offers basic structural concepts to capture system relationships and dynamics. Over time, many of the major CFT theories have made contributions to these. Although some have peaked and fallen into disuse (see Lee, Nichols, Nichols, & Odom, 2004), others have stood the test of time. Couple and family therapists must know them. Supervisors may wish to construct a table of what they and others consider essential systemic concepts. This can be updated as they and their trainees see fit, and with changes in the National Licensing Examination in MFT (Association of Marital and Family Therapy Regulatory Boards, 2020). We consider the following systemic concepts essential. They have proven valuable to relational therapists and researchers over half a century.

- *System and cybernetic concepts*: wholeness, homeostasis, negative and positive feedback, first and second order change, circularity, recursivity, reciprocal influence, open and closed systems, morphogenesis, equifinality. For detailed explanations to use with trainees and others, see Becvar and Becvar (2012), Midori Hanna (2019), and Wright and Leahey (2009) as well as Chapter 8 in this volume.
- *Structure*: system, subsystem, hierarchy, alliance, boundaries, triangles.
- *Tools for assessing systems*: active listening, circular questioning, multiple realities, frames, exploration of diversity and context, co-construction.

Caldwell and Claxton (2010) provide examples of methods for helping trainees learn system concepts as do Becvar and Becvar (2017).

Development of a Therapy Approach

One of the most important tasks of learning therapy and supervision, in our opinion, is the development of one's own approach. There are many singular models of CFT (e.g., Bowen, 1978; Minuchin, 1974), integrated approaches (e.g., Structural/Strategic, Stanton, 1981), and evidence-based approaches (e.g., Emotionally Focused Therapy, Johnson, 2008). We find that beginners who stay within one theory and later expand (e.g., begin with structural and then add multigenerational) report less confusion. In any case, whether a therapist learns the approach of the supervisor or one of their own choosing, we have found it important for trainees to be able to articulate their approaches and to apply them to their clinical work.

Bitar, Bean, and Bermudez (2007), in a grounded theory pilot study, described two domains that influenced CFTs' selections of the therapy they eventually practiced: personal and professional. Within the personal domain, themes that emerged included personality factors, personal philosophy, family of origin, their own therapy, and their own marriages. Professional contextual factors included the influence of undergraduate classes, graduate training, their clients, professional development, and clinical sophistication. It seems potentially useful for supervisors to consider these same factors as they develop and articulate their own philosophies of supervision. Further, this conceptualization could be quite helpful for supervisors who lead their trainees through a process of theoretical development.

Supervisors may want to be even more proactive about helping trainees develop their personal ideas about therapy. Piercy and Sprenkle (1986, 1988) listed some very pointed questions for trainees to consider as they develop their own approaches. Further, Nelson and Prior (2003) conducted a study on theory of change projects in CFT graduate programs. They documented both the areas of inquiry and the processes used as students learned and articulated their own approaches.

Nelson and her students (Appendix A) developed Marriage and Family Therapy model charts. Although not complete, the document lists each of the seminal, so-called "traditional" systemic approaches, plus two postmodern approaches (Narrative and Solution-Focused) and two integrative approaches (Emotionally Focused Therapy and Gottman Method Therapy). These charts lay out important leaders of the approach, assumptions, concepts, goals of therapy, the role of the therapist, what is assessed, interventions, how change is viewed, how termination of therapy is determined, perspectives on self-of-the-therapist, and evaluation of the approach as well as seminal and useful resources. Supervisors are finding that these charts are useful for both their own ideas about change and therapy as well as their trainees'. Approaches can be cross-checked for assumptions so that the therapist is not working against her or himself. The charts also may be useful for studying for the national MFT exam. Finally, supervisors and trainees may duplicate one of the charts, omitting details of the approach, and use it to delineate and clarify their own approach to couple and family therapy.

Pragmatics of Getting Started

Those who supervise individuals new to relational therapy have several issues to consider.

Screening: Readiness for Supervised Clinical Experience

Prospective supervisors have the right to expect and be given trainees equipped to be able to remain in the treatment room cognitively, emotionally, and behaviorally (Nichols & Everett, 1986). This capacity is a function of personal maturity characterized by good-enough boundaries, social judgment, self-observation, and self-control. This is important to all supervision, but of extreme importance if initial supervision sessions are not live observations of therapy.

Prospective supervisors also have the right to expect that trainees have the foundational tools of relational therapy, namely, a generic overview of what therapy is, active listening skills, and understanding of basic systemic constructs. *These are the unique tools of the CFT profession.* Prospective trainees should be able to define basic systemic concepts and see them in their training group, themselves and their own families, and in live and videotaped clinical presentations.

It is useful to have formal contingency plans (that is, what to do in case of fire, dangerous weather, and potentially dangerous client states, to name a few topics). Similarly, supervisors may provide or co-develop decision-making checklists with trainees for assessing potential lethality toward self or others, or regarding civil commitment (see Chapter 14). These administrative devices help members of the training system manage their emotions while giving important directions under times of duress. They also are invaluable in contracts and policies and procedures manuals when quick access and/or documentation is critical.

Protections Necessary for Supervisors, Training Institutions, and Communities

There will be times of clinical duress, or when someone alleges malfeasance, or when supervisors must evaluate progress. At such times, relevant parties need access to data from which they can determine what may have been done and its reasonableness. Legal advisors commonly observe, "If it isn't written, it doesn't exist." An adequate documentation package protects supervisors, their trainees, and the institutions in which training takes place. If there is a formal policies and procedures manual, trainees need to read, comprehend, and accept its specifications and affirm this understanding through signatures and dates. Documentation packages and other administrative needs will be touched upon in later sections of the text. However, two matters are required at the start of any course of supervision: supervision contracts and progress notes.

Supervision Contracts

Contracts are written documents that specify expectations and obligations of both the supervisors and their trainees. Their terms protect both parties as well as the training institution. These contracts must be signed and dated by supervisors and trainees. Contracts serve not only to alert both trainees and supervisors to expectations and responsibilities but are useful for anticipating actions in certain circumstances such as for contacting the supervisor during crises, or consequences should the supervision be terminated prematurely. Dated signatures document agreement with the contract and what it specifies.

Supervision contracts may be unilateral statements of structures by the authorities involved or, to some extent, negotiated. These contracts need to be timely, that is, they are based on the developmental levels of the supervisor and therapist, and they also are informed by the values and norms of the settings in which supervision and therapy are being practiced. Therefore, they will include the most current requirements of ethical and legal regulatory systems: organizational and legal codes of ethics and standards of practice; legal requirements governing electronic communication, record keeping, and provision of services (see Chapters 11 and 12).

Beyond these mandatory requirements, the following are the basic ingredients of supervisory contracts (largely adapted from Bernard & Goodyear, 2019; J. T. Thomas, 2010; see also Smith, Cornish, & Riva, 2014, for considerations involved in group supervision):

- Supervisor's background: training, license, therapy, and supervisory credentials.
- Supervisor's methods: the contract should specify the mechanisms of supervision: group or individual; based on case presentations, recordings, or live viewing. It is crucial that the mechanisms of providing access to raw data (live viewing, recordings, case notes) be specified, the amount required, and sanctions when raw data are not made available.
- Confidentiality policies: who will and will not have access to information revealed in supervision under what circumstances, and what kind of information will be kept confidential.
- Financial issues and policies.
- Requirements for documentation of clinical and supervisory hours as well as clinical and supervision notes.
- Risks and benefits of supervision.
- Goals of supervision and how often and how they will be determined or reviewed,
- Evaluation instruments and procedures; clinical versus administrative evaluation differences; formative as well as summative evaluations; criteria for evaluating progress; consequences of various levels of evaluation.
- Duration of the contract and criteria for termination.
- Expectations for knowledge of state/provincial requirements to do therapy and ethics codes.
- Supervisor's responsibilities: what the trainee can expect from the supervisor such as cancellation notification, availability, directiveness levels, confidentiality, and so forth.
- Trainee's responsibilities: what the supervisor expects from the trainee such as notification of cancellation, preparation for supervision, notification of ethical or legal situations, and so forth.
- Supervision session content: form of preparation and presentation, time allocation.
- Supervisor accessibility and contact information.
- Agreement to keep supervisors informed about:
  - Disputes with clients or impasses in therapy;
  - Allegations of unethical behavior by clients, colleagues, or others (e.g., clients' family members);
  - Threats of a complaint or lawsuit;
  - Mental health emergencies requiring immediate action;
  - High-risk situations and cases in which clients evidence suicidal thoughts, gestures, attempts, or a significant history of attempts, or those presenting with a history of, propensity for, or threats of violence;

- Contemplated departures from standards of practice or exceptions to general rules, standards, polices, or practices;
- Suspected or known clinical or ethical errors;
- Contact with clients outside the context of treatment, incidental or otherwise;
- Legal issues such as possible reporting obligations related to suspected abuse or neglect, or ethical violations by other professionals.

- Ethical considerations: the contract specifies what professional codes of ethics will govern the supervision. There is much overlap among the dictates of professional CFT, social work, psychology, and counseling. But there are important differences (e.g., CFT specification of the "client" as a relationship versus an individual). The contract also states that trainees' clients are told that their therapists are under supervision and by whom. Supervisors may wish to specify particular things necessary to a specific context, such as management of multiple relationships.
- Requirements or recommendations about therapy for trainees.
- Financial arrangements and consequences for neglect.
- Specification of the circumstances under which the supervision may be discontinued and how it is done. This is a good place to state that under certain circumstances, the supervisor may report the reasons for terminating supervision to subsequent supervisors or licensing boards.
- Due process: several of the above topics—responsibility, methods, financial, ethical conduct, and evaluation issues—can result in disagreement. Therefore, contracts should describe how disagreements between supervisors and trainees can be explored fairly.

Thomas (2007) cites a number of areas that she believes are essential in supervisory contracts. This list is shorter than the above yet covers the bases quite well and may be preferable for some supervisors:

- Supervisor's background.
- Supervisory methods.
- Supervisor's responsibilities and requirements.
- Trainee's responsibilities.
- Potential supplemental requirements (e.g., reading material or assignments, personal therapy if necessary, assessment for medical problems, substance use, or mental health concerns).
- Confidentiality policies.
- Documentation of supervision (hours, type, and content).
- Financial policies.
- Risks and benefits.
- Evaluation (criteria and process).
- Complaint procedures and due process.
- Professional development goals.

- Endorsement (verification of hours; conditions for informing others of concerns).
- Duration and termination of the supervisory contract.

Thomas emphasizes, as do others, that including as much as possible in the contract prevents conflict later on in the supervisory process.

Documentation of Therapy Sessions

At a minimum, the supervision contract for entry-level trainees must require access to raw data. This may be through live observation through a one-way mirror, in-room observation, or audio or video recordings, and, in some places, client charts. The contract must also require comprehensive progress notes by trainees of their sessions and by supervisors of the supervisory sessions. Supervisors should be especially motivated to describe supervisory or clinical events that involve safety issues (that of the clients, therapist, others, institution, or community). Such notes describe the event, the basis for decisions (see Chapter 12 for our ideas about ethical decision-making procedures), what was done or not done and why, and why the remedial steps could stop (that is, the basis on which it will be decided that the problem situation ceases to exist).

The Form of the Supervision

It has been customary for accreditation or regulatory bodies to specify the kinds and amount of supervision required for an accredited degree or license to practice therapy independent of supervision (see, for example, Sturkie & Paff-Bergen, 2000). Such matters are susceptible to change. However, supervisors and their institutions are held liable for alleged errors of their trainees. Therefore, there needs to be some means for supervisors to see what their trainees are doing first-hand. Live supervision is the most logical means, but it often is not practical. Therefore, trainees must be informed and then strictly required to abide by the supervisors' requirements for access to therapy data. Trainees should be instructed that not abiding by these rules is grounds for terminating the supervisory relationship.

Information should also be provided to trainees about how the supervisor intends to use data: what the supervisor will be looking for in case notes and what kind of feedback to expect, how the supervisor will supervise with a recording, or what will happen in a live observation in the room, behind a one-way mirror, or viewed through closed-circuit technology. Information about live observation should include circumstances for calls in to the therapy room or requests for the therapist to leave the therapy room for consultation. Much of this is formed as part of the supervisor's personal philosophy of supervision, and some may be dictated by the training setting.

Fundamental Processes of Supervision

Supervision flows easily and incurs the fewest difficulties when the supervisor follows a systematic process. This typically includes an interview to determine trainees' goals for supervision, their preferred approaches to therapy, and whether there is likely a good enough fit between the trainee and the supervisor for supervision to move smoothly toward the ultimate determined goal.

Supervision follows good-enough education, which may be introductory in terms of system concepts, CFT principles, and basic interviewing skills. Supervision is the training arm of the applied family science process. Trainees first learn about families and relational dynamics, and then supervisors coach them in the effective use of these data. If trainees do not come to supervisors with the necessary knowledge base, supervisors must supply this or require further education on the part of the trainee. Public agency supervisors often find themselves in this situation when human resource personnel recruit newly graduated holders of bachelor degrees, generic counselors, and therapists other than graduates of CFT graduate training programs.

In the Basic Family Therapy Skills project (e.g., Figley & Nelson, 1989, 1990; Nelson & Figley, 1990; Nelson, Heilbrun, & Figley, 1993; Nelson & Johnson, 1999), Nelson and her colleagues identified five domains of goals and activity, based in part on Tomm and Wright's earlier (1979) work. These domains include conceptual, perceptual, executive, evaluative, and professional skills. The trainee begins with a knowledge base that includes basic concepts (e.g., triangles, reciprocity, hierarchy), gathers data through interviewing and watching client families, and then uses those concepts and perceptions to craft interventions in the therapy room. Leading trainees through this process in a systematic way assists their learning in all areas.

Cultivation of professional skills is woven throughout the whole of supervision. Even so, the next logical step with beginning trainees is to evaluate predetermined goals and criteria for therapist skills and therapy outcomes. In this regard the American Association for Marriage and Family Therapy (AAMFT) Core Competencies (AAMFT, 2004; Nelson et al., 2007; Appendix B) are useful and, in many settings, required. They offer reasonable and logical goals with regard to the process of clinical work with clients: admission to treatment, assessing client systems, determining treatment plans, and so on. The Core Competencies offer supervisors a common-sense and systematic process for conducting supervision and its evaluation. Northey and Gehart (2019) condensed the Core Competencies into fewer items, which may be more useful for some supervisors and trainees.

Virtually all prospective supervisors have an understanding of the most favorable ways of proceeding (Anderson, Schlossberg, & Rigazio-DiGilio, 2000; Hicken, 2008; Hildebrandt, 2009). All prospective supervisors have at one time been consumers of supervision and they have their own ideas about their roles based on those experiences (Anderson et al., 2000). They know what they have experienced as helpful, indifferent, and off-putting. Some of these memories involve their supervisors' personalities, social sophistication, attitudes about power and authority, theoretical and other biases, pedagogical ways and means, and work habits. Prospective supervisors have found the recognition and processing of these insights to be very valuable when thinking about the process of supervision and their part in it. Recognizing what they already know about supervision makes them less anxious, gives them a sense of direction, and is a first step toward identifying the self of the supervisor.

Supervisors of beginning students typically find that trainees begin with anxiety about therapy and, although dependent on their supervisors, are very sensitive to what they perceive to be evaluative comments. Indeed, although they may ask, "Did I do this okay?," their underlying question has to do with their supervisors' opinions of their capacities to become therapists. If all goes well, the training team over time will see increasingly appropriate therapist autonomy. Since autonomous practice is the training system's overarching goal, it will need to recognize and address where this does not happen. However, the training system must be alert to premature independence. This typically happens when supervisors have too many trainees and other responsibilities, their institutions take on new clinical tasks, trainees' personalities intervene, or supervisors are too eager for their trainees to do well.

It may prove useful to recognize that both supervision and therapy are created social systems and therefore many of the same beneficial dynamics may be found in both:

1. There is a solid working alliance with mutual goals and a facilitating relationship. Supervisors' priorities in any situation, except client emergencies, is their relationship with their respective trainees and the goals on which they are working.
2. Focus on process rather than content.
3. Focus on developmental growth of the trainee.
4. Recognition of systemic training in all parts of the training system.
5. Systems-based conceptualization of and communication about data, interventions, and outcomes are a primary shared goal.
6. There is sensitivity to and acceptance of multiple realities.
7. Both are settings that are light on advice, but characterized by an exciting climate of discovery, social relatedness, and the inclination of all to actively listen and appreciate others—unless the process bogs down. Then, direction may help folks get unstuck.
8. Group and relationship processing are continuous so that all participants can stay in the room cognitively, emotionally, and behaviorally.
9. Supervisors and trainees are always able to relate interventions to the issues at hand; for example, "I am asking about our relationship because, if we are not working as a well-oiled team, it will affect your work with your clients."
10. Good interviewing technique is continually stressed and cultivated.
11. The participants engage in mutual and effective goal setting.
12. The members assume appropriate responsibility for affects, beliefs, actions, and change—but also continually look for reciprocities and recursion.
13. Both groups have appropriate boundaries such that they are able to obtain and use consultation from the larger training system in which they are embedded.

Therapy and supervision differ in that the former is primarily concerned with ascertaining systemic dysfunctions and remedying them, instead of being preoccupied with professional growth. Supervisors, of course, have an eye out for areas about which trainees need to be concerned, but their focus and goals are typically more directed toward cultivating clinical resources for the trainee.

Indeed, supervisory relationships ideally result in collegiality (Nichols & Everett, 1986), which is not a goal of therapy.

The theoretical construct of *isomorphism* is an important training system dynamic. Isomorphism sometimes is mistakenly characterized as parallel processes throughout the training subsystems, while others reduce it to social modeling (see discussions by White & Russell, 1997 and Koltz, Odegard, Feit, Provost, & Smith, 2012). At the very least, it maintains that supervisory process dynamics overlay therapy in terms of patterned dynamics. Therefore, if supervision uses a directive pattern with trainees, trainees are likely to be directive with their clients. If supervisors practice active listening and do not ask clarifying questions, therapy dynamics are likely the same. Trainees of supervisors who are not systemic in their observations, explanations, and interventions are themselves likely to grow more "individual" with their clients. When supervision is dominated by supervisors' needs to be successful with their trainees, trainees' therapy sessions will be dominated by their need to "make a difference" with their clients. If the client system is marked by anxiety or chaos, this pattern may be repeated in therapy and/or supervision. And so on. Isomorphism can even be extended to the accreditation process. For example, both of us have done CFT training program site visits for the Commission on Accreditation for Marriage and Family Therapy Education, an arm of the American Association for Marriage and Family Therapy. We have found many situations wherein the CFT training centers were not doing substantial family or couple therapy. They were admitting, diagnosing, and intervening mostly with individuals and not always from a systemic perspective. When this was brought to the supervisors' attention, the following years saw individual sessions diminish in frequency compared to couple and family sessions. Further, sessions with individuals became more systemic, taking into account other family members and aspects of clients' contexts.

A Minimalist Way to Begin Cases

In the best of all training worlds, initial cases should be those that promise the least amount of challenge and the highest probability of success. Here are two scenarios used by the authors, each based on the trainee's therapy approach:

1 The trainee begins with the question, "Why are you here?" The trainee then practices active listening. In this and future sessions, to the extent that poor social skills pose a barrier to productive interaction, the trainee intervenes. Clients then identify the behavior as a problem needing attention, work it out, and move on. Later, to the extent that having listened, clients have not heard, or having heard, but do not take action, an appropriate CFT approach is employed to address the situation.
2 The trainee begins with the question, "Why are you here?" The trainee then practices active listening. After an appropriate period of time, the trainee introduces an elementary solution-focused sequence of questions (De Jong & Berg, 2013) such as, "What's been better since you called for an appointment?" "When things are going well, what are you (all) doing?" "What is going on that you want to keep?" "When all is resolved, what difference will

that make to you and others?" "How will you know that this session was worth your time?"

Direction for any scenario that occurs after the opening question is best determined by connection to an articulated approach to therapy. Beginning therapy with "fly by the seat of the pants" practices seldom results in effective and efficient training for therapists. In fact, in the second author's training program, beginning therapists were given only three directives for their first ever sessions with clients: 1. Show up. 2. Ask at least one question. 3. Don't throw up. With live supervision, beginning therapists can have some confidence that they will get through the first session alive, without having harmed their clients, and not embarrassing themselves.

Beginnings go best when agreed upon between the supervisor and trainee. Questions such as, "How do you like to start therapy? What are your goals for your first interviews with clients?" will likely result in better supervision than when supervisors direct therapy from the onset of a case.

Exercises

1 Do you agree with our definitions and differences among education, training, and experience? How do your ideas differ?
2 Beyond the ideas we present as foundational to CFT, what others can you think of that you want to include in supervision?
3 Which system concepts are most important in your therapy and supervision work? How will you help trainees develop a sense of system thinking?
4 What issues do you think are essential for good supervision contracts? How do you plan to develop and deliver those contracts? What are some consequences, should trainees breach points in the contract?
5 What other elements can you think of as essential for supervision to get off to a good start?

4 Screening, Contracts, Core Competencies, Evaluation, and Feedback-Centered Supervision

Starting at the beginning is the best place to start—most of the time. However, when learning a new skill (such as supervision) or teaching competency (such as performing CFT), it often is wise to start at the end: What will a successful accomplishment look like? How will we know we have succeeded? Then, how will we know that we are on the right track? In therapy, we have ideas about what success looks like. It is tied to some goal for change that will be obvious in some way. The same is true in supervision; although change typically is not related to dysfunction or unhappiness, the goal is change in the therapist from neophyte to increasingly competent therapist. Therefore, much of this chapter is related to the goals that were discussed in Chapter 2.

Goals in supervision include both long term (e.g., help the trainee become a competent therapist and an ethical professional) and short term (e.g., create a safe space for exploring potentially difficult topics; help the trainee develop basic interviewing skills; cultivate a systemic epistemology). Some are general across all or most relational therapies; others are unique to a particular trainee, supervisor, training setting, or therapy approach. Therefore, it is important that readers revisit this chapter after developing and articulating a personal philosophy of supervision that includes clear roles and goals. Those roles and goals will guide the development of screening and evaluating devices and procedures. In addition, as you evaluate trainee competence and the process of supervision, your goals and evaluating ideas are likely to change recursively.

Screening

A relational therapy supervisor is wise to evaluate trainees' skills, competencies, and potential at the beginning of the supervision experience. The purpose here is to (a) determine whether a supervisory relationship is appropriate and (b) determine what skills and competencies may require further development, in what order, and in what ways. Screening should also include some determination of "fit" between the supervisor and trainee in terms of philosophical approach to therapy, desired goals, working style, and personal sense of fit. If that is missing, it is typically a good idea for the supervisor to help the trainee find a different supervisor. If that is not possible, the trainee and supervisor should have careful conversations about how to proceed so as to benefit everyone, including clients and the rest of the training system, as much as possible.

DOI: 10.4324/9781003099833-5

Screening may use the same instruments, devices, and processes that are useful in evaluating progress. Pre- and post-test evaluations provide both information about what learning is required and documentation that can be used to guide the supervision. This documentation can also be used to demonstrate progress, justify remediation, and—where necessary—to terminate the supervisory relationship (see Chapter 14).

Philosophy

In addition to screening or evaluating new trainees for competence in critical areas, it is important that supervisors and trainees talk about their philosophies of therapy and of supervision. Some supervisors wish to supervise trainees who are learning only specific approaches to therapy. For the most part, supervision according to these therapeutic models is consistent with the concepts and methods specifically involved in the therapy they do. Some of the models currently most prominent in training programs are Emotionally Focused Therapy (Johnson, 2019), Brief Strategic Family Therapy (Szapocznik & Hervis, 2020), Transgenerational Therapy (e.g., Boszormenyi-Nagy & Spark, 1973; Bowen, 1978, 1985), Solution-focused Brief Therapy (e.g., de Shazer et al., 2007; Nelson, 2019), and Integrative Systemic Therapy (Pinsof et al., 2018). There certainly are others.

In these instances, both the supervisor and the trainee need to know at the onset whether the model is an appropriate fit for them. Supervisors who are able and willing to help trainees learn a singular or an integrated approach must similarly understand the trainees' goals in order that supervisors may determine trainees' ability to work within supervision. For example, a supervisor may be comfortable supervising solution-oriented therapies but not intergenerational therapy. The trainee may wish to focus a great deal on his or her own family of origin dynamics and self-of-the-therapist factors. Is the supervisor able and willing to help the trainee do this?

The supervisor and trainee must also determine the extent to which there is a fit between them with regard to supervision philosophy in general. Although developmental perspectives suggest that new trainees benefit from teaching and hierarchical relationships (see previous chapters), the overall philosophy of the supervisor is important. Trainees who wish for generally collaborative relationships with their supervisors are not likely to do well with a generally hierarchical/directive supervisor and vice versa. Selicoff (2006) called for supervisors to examine the fit between collaborative and hierarchical supervisory styles and, from a postmodern perspective, encouraged supervisors to embrace a both/and rather than either/or approach to this aspect of their supervisory roles.

General Fit with Relational Therapy

This may seem obvious, but we have learned that, try as we might, we are not always able to determine in a screening process whether a prospective trainee is suited for individual therapy or for relational therapy, or for work with us. Screening for this kind of potential or competence is likely more subjective than many of the competencies listed in the American Association for Marriage and Family Therapy's Core

Competencies (AAMFT, 2004; Nelson et al., 2007; Appendix B; discussed below) or elsewhere. For this purpose, the supervisor must use his or her own subjective sense about the person's potential as a relational therapist. We caution supervisors, however, to not be too quick to judge someone based on first impressions or personality fit. Many supervisors have had experiences where they were not successful at helping particular trainees develop important skills but other supervisors were able to do so.

Values

It is important for trainees and supervisors to be able to accept, if not share, each other's values. There may be certain areas, however, that preclude a particular supervisory relationship. Such areas may include values around reproduction or reproductive rights, sexuality and sexual expression, and even the rights of a person to determine his or her own future. Heartfelt discussions about such areas are beneficial to both trainees and supervisors, and should include scrutiny of codes of ethics as well as literature (e.g., Caldwell, 2011). However, outright clashes could lead to situations in which trainees begin withholding information from supervisors or supervisors become too judgmental for constructive progress to occur. Curiosity and discussion about values and how they develop tend to work better than confrontation.

Pragmatics

Again, this may seem obvious, but screening conversations should include talk about the pragmatics of supervision and whether the trainee and supervisor agree on them. Clear expectations for supervision fees, schedules for meeting, the format for supervision, setting goals, evaluating the supervision as well as the trainee's progress, and procedures for emergencies will help trainees and supervisors determine the extent to which there is sufficient agreement for them to proceed with supervisory relationships. Within this part of the process, the expectations and requirements of the training setting, whether a graduate program, agency, or licensure requirements, must be clear and agreed to, as well as understandings about modalities for supervision (see Chapter 5), and what statements about supervision and confidentiality will be included in clients' informed consent to treatment document.

Contracts

We discussed specifics about supervisory contracts in detail in Chapter 3 of this text. However, at this point—screening—it is useful to have goals, procedures, and pragmatics of supervision in written form. This helps trainees and supervisors determine whether a supervisory relationship is appropriate for them as well as to provide documentation to which to refer for evaluation or repair purposes. It is very different to have a conversation that starts with, "We agreed to weekly meetings ..." than to get frustrated and even angry about no schedule, emergencies that could have been avoided with regular supervision, or insufficient supervision overall. The contract also can specify the criteria for changing the contract or ending the supervisory relationship, whether that is based upon time (e.g., a semester, a year), when the trainee has mastered certain competencies or mastered them to a stated level, or even in the circumstance of unacceptable evaluations. Regardless of details, clarity about these matters can go a long way to helping determine whether a supervisor–trainee relationship is likely to be appropriate for both.

Core Competencies

A major goal of relational therapy supervision is the development of a competent therapist. The AAMFT supported the development of a list of marriage and family therapy Core Competencies (CC; AAMFT, 2004; Nelson et al., 2007; Appendix B) to guide trainees and supervisors toward a goal of "competent therapist." This list was designed to describe a therapist who is ready to do therapy independent of supervision, typically at the time of licensure, which often is about two years after master's-level graduation. Many have expressed concern that it is not possible for students and seem to forget that the CCs were not designed to be mastered in graduate school.

Northey and Gehart (2019) have provided a condensed list of Core Competencies. It is based on the original list but, because there are fewer items, educators and researchers may find it easier to use in setting goals and evaluating trainee progress.

The fact is, most of the items on the list may only be introduced during graduate training; the remainder are the focus of postgraduate supervision and training. The CCs are divided into six domains (Admission to Treatment; Clinical Assessment and Diagnosis; Treatment Planning and Case Management; Therapeutic Interventions; Legal Issues, Ethics, and Standards; and Research and Program Evaluation). These domains, which begin with a logical approach to treatment and also include contextual factors or diversity factors, are further divided into subdomains: Conceptual, Perceptual, Executive, Evaluative, and Professional Skills (see Nelson & Johnson, 1999). Although the Core Competencies comprise a daunting list of 126 items, most relational therapists and supervisors who spend a few minutes with the list can easily see the logic of the domains, subdomains, and items, and easily can evaluate themselves on many items. They then begin to see patterns: areas of competence and areas ("growing edges") that may need focus for improvement. These patterns subsequently can be used to guide the course of supervision. Areas of competence can be used to enhance learning in other areas.

Supervisors may use the list itself as a guide for screening therapy trainees into supervision. Many use a simple Likert-type scale to ask potential trainees to rate themselves on each item or a selection of items that the supervisor believes are critical for this purpose. A conversation may ensue that includes the trainees' ideas about details that merit a particular score. Supervisors may devise questions to help them ferret out information that also will help them rate a current or potential trainee. This approach may result in an overall sense of the trainee's competence in critical areas (perhaps graphically presented as a profile) and used to help determine direction. This assessment also may illuminate the suitability of a match between a particular trainee and supervisor. For situations where the supervisor has grave concerns, such documented information can be used in conversation with others in the training context (trainees themselves, other supervisors, faculty, and/or administrators) to determine courses of action. At heart, however, the CC screening should help determine a supervision plan for the development of specific competencies or areas of competence.

Some supervisors may not wish to use the entire list of Core Competencies or even Northey and Gehart's (2019) items to guide their screening or supervision. In those instances, we encourage supervisors to use other, more suited lists for their situations or to develop their own. We believe that such lists minimally should include trainees' knowledge in critical areas such as system thinking and concepts for particular approaches to therapy, psychopathology, basic understanding of ethics and appropriate laws, training program requirements, and agency policies.

Evaluation

Many of us have found ourselves in situations where we knew we were being evaluated or evaluating someone else without specific knowledge about either the criteria for evaluating or the process involved. We believe that this is both unfair and potentially crazy making in the context of relational therapy supervision. It is unfair because, regardless of how collaborative a supervisor may believe himself or herself to be, there is an important hierarchical nature to supervision. Supervisors have power over trainees in terms of their careers and day-to-day lives. They also have responsibilities to the clients of their trainees as well as to the training context and larger communities. In addition, they have obligations to their states or provinces and to their professions. Lack of clarity about this can put a trainee in a bind that could be confusing unless the evaluative process can be talked about explicitly.

It would be nice if we were able to write extensively about evaluation instruments for assessing therapists' competence. What was said about screening tools applies here and the same instruments can be used. We provide some discussion below. However, as Perosa and Perosa (2010) observed, we fall short as a field and need to develop more and better instruments and processes that are valid and reliable for determining therapists' competence. In our experience, some of what is discussed below has been helpful to supervisors and others evaluating trainees. However, most supervisors are likely to develop their own devices and methods that suit their unique situations, perhaps by modifying one of the instruments described above and to follow. Such devices should reflect goals for trainees that are observable, specific, concrete, measurable, and realistic (see Nelson, 2019, for more discussion of well-formed client goals that may be useful for trainee or supervision goals).

Formative Evaluation

Formative evaluation occurs "along the way" during the development of trainees' skills and professional identities. That is, at some intervals—regular or irregular—the supervisor helps the trainee evaluate progress since the beginning of their supervisory relationship and/or since the most recent evaluation. These evaluations help supervision by offering flexible baselines or touching points for revising a supervision plan. Areas that are well developed may fade into the background, and new areas may present themselves as opportunities for focus. We believe that this best occurs in a developmental context so that trainees are not measuring themselves against "master" therapists (whatever that means) but against themselves in their own progress, or against therapists at similar developmental levels. Formative evaluation is also done in the context of marking and documenting milestones in training (Miller, 2010). This serves to both inform the process of supervision and celebrate the demonstration of competence.

Formative evaluation can take place in an ongoing way as supervisors listen to trainees report on cases, observe or listen to therapy recordings, and observe therapy as it occurs. Indeed, we believe that one of the main purposes of supervision is for this kind of evaluation to occur in a thoughtful way during all of supervision. We believe that supervision progress notes help supervisors to be more aware of their evaluations. Such notes not only facilitate discussions with trainees and record interventions or topics of discussion, but also inform their observations of themselves as supervisors. Schur (2002) wrote about a particular way for supervisors to think about their decisions, even in the moment, and to reflect upon their own processes and ways of reaching decisions about what they do in supervision. This suggests to us that it is useful for supervisors to be aware of their personal thoughts and feelings as they evaluate trainees' therapy behaviors, and their own subsequent decisions and actions. This kind of recursive process can serve to help supervisors keep trainees' developmental stages, prior demonstrated skills, and present skills and difficulties in mind as influential aspects of supervision, and take corrective action where needed.

Miller and colleagues (Miller, 2010; Miller, Linville, Todahl, & Metcalfe, 2009) discussed the use of Objective Structured Clinical Exercises (OSCE) to help trainees demonstrate and supervisors evaluate progress outside actual client contexts. Role plays are set up that specify particular competencies that are to be demonstrated, during which supervisors observe the trainee practicing that competency or skill. These observational evaluations can be scored or commented upon using rubrics (e. g., Gehart, 2017) and serve many purposes including documentation of competence and/or progress; ideas for areas of focus for the next part of supervision; progress reports for subsequent supervisors, graduate programs, or administrators; and areas for discussion between supervisors and trainees. Family therapy educators at the University of Rochester (Le Roux, Podgorski, Rosenberg, Watson, & McDaniel, 2011) developed their own OSCE (the Rochester OSCE) to evaluate trainees in developmentally appropriate ways. Using the OSCE way of evaluating competence may be less likely for supervisors and trainees in postgraduate settings, since the process calls for actors as clients. This suggests to us that live, video, and/or audio data are most important for evaluating trainee competence.

Sparks and her colleagues (Sparks, Kisler, Adams, & Blumen, 2011) use the Outcome Rating Scale (ORS; Miller, Duncan, Brown, Sparks, & Claud, 2003) and other brief devices in a process called Outcome Management (OM). Using OM provides a unique way for trainees to learn from their clients, who fill out appropriate instruments to provide the feedback.

In addition to evaluating trainees' progress and therapy behaviors in the context of specific therapy or role-play situations, paper-and-pencil instruments can be used to evaluate trainees at different stages of their development of skills. One way to use the AAMFT Core Competencies or Northey and Gehart's (2019) condensed version is to attach a Likert scale to each competency. For example, Gehart (2017) has written an entire text based on the Core Competencies, with each chapter focusing on a different set of skills. The chapters include ways that trainees can be evaluated using the Core Competencies list.

Nelson and Johnson (1999) used the basic family therapy skills research of Nelson and Figley (Figley & Nelson, 1989, 1990; Nelson & Figley, 1990; Nelson, Heilbrun, & Figley, 1993), which focused on beginning family therapy students, to develop the Basic Skills Evaluation Device (BSED). The device condenses basic family therapy skills into conceptual (knowledge based), perceptual (connecting knowledge with observed behaviors), executive (what is done by the therapist in therapy), evaluative (evaluating both the therapy and oneself as a therapist), and professional (supervision, ethics, working with ancillary professionals) skills. Each area has substantial specificity within it, yet is much shorter than the complete list of either basic skills (e.g., Figley & Nelson, 1989) or the Core Competencies.

Using the BSED or a similar tool of their own devising, supervisors and trainees can capture competence in broad areas rather than specific skills or items. Details can be added in comments sections. Readers of this text are encouraged to both search for and experiment with various ways of evaluating trainees as they progress, and evaluate these different ways for the best fit with their own work.

For example, one of us (Lee) has advanced trainees specify goals for their predetermined course of supervision. These goals are prioritized and each is carefully defined in terms of observable behaviors. The goals are written on a worksheet in rank order, with a 10-point scale alongside each. The trainees then place a mark on that scale where they perceive themselves at the time. In follow-up discussions, they are asked what progress on one such trait might look like and what will tell them they are making progress. At the end of the course of supervision, they evaluate themselves again and discuss the ramifications of their evaluation (e.g., "Good enough," "Needs more work," etc.).

Summative Evaluation

As Lee's example indicates, all of the formative ways of evaluating trainee progress can be used as summative evaluations as well. Summative evaluations tend to be more formal, providing documentation for determining the level of success of the trainee at the end of a predetermined supervisory process. This might be at the end of a semester or training period in an agency, at the end of a graduate program, or as a way of evaluating a trainee's suitability for licensure or independent therapy practice. In these cases, it is even more important that the evaluation include a paper trail. However, it might also include recommendations for further training or amelioration of difficulties that might be present. These recommendations might be used by the same supervisory system. They also might be used by further supervisors or training contexts.

Evaluation of Supervision

Along with a responsibility to use appropriate trainee evaluation procedures, we believe it is important for supervisors to develop procedures that trainees can use to evaluate supervision. In addition to researching and possibly using forms and procedures that have been developed for evaluating supervision, we believe that the best evaluations are developed at the beginning of supervision and are based on criteria that supervisors and trainees have agreed on. These criteria should be related to the goals set forth for supervision, and they and the methods for evaluating progress toward these goals should be established in the written supervisory contract. Williams (1994) has developed a Supervision Feedback Form that allows trainees to evaluate their experience in supervision and its helpfulness on various factors. Information from this form may help supervisors fine-tune their supervision for particular trainees, particular practices, or overall.

Supervisors need explicit ways to evaluate their supervision so that they can improve their supervisory skills and be more helpful to trainees. Progress and helpful supervision with one trainee might not be as helpful to a different trainee. The only way a supervisor can know that is if the trainee has a way of explaining it and feels safe to do so. Trainees can be very helpful in this process, giving both formative and summative feedback to supervisors about the content and process of their supervision. In this way, the supervisory system can make course corrections to the benefit of all involved by providing information for revising goals for supervision as well as establishing new ones.

Trainees who have moved through various stages of clinical training and supervision need to have developmental changes that occur with experience acknowledged. Feedback about their experiences can help supervisors alter their supervision styles considerably to be more in sync with their trainees' competence level, developmental stage, and learning needs.

Feedback-Centered Supervision

Feedback from the training system has sharply increased in the past 15 years. Informal data gathering of process observations and wishes from clients and their therapists has become popular. Since interest in common therapeutic factors and, especially, the therapeutic alliance, has also been prominent in this era, there has been a modest climate change, namely, behavioral health educators and trainers are now privileging the voices of the consumers alongside those of theoretical model builders.

For the sake of clarity, consumer feedback can be classified either as (a) client scores on formal omnibus inventories focused on presenting problems, designated by formal classification systems or client statements, or (b) replies to somewhat informal and brief surveys and open-ended queries intended to encourage recursive dialogues ("checking in") within the training system. The nature of the consultation can privilege the concerns of supervisors, therapists, and/or client units. These allow the training team to consult with a client before, during, or after a session, or any other time in the course of treatment.

Systematic and Standardized Feedback Systems

Carefully crafted and standardized client self-reporting systems have been developed to routinely and consistently track the goals, facilitators, and barriers of the training system. Such systems characteristically include the components of the therapeutic alliance with the AAMFT Core Competencies. Two exemplars of what are commonly termed "systematic client feedback systems" are described below: The Partners for Change Outcome Management System and the Systemic Therapy Inventory of Change.

The Partners for Change Outcome Management System (PFCOMS)

The PFCOMS is the latest iteration of an ongoing, evolving, systematic, and integrated program of scholarship (Duncan, Miller, & Sparks, 2004; Sparks et al., 2011; Sparks & Duncan, 2018). From the beginning, its goal has been to develop

> a valid, feasible option for alerting clinicians to not-on-track clients, allowing time to respond to prevent treatment failure. A hallmark of the system has been its valuing of client voice and related collaborative interpretation and integration of scores into ongoing therapeutic conversations.
>
> (Sparks & Duncan, 2018, p. 800)

It has been used extensively with couples and families. It employs statistically robust measures of client change that are in keeping with the AAMFT Core Competencies in order to continually monitor client progress throughout treatment (Sparks et al., 2011). In fact, review of the instruments is an integral part of live supervision sessions. Normative data allows the training system to recognize when the therapy is not on track and when there is risk of client drop-out. A recent meta-analysis of 18 process and outcome studies using the PFCOMS (Ostergard, Randa, & Hougaard, 2020) indicated that its overall impact has been mildly beneficial. However, their meta-analysis process has been criticized (Duncan & Sparks, 2019). Therefore, further assessment of the PFCOMS' efficacy may be needed.

The Systemic Therapy Inventory of Change (STIC)

The Systemic Therapy Inventory of Change, or STIC (Pinsof et al., 2018), has been described by its developers as "the first tool to assess change across multiple relationships and multiple domains of functioning, so it can be used in individual, couple, and family therapy" (Zinbarg & Goldsmith, 2017, p. 2). It originally was expected to be a valuable research tool. However, its developers also discovered that it could be used for goal setting and quality control as a supervisory tool. It is important to note that the STIC did not inquire into the therapeutic alliance or seek responses from the therapists. Instead it focused on the strengths and vulnerabilities existing in the relationships of the clients within their family units.

What began as an omnibus paper-and-pencil questionnaire evolved over time into a sophisticated web-based questionnaire and reporting system. In practice, supervisees were expected to have their clients complete the STIC surveying between sessions and then to bring the results to their supervision sessions. These results were used to inform the supervisees' initial assessments, case formulations, and treatment planning. The data would also help them monitor their clients' progress, and aid in termination.

It was expected that clients who completed the STIC measure and whose therapists received feedback about how they were progressing in therapy would have more optimal outcomes than clients who received therapy without completing the STIC measure and whose therapists did not receive feedback. This information would allow therapists to make changes in the therapy so that it would be more beneficial. This hypothesis was tested in a randomized clinical trial (reported by Zinbarg & Goldsmith, 2017) and achieved modest but statistically significant support. With regard to the therapists (see McComb, Diamond, Breunlin, Chambers, & Murray, 2018), those trainees who were least experienced appreciated the STIC because of the structure it provided them. The more experienced the therapists were, however, the less useful they considered it.

"Checking In"

An example of less elaborate "checking in" with clients is the Client Feedback Note (CFN; Haber, Carlson, & Braga, 2014). After each session, clients are asked to consider four questions addressing feelings, learning, problems, and wishes: *What are my feelings about the session? What did I learn? What did I not like? What do I wish would have happened?* Of course, when the training format is live supervision, supervisors also can enter the session and check in with the clients on behalf of their therapists (Dwyer, 1999).

Generally Speaking …

With regard to the larger client feedback mechanisms, it is good to consider that a specific training system's goals may be diverse depending on the setting in which they are situated and what the trainees basically want to achieve (Jensen Oanes, Karlsson,

& Borg, 2015; Tilden et al., 2021). Professional colleagues as well as the trainee body may differ in the extent to which they prioritize these tools and this is directly associated with the consistency of their application (McComb et al., 2018). Entry-level trainees have positive attitudes toward omnibus inventories because the information helps them conceptualize their cases and develop treatment plans. However, these inventories seem to become increasingly less popular as a function of supervisees' professional experience. More experienced trainees want to invest their supervisory time in matters of personal professional growth (e.g., Stoltenberg & McNeill, 2010; Tilden et al., 2021). Consequently, their cooperation in the use of sophisticated client-centered tools, for example, the STIC, typically drops off over time. It remains to be determined if briefer psychometric client feedback devices that are process-specific, for example, targeted to ongoing assessment of the therapeutic alliance and motivation for change, and empirically found to be associated with positive therapeutic outcomes (see Owen, 2012; Whipple et al., 2003) will find more favor in a wider range of training systems than do the omnibus systems (PFCOMS, STIC). One concern that has been voiced by a majority of the supervisees who employed them is that the omnibus inventories require too much time and attention to be practical with group supervision formats (Stoltenberg & McNeill, 2010).

In summary, the professional literature suggests that post-session surveys are more likely to be consistently used if they are user friendly, to wit, they are brief and otherwise easy to complete, targeted to your supervisees' interests, and enjoy both face and empirical validity with regard to outcomes. In fact, Sapyta, Riemer, and Bickman, (2005) compared the efficacies of the many ways of obtaining feedback from clients for therapists and found that the most useful contain new information, the source of the feedback has credibility, and the feedback is timely with regard to the case at hand. Moreover, the feedback is positive rather than negative—although accuracy trumps valence—and addresses the therapists' actual behaviors.

The reader will find that the focus of the feedback-guided supervision methods described above all have to do with what the clientele has to offer—in terms of their own opinions or that of theoretical experts—that would inform the therapy and keep it on its desired course. The authors believe it is reasonable to extend this guidance to the supervisory relationship. In fact, they believe that the factors inquired into with regard to the clients also are central to their therapists and to their supervisors—be they specific to major models, common therapeutic factors, or compilations of desired outcomes. In the current technological parlance, *system feedback* should be a central heading on the dashboard of every member of the training system. It also is reasonable to assume that, if something occurs at one level, it will permeate the training system and eventually establish itself throughout as all parties adapt to/incorporate it.

Concluding Thoughts

So, we began at the end and now we end at the beginning: The recursive relationship among goals, formative evaluation, and summative evaluation is systemic in nature and therefore isomorphic between therapy and supervision, and between supervision and other parts of the training system. We encourage readers to be flexible in their supervisory processes and thereby to accommodate the inevitable changes that occur as trainees (and supervisors) develop.

Exercises

1. What are some important factors for you for screening trainees? What criteria might you use for deciding to accept or not accept someone as a trainee? How will you work with trainees that you are assigned with no choice, yet have some concerns about as therapists?
2. Look at the Core Competencies and choose just one domain and subdomain. How do you think you might assess a new trainee for competence in that area?
3. What things will you look for to determine whether there is a good fit between you and your trainee philosophically?
4. What values do you think you might have that will clash with your trainees? How will you work in those situations?
5. Based on this chapter, what are some things you will include in your supervision contracts concerning evaluation, both formative and summative?
6. What are some things you would like your supervisees to tell you—and evaluate—about your supervision? In what ways might that be expected to be helpful across the entire training system (that is, influential to you, the supervisee, the clients, and the diverse contexts in which you all are situated)?

Part 2

Relational Supervision Practices

An Overview

DOI: 10.4324/9781003099833-6

5 A Closer Look at Supervision Formats

Supervision may take place in an educational clinic, agency setting, or private office. It may take place in a room, over a telephone, or using the Internet. It may be a written interchange (real-time messaging or email). It also might be a face-to-face interchange in the same location or at a distance. Each of these formats has its own logistical, ethical, administrative, and legal concerns. These will be explored below. However, fundamentally, they all are manifestations of two formats: dyadic and group supervision, and two methods: namely, live supervision versus retrospective consideration of recorded live data or case presentations.

Individual and Group Approaches: Advantages and Disadvantages

Dyadic supervision, sitting face-to-face, or watching the trainee with the clients and the supervisor behind a one-way mirror, may seem idyllic. It bespeaks a private, tailor-made, and safe relationship with a personal trainer or coach. Nevertheless, professional CFT's accreditation body defines individual supervision as a supervisor and one or two trainees and group supervision as fewer than eight trainees with a supervisor (Commission on Accreditation for Marriage and Family Therapy (COAMFTE), 2017). Trainees must receive at least one hour of supervision each week they see clients, and at least 50 hours of the 100-hour minimum requirement must use observable data. Just as therapeutic groups offer opportunities for growth that may not be matched by conjoint therapy (e.g., a social laboratory, discovery that one's issues are universal, and so forth; see Yalom, 2005), group supervision is thought to offer different opportunities and challenges than dyadic supervision (Mastoras & Andrews, 2012, and below). Although training contexts limit what can be and is done (Lee, Nichols, Nichols, & Odom, 2004), most would agree with Lee and Everett (2004) that the "gold standard" employs a mixture of dyadic and group supervision, and live and retrospective approaches. The relative strengths and concerns of dyadic and group supervision formats are delineated below.

DOI: 10.4324/9781003099833-7

"Individual" Supervision

Many years ago, some authorities paradoxically declared that "individual" supervision was not necessarily individual (one supervisor and one trainee): it could include two trainees. Since the presence of a second trainee constitutes a small group and presumably changes the dynamics of the supervision process, it seems unwise to discuss "dyadic supervision" if it involves more than one trainee. Having said that, we note that the COAMFTE and many states have defined individual supervision as one supervisor and one or two trainees (COAMFTE, 2017). In this section, we define "dyadic" supervision as one supervisor and one trainee. One-on-one supervision is expected to enhance the experience of live and retrospective supervision in significant ways.

A Personal and Safe Place for Learning

Dyadic supervision maximizes attention on trainees. It is focused solely on the unique training needs of one individual. Time and energy do not need to be distributed among several participants and their respective caseloads. Moreover, trainees may feel safe given the absence of an audience of their peers, and perhaps will feel less inclined to compare themselves to others. Moreover, beginning trainees often complain that they are confused by the multiplicity of perspectives—theories, assessments, and interventions—that can be brought to bear on cases. Dyadic supervision reduces the number of voices in the room and supervisors can focus on the unique training needs and learning styles of each trainee. The relative privacy of dyadic supervision may facilitate more open and profound reflection on evaluative issues, interpersonal dynamics, self-of-the-therapist, and professional issues. Concurrently, supervisors may feel freer to challenge and/or support trainees in this private setting.

A Haven

Some trainees have observed that dyadic supervision is not only a place for learning; it also is a haven in which they can repair (see Holloway, 1995). It can be a quiet and nurturing space in which they may express doubts, vent emotions, gain new insights, and refresh their energies. This kind of safe setting, conducive to quiet reflection, may especially be useful for supervision that will focus on what can be learned from the supervisory relationship.

Some Limiting Aspects

Conversely, the potential benefits offered by dyadic supervision may be accompanied by less desirable features. Dyadic supervision, with its privacy, seems to connote a safe place for learning. However, participants may not experience it that way. Privacy means relationships and power differentials may be experienced as intense, boundaries between personal and professional selves may become blurred, and there are no witnesses. Some trainees may feel less safe in dyadic supervision when they cannot escape or "pass" by letting other trainees garner supervisors' attention and they must be involved. It is more difficult to hide unpleasant feelings. They may feel intimidated or perhaps become overdependent on the supervisor. Indeed, the potential intensity of the supervisory relationship may lead to problematic collusion between partner (Anderson, Schlossberg, & Rigazio-DiGilio, 2000; Nichols & Everett, 1986). For example, particularly anxious and dependent trainees may elicit protective responses from their supervisors. This protection may inhibit professional growth while blurring the boundaries between supervisory and therapeutic relationships.

Supervisors must be extremely sensitive to power differentials and attitudes in relation to gender (Nelson, 1991; Schiavone & Jessell, 1988), sociocultural identification, and evaluation, and be alert to microaggressions (Sue, 2010/2020). Supervisors are advised to cultivate ongoing attention to the working alliance from the first meeting onward. We suggest that supervisors, in their first meetings with trainees, explicitly predict potential issues and mutually consider how they might be handled.

Group Supervision

Group supervision may provide a correction factor for many of the concerns raised about dyadic supervision. It is less private, the intensity of the relationships between supervisors and trainees may be diluted by being spread across several individuals, and group support is available to both trainees and supervisors (Riva & Cornish, 2008; Smith, Riva, & Cornish, 2012). However, group supervision is an important training resource in its own right. In fact, so many benefits may be attributed to the group approach that it is surprising it may be declining in use, especially outside of training centers (Lee et al., 2004).

Economies of Group Approaches

Group supervision is economical, both financially and in terms of individual energies and time. Financially, the hourly fees of privately contracted supervision can be divided among the participating trainees. Where supervisors are employees of agencies, schools, and institutes, they may supervise several individuals at the same time, maximizing agency resources. Supervising individuals in groups makes possible other important economies.

Trainees learn in both direct and indirect ways. Although the focus may be on one individual trainee, non-participants, including those on the periphery of the group, are discovering much that is relevant to them. Ambivalent recruits look on and obtain diverse conceptualizations, didactic explanations and instructions, and role modeling. Concurrently, they can see how atmosphere and safety are explored as group processes. Peripheral members can come to appreciate how a productive consultation process is constructed and may gradually be socialized further into the group.

Individuals who are not the focus of the group can always benefit indirectly. For example, they can be prepared when something occurs in their own professional lives because they have already learned about it through the experiences of other trainees. Exposure to the variety of perspectives in a group also helps in the learning of therapeutic and critical thinking, as well as professional socialization. Equifinality, the systemic notion that there are many ways to accomplish something, becomes very evident in group supervision. The setting allows everyone access to many ideas that may be helpful.

Supervisors as well as trainees appreciate the economies of group approaches. They do not have to do all the teaching, supporting, and auditing because, as noted above, the group members learn directly and indirectly from each other's experiences. Members comment on each others' work and clarify and consolidate what they know by teaching it to others. This is done by answering questions about their own cases and by being consulted by other group members.

Not only does this process build confidence and professional identity in the group members, but supervisors do not have to be expert with regard to all things at all times. Moreover, supervisors discover that they do not have to be the only, or main, sources of support. In constructive groups, the members take care of one another. They consult on cases, listen to concerns, and provide reality checks, humor, and hugs. In this process the participants have the corrective emotional experiences of discovering that their "personal" issues in fact are somewhat universal. They find that they have the same concerns about their professional work, their educational and training experiences, and the often-conflicting demands of their many professional and personal roles.

A Rich Environment for Learning

In addition to the economies afforded by group supervision, group supervision provides richness to training experiences (Bernard & Goodyear, 2009; Holloway, 1995; Proctor, 2000; York, 1997; oral reports of participants in supervision classes and postgraduate supervision and workshops). The foremost aspect of this may be the level of diversity that informs the training processes. Trainees typically are diverse in who they are personally (and perhaps professionally) and often are at different stages of professional development. They each bring many clinical cases, and these cases differ one from another, as do the trainees' ways of conceptualizing and treating them. Too, the members may represent practices in diverse clinical settings. Diversity among group members enhances the learning of all members by providing multiple perspectives on context, therapy approaches, and meanings.

There has long been a debate in the field whether or not supervision groups should be homogenous with regard to the aforementioned factors (e.g., York, 1997). Recognition of multiple realities may render this debate moot. We contend that groups cannot be homogeneous because there always will be differences among group members. Groups offer a mix wherein diverse individuals open themselves and their work to others. This experience provides insight into contextual issues that cannot be obtained from books. The training system is empowered by increasing awareness and acceptance of differences in values, styles, conceptualizations, emotions, and techniques. If group membership includes members at differing professional levels, veterans can be important sources of hope and support for newcomers. Veterans once were anxious beginners, but now they are professionals with confidence; that is, their sense of professional competence is based on social and professional tools and success in realistic treatment and life plans.

A Social Laboratory

Groups are social laboratories in which members experience and are shaped by the group process, learning more about themselves and themselves as therapists. They can learn social and therapeutic skills directly. Members can ask each other about how to do something or even how they come across interpersonally and receive multiple perspectives. They can copy what they see and hear. They can practice therapeutic communication, de-escalation techniques, and systemic interviewing through role play. Groups also are good for demonstrating constructive challenges as well as social support in the face of them. Members can struggle with authority, voice their doubts and fears, test hypotheses and perceptions, and plan strategies.

Groups also are often helpful for trainees who are learning about themselves as therapists and how past experiences impact current therapy. Self-of-the-therapist work often may be done when trainees feel safe with each other, can kindly confront each other, and can explore the myriad potential meanings of family of origin or other experiences and their impact in therapy.

A Haven

Membership in a supervision group is said to have a restorative, refreshing function (Holloway, 1995). Trainees spread thinly by their professional and personal obligations have spoken appreciatively of the social support and professional networking provided by regularly scheduled participation in their supervision groups. They report a sense of common mission, concern, and caring. They say that they emerge from supervision sessions confident and stimulated; they felt heard, were reminded of their strengths, and perhaps were given some new ideas (Lee, Eppler, Kendal, & Latta, 2001).

How Benefits Are Maximized

The key to good group supervision is careful monitoring and maintenance of the group process through which working alliances take form and are audited and maintained. Supervisors do this by obtaining mutual agreement on immediate and long-term goals, the strategies most likely to meet them, and the ways in which the group is a primary and rich resource. While doing this, supervisors model good communication and interviewing skills, and let the group do the work unless a barrier arises. The supervisors then use their executive roles to help the group identify barriers to constructive processes, appreciate them as opportunities, and devise plans to deal with them. Having done this, supervisors move back into their observing/auditing posture. Supervision groups often are very good places for trainees to talk about their preferred therapy styles and approaches and to benefit from listening to other trainees talk about theirs.

The foregoing does not imply that this is *all* that group supervisors do: Like all supervisors, they also have the roles of teachers, consultants, colleagues, and administrators, often with individual trainees in turn as they report on and discuss clinical cases. However, with regard to construction and maintenance of constructive group processes, that is, beneficial milieus for learning, supervisors would do well to review the classic treatise on group therapy (Yalom, 2005) and take advantage of this process, particularly in helping trainees develop professional maturity, as well as focusing on theory, interventions, and evaluation.

Caveats

As with dyadic approaches, there are limitations to group supervision. A primary one is the limited amount of time and detailed continuity that can be given to one case or trainee. Rationing the amount of time available to an individual may be necessary. Some groups focus on different trainees and cases each session. However, there are emergent circumstances—for example, a crisis in a case or with a trainee, or a major problem in the group process—that may override any attempt at equitable parceling of time and energies.

Sometimes a case or an enthusiastic member is allowed to dominate the group. This may be because the members and/or supervisor are tacitly allowing this. For example, focus on one member or one case may facilitate not exposing others. Over time, all members of the group should be able to shoulder both the privilege and responsibility of being focused upon and interacting in the group.

Another concern is the lack of safety found in some groups. Confidentiality may be a continuing risk in some settings. Fellow group members may be experienced as competitive, aggressive, microaggressive, hostile, or perhaps as needy and dependent. Subgroups may form. Trainees may seek consultation from each other or privately from their supervisors to avoid bringing matters up in the group.

The use of group supervision will be most effective to the extent that supervisors and trainees together attend to the atmosphere of the setting and, specifically, the group process. Group supervisors must also attend to many supervisory tasks: developmentally appropriate case consultation; integration of theory, assessment, and technique; increasing emotional awareness, acquisition of self-evaluative skills, and cultivation of social support; social learning; and professional socialization.

Blending Individual and Group Approaches

In some settings, dyadic and group approaches are not mixed. Trainees are in one or the other. The rationale is that, otherwise, trainees would bring concerns from one setting into the other instead of resolving their concerns where they arose. Currently, although settings may limit that which can be offered, educators, trainers, and trainees—given the luxury of doing whatever they wish—are free to think about the optimal proportion of dyadic and group supervision for a cohort of trainees. If trainees are exposed to both approaches, supervisors consider the best ways for the trainees to move back and forth between them. For example, personal issues processed in dyadic supervision may need to be taken into the group setting (with permission) and inform the work there. Similarly, supervisors need to monitor how issues raised in group settings inform what takes place in the dyadic work. If a team of supervisors is working with trainees placed in both forms of supervision, the supervisors need to develop protocols for consultation and feedback so that they share training information responsibly and avoid being triangled or triangling each other and/or trainees.

Live and Retrospective Approaches: Advantages and Disadvantages

Live (or "Direct") Approaches

Civil law precedents, many state statutes, and common sense obligate supervisors to have first-hand knowledge about their trainees' therapy, on the one hand, and the trainees' developing clinical resources, on the other. Supervisors are held liable for the actions of their trainees and the outcome of the trainees' cases. Therefore, they must have knowledge about clients and what is taking place in sessions. Moreover, if they are to be maximally effective, supervisors need to construct their own realities of cases instead of relying solely on trainees' reports. Therapists focus on some things and, for diverse reasons, ignore or minimize others. Therapists and their supervisors differ in how they view themselves, the clients, and interactions and this affects what they see and what they deem important in therapy. Although there is no evidence to date that live supervision provides better therapeutic outcomes than do other forms of supervision (Bartle-Haring, Silverthorne, Meyer, & Toviessi, 2009; Tanner, Gray, & Haaga, 2012), there is no denying that besides satisfying supervisory obligations, live approaches have much to offer training systems.

In our supervision training workshops, participants have commented that they would like to do live supervision, but do not have resources for one-way mirrors. Others have immediately presented alternative methods for live supervision: closed-circuit viewing, co-therapy, and sitting in the room with the therapy system. Using safe and secure Internet platforms, supervisors can remotely "be" in the therapy room or Internet session.

The typical format for traditional live supervision has been for the supervisor to sit behind a one-way mirror (or in front of a TV monitor with closed-circuit technology) and to call in via a phone; ear piece; most recently, electronic tablet (Machua, Johnson, & Moro, 2015), or other communication device (being careful that such devices maintain confidentiality), or to call therapists from the therapy room for consultation. They usually have pre- and post-session discussions about plans for the session and to debrief the session and provide feedback. The relative influence of these communication methods on therapists' behaviors, both immediately and sustained, is to date uncertain (see Probst et al., 2018; Thurber, 2005). Also, clearly, there are a number of different formats in which trainees and supervisors do live supervision. For example, Chang (2010) and Lowe, Hunt, and Simmons (2008) described reflecting teams and their use in live-observation training. Such approaches allow cases to be conceptualized from broadly different perspectives, thereby allowing rich discussion of multiple perspectives.

Relative Benefits of Live Approaches

Beyond the obvious mandate for live supervision, supervisors and trainees agree that the following advantages accrue (participants in workshops and roundtables facilitated by the authors; Jordan, 2000; Woodside, 2000):

1. Live supervision parallels therapy; namely, it is action-oriented and focused on "what is happening here, right now." Feedback is immediate. Supervision can seize upon data as they are immediately perceived before they are distorted or forgotten over the passage of time. Supervisors and trainees also have immediate access to subtle features that trainees may overlook in retrospective supervision. Trainees benefit from relatively instantaneous corrective feedback as they proceed with their cases. Moreover, supervisors gain credibility when they are paying immediate and close attention to the clinical work.
2. Supervisors can ask trainees about what is happening when it is immediate and process the trainee's approach or suggest/codevelop other approaches. This allows the trainee to experience shifts in therapy due to even slight changes in their behavior.
3. Supervisors may feel reassured that clients are being afforded responsible, good-enough care. If necessary, they can help trainees recognize and explore potential safety or legal concerns and intervene appropriately in crises.
4. Beginning trainees, realistically anxious and lacking in know-how, may appreciate real-time and post-session clinical and emotional support. They may draw comfort from knowing that their supervisors are close at hand. They often look forward to mid-session breaks. This break provides a "time out" and an opportunity for additional direction, such as advice about handling emotion or an impasse.
5. Trainees and supervisors together observe the immediate effects of implementing interventions based on their clinical assessments.
6. Constructive observations by supervisors can be antidotes to trainees' unrealistic goals, self-denigration, and expectations of blame from supervisors. Moreover, other trainees who are observing can learn from what they are seeing take place "on both sides of the mirror." Vicarious learning can be powerful (see Truax, Shapiro, & Wargo, 1968).

These benefits are crucial to responsible and productive supervision. However, there also are down sides:

1. Live supervision may contribute to performance anxiety, perhaps for every member of the training system: supervisors, trainees, clients, and administrators.

Perhaps even more important, "here-and-now" presence of the training system may tempt supervisors to become more active in the treatment and undermine the training goal of building trainees' confidence and self-sufficiency. In addition, the observable presence of more actors than the clients and their therapists may lead to dilution of and other complications in the relationships between trainees and their clients.

2 Focus on live data alone may actually serve to distract the training system. For example, focus on single sessions may impair views of a bigger clinical picture (see Wetchler & McCollum, 1999). Moreover, since there is no replay available, trainees and supervisors may miss important issues or cues and thereby be limited in future reviews. Too, focus on live issues in immediate sessions may bypass a more comprehensive assessment of the client system. Microskill development may take precedence over theory development and professional growth of trainees.
3 Facilities for traditional live supervision are not present in most postgraduate practice settings (e.g., in-home, private offices, and many agencies).
4 Live supervision requires supervisors to spend an entire hour observing and perhaps another hour processing one case. It is not suited to supervising large caseloads or many trainees on top of other responsibilities. Moreover, if not enough time is taken for reflection about the dynamics of clients, therapists, and supervisors, the probability increases for isomorphic replications of dysfunctional patterns throughout the training system.

Clearly, the benefits of live supervision cannot be ignored. Some supervisors recommend co-therapy as a means of providing it where it otherwise would not be possible (DeRoma, Hickey, & Stanek, 2007; Romans, Boswell, Carlozzi, & Ferguson, 1995; York, 1997). Co-therapy, of course, brings its own dynamic complications, especially when the partners are not equals and one is an authority (see the discussion of cotherapy and illustrative vignettes in Falke, Lawson, Pandit, & Patrick, 2015). Such training systems might benefit by having the cotherapy itself reviewed live or after the fact: live, by closed circuit technology or webcam; later, by review of video recordings. Whatever the method employed, the images onscreen must include both cotherapists as well as the clients as much as possible.

Lessons Learned

Despite its importance, live supervision is being practiced less and less (Lee et al., 2004). This perhaps corresponds to logistic and economic difficulties in contemporary settings and the demise of major CFT theories (e.g., structural and strategic) that privilege live observations. Moreover, many of trainees' best and worst supervisory experiences seem to involve live supervision (Wark, 2000). For the past 30 years, supervisors and former trainees (Anderson et al., 2000; Boston, 2010; Carpenter et al., 2012; Liddle, 1988; Storm, 2000a; White & Russell, 1995) have consistently offered constructive observations about how to get the most out of live supervision. These observations, of course, apply to all supervisory situations. Our personal experiences and take on the literature can be summarized as a version of the Golden Rule: Supervisors and trainees should relate to each other in ways that they would have trainees relate to clients.

1 Foremost, supervisors and trainees should have a basic understanding and acknowledge the presence of isomorphism across the training system. What happens between supervisors and their trainees is likely to be similar to patterns in the trainee-client and clients-plus-significant others' subsystems. Therefore,
2 Supervisors must actively listen to and validate their trainees, and stay connected emotionally and cognitively to them and what is going on in their cases. Supervisors need to have a high tolerance for their own anxiety and uncertainty, be able to separate their own needs from the trainees' and clients', and be flexible. Again, trainees offer the therapy, supervisors provide supervision to trainees. Think of the "supervisor as pit crew" metaphor.
3 Supervisors should recognize that offering critique in a live setting particularly with other trainees and perhaps even clients watching can be either helpful or destructive to all parties. The process—how it is done—may be much more influential than that which is said. Accordingly, supervisors should be personable, respectful, and humble. They should acknowledge supervisory mistakes, engage in good goal setting (realistic, positive, observable, etc.; see Nelson, 2019), offer concrete suggestions, and explain the reasons behind their suggestions in terms of both immediate and long-term gains. They should invite feedback. In short, they must understand that they are facilitating and participating in the construction of a therapeutic milieu. Supervisors must be expert in identifying signs of anxiety throughout the training system and understand that levels of anxiety that are too high can get in the way of learning and doing. This also is true of criticism combined with disrespect.
4 Supervisors should not ask trainees to understand and to do things that are not in keeping with their professional development.

Retrospective Approaches

Retrospective approaches are the most commonly used (Lee et al., 2004). But they also may be the most under-appreciated (McCollum & Wetchler, 1995). These approaches typically involve the review of live data taken from video and audio tapes, reviewing case notes, or interactions based on therapists' reports of cases.

Audio and Audiovisual Recordings

Access to live data may be provided by audio, video, or digital recording. Audio recordings provide interesting information. For example, they may be used to uncover subtle emotional nuances that might be over-ridden by visual cues (e.g., Nichols & Everett, 1986). They also provide supervisors access to live data in settings where no other access is possible. When the last survey was conducted 16 years ago (Lee et al., 2004), 53% of all AAMFT Approved Supervisors were using audio recordings at least part of the time.

Audiovisual recording employing high-resolution visual images and clear voices is the recording method of choice. Data are not useful if they cannot be seen or heard clearly. Images should include all individuals present in the therapy room including the trainee.

Although supervision based on audiovisual recording clearly is much like live supervision, it has several strengths that live supervision does not. For example,

1 Supervisors and trainees do not have to have access to the therapy site at the same time. Recordings also allow distance supervision more easily. Moreover, review of therapy recordings can be done to suit the schedules of the training system, or if special time is needed, to provide ample reflection and discussion.
2 Audiovisual recordings provide economies of time. For example, an entire session does not have to be reviewed. Prior to supervision sessions, specific parts of sessions can be bookmarked, for example, interesting behavioral patterns, apparently pivotal moments, escalations, stuck spots, and so on: whatever the trainee or supervisor wishes to focus upon.
3 Audiovisual recordings also can be used to aid recall and correct bias by presenting moments or dynamics that were originally forgotten and minimized by any of the participants. Audio can be muted to allow the training system to focus exclusively on visual data, such as body language and nonverbal interactions. Moreover, audiovisual recordings can be used to freeze moments in time so that they later can be explored; a small event can be scrutinized in detail. Conversely, used as time-lapse photography, composite recording can recap months of therapy.
4 Audiovisual recordings allow trainees to see themselves in action. Supervisors and trainees are given the opportunity to look at not just clients' but also the trainees' behavioral cues, such as a lack of fluency in speech, tonal shifts, body language, and interaction patterns. When trainees can look over their own shoulders and observe themselves, they and their supervisors can mutually identify and explore self-of-the-therapist issues as well as track interactional recursion (that is, how clients and trainees continuously provide cues to each other that shape their interactions).
5 Supervisors can use recordings to focus selectively on those parts of therapy sessions that highlight special training or clinical concerns. For example, audiovisual recordings might be used to help therapists reflect on their personal and professional roles by discovering common behaviors with selected clinical incidents or types of clients. In fact, audiovisual recordings may be used as a reality check; because they offer a replay and also provide distance from the emotional process of sessions, trainees may discover that they selectively remembered aspects of events during a session. They also might discover that things they thought went well did not, or vice versa.
6 Trainees can review their audiovisual recordings to meet personal and training needs. Audiovisual recordings may be used to provide vicarious learning for

other trainees, alone or in groups. Moreover, as many have discovered, clients also can benefit from reviewing audiovisual recordings of their sessions.

7 However, there need to be explicit, written rules and auditing procedures about how recordings are to be reviewed and by whom, stored, destroyed, and transported. Client confidentiality must be iron-clad (except as required and/or allowed by law) and clients informed on how the recordings will be used and the safety procedures for ensuring confidentiality. More than one institution has faced the dilemma of having allowed trainees view their recordings at home, and then having one lost somewhere outside of the clinic setting. Labels on recordings must contain no identifying information, and recordings should be stored in safe places under lock and key. Storage using an internet cloud service or external hard drives should be encrypted and perhaps password protected. Unless archived (see below) or kept for specific purposes, all recordings must be effectively destroyed after their use.

8 If archived, audiovisual recordings can be consulted over time, or reviewed repeatedly, to explore patterns, provide illustrations for other trainees, and document the growth of trainees and/or clients. Security concerns remain and all recordings should be protected for security and confidentiality no matter how long they are kept. Archived recordings can be used for research with appropriate client and institutional review board approval. One of us (Nelson) directed several master's thesis projects that involved trainees' developing checklists of their own interventions and actions, and then viewing and coding recordings of their therapy sessions (Withers & Nelson, 2015). This information was then used by the therapists to review their ideas about their own work, making decisions about their approaches based on the patterns they had observed (evidence-based practice).

Technologies for different ways of recording case sessions are booming and range from simple, small recorders to elaborate systems that store data on secure networked servers or in the cloud so that supervisors can view the recordings on any computer that has access to the recording. Potential consumers of this new technology must first consult with their legal and information technology advisors. This is a matter of confidentiality and privilege, among other things. Most states include this privilege in their licensing or related statutes. Violation therefore is a criminal offense and also fertile ground for civil litigation (see Chapter 11). The AAMFT's (2015a) most recent Code of Ethics allows for the use of electronic technology as long as it is kept confidential, is secure, and the user has training in appropriate procedures and requirements. The most recent *AAMFT Approved Supervisor Designation: Standards Handbook* (AAMFT, 2014) also reflects recent changes approved by the AAMFT Board of Directors regarding the use of technology for supervision and supervision mentoring using the same ethical codes. Some states also are beginning to allow the use of telephone and Internet technology supervision under certain circumstances (see further discussion of technology-assisted or remote supervision below).

Caveats about electronic facilitation aside, many of the guidelines offered in support of live supervision, namely, social skills, support, and grace, also apply to retrospective supervision. Beyond these basics, the probability of desirable outcomes is likely to be enhanced when supervisors and trainees discuss how the recordings will be used in the context of supervision. Trainees and supervisor candidates have told us that review of recordings produces less anxiety when it is informed by specific questions, most often raised by the trainees themselves.

Trainees sometimes feel uncomfortable about informing clients that sessions will be recorded. However, fully informed consent is mandated by the AAMFT Code of Ethics as well as many state and provincial laws and decency. Discussion of this mandate may provide relief to therapists (Protinsky, 1997), especially if that discussion includes the clients. In any case, this discussion needs to be grounded in trust and integrity. Therefore, it helps to make both therapy and supervision safe places so that concerns can be voiced and addressed.

Policies about what should be recorded need to be very clear. In some instances, all sessions must be recorded; in others, trainees may decide which sessions to record. Supervisors may be comfortable with case consultation after a time but want a trainee to record the next session so that what they have discussed and determined as a course of action can be observed. In any case, the requirements need to be clear to trainees.

Supervisors seek those segments of recordings relevant to trainees' learning issues. However, supervisors use their own powers of observation and diplomacy to counteract trainees' tendencies toward detecting deficiencies and doubting themselves. It also makes sense that supervisors ask for examples that their trainees feel good about. Nevertheless, supervisors must also use their executive functions to raise important questions or visit segments of recordings that challenge defensive or naïve trainees.

Supervisors might vary how the recordings are used. Sometimes they might view a recording as it unfolds and ask about moment-to-moment dynamics. Other times, perhaps at a therapeutic impasse, the recording could be stopped and the trainees invited to just sit, reflect, and share their thoughts and feelings. Trainees could also be asked to relate what they have just seen to theory or their ongoing assessment and treatment plan. For example, Quinn, Nagirreddy, Lawless, and Bagley (2000) have developed innovative ways to involve clients in supervision sessions using recordings. Their methods are meant to help trainees discover and reflect upon their internal processes while engaged in therapy. No matter how recordings are employed, supervisors should not require recordings and then not use them in a comprehensive fashion (Todd, 1997). To do so is a violation of the supervision contract, a loss of important data, and a potential wound to a supervisor's credibility.

Trainees generally have admitted to being ambivalent about videotaping (e.g., Routon, 2018). They are excited by recorded evidence of their professional growth. But they are worried about the evaluative component used in supervision. Consequently, trainees may "forget" to record a session or bookmark a recording in advance of supervision sessions. When recordings are a requirement of supervision, supervisors may find it useful to regard their absence as an indicator of learning issues. Instead of challenging trainees, supervisors may collude with them (Todd, 1997). Perhaps both parties in such a circumstance are fatigued or distracted. Perhaps it is a matter of other interlocking dynamics between the trainees and their supervisors or others in the training system. In any case, this situation needs to be explored.

Case Presentations

Despite the critical importance of access to live data, versions of verbal and written case review have been the most frequently used of contemporary approaches to supervision (see Lee et al., 2004). Case reviews traditionally have been based on verbatim session notes, structured progress notes, overall case summaries, or unstructured verbal reports. It is easy to understand the popularity of these approaches.

1 This method is very economical. Case presentation approaches require neither special equipment nor setting. They can take place in person or electronically. They allow supervisors to stay current with large numbers of trainees and their cases.
2 Case presentations typically involve the consideration of a particular session within the context of larger clinical pictures (e.g., Wetchler & McCollum, 1999). Of equal importance, within the parameters set by diverse supervisors, case presentations are constructed by the trainees, perhaps via structured formats required by supervisors. Therefore, on the one hand, there is a setting in which family therapy theories can be discussed as they apply to the material at hand, including dynamics that certain theories would highlight or ignore.
3 On the other hand, there is an opportunity to explore self-of-the-therapist variables. For example, the supervisory team can be alert to what is being talked about and what is not; what questions have and have not been asked; what theories and techniques seem to be more comfortable for the therapist than others. Such conversations may be entryways into discussions of gender, ethnic and class membership, sexuality, power, violence, and religious involvement. Presumably growing awareness and integration of all of these factors—theory through contextual issues and case content—would inform the development of trainees' integrative models of therapy.
4 Case presentation approaches are the least intrusive to the therapy process itself. Trainees are on their own with clients. This seems important if trainees are to become self-sufficient clinicians.
5 Because trainees construct and present their cases after the fact, they may have less performance anxiety in the therapy sessions. They are not on stage with an audience, seeing (and evaluating) the good, the bad, and the ugly.
6 Concurrently, because they are on their own, they must learn to write accurate case notes that use the clients' language and reports rather than their own interpretations except when noted as such.
7 Finally, some aspects of case presentation approaches are especially useful to beginning trainees. These approaches push trainees to pay attention to the details and process of sessions and to present their thoughts and rationale for interventions. Often, case presentation outlines and structured progress notes are employed to help beginners obtain competency in putting together a

clinical pictures and interventions. This kind of structure forces individuals to think and reflect in ways simple review of live or recorded sessions does not.

Caveats about Retrospective Case Presentations

A foremost concern of supervisors using these approaches is that they are relying—in many cases, solely—on trainees' constructions of the content and process of sessions. Given supervisors' liability in the civil court and the statutes of most states, this is an incredible vulnerability. No matter how conscientious trainees may attempt to be, it is likely that important details may be lost in the retrospective reporting of a case. Moreover, case presentation approaches are heavily dependent on therapists' writing and verbal skills. Finally, the validity of what has been written may be inversely proportional to the time that has elapsed between a session and the written process notes. Process notes written more than a day after a session may be largely fiction.

When training is largely based on case presentations, more attention may be given to theoretical development and conceptualization than to skill training, and thoughts and feelings of trainees as they actively engage in therapy. Supervisors and trainees must get creative about the delivery as well as conceptualization of interventions.

In retrospect, case presentation approaches, the document package (intake and process notes, case summaries) is privileged above what actually happens in session. However, no matter how detailed these documents are, all of the requirements delineated in this chapter must be met: fully informed consent for treatment, privileged communication and its limitations, identifying information, and secure storage and transportation. In the past it has not been unusual for trainees to lose case files outside the treatment office, and even briefcases full of them. This issue is ameliorated to some extent by digital files and storage, but care must be taken to protect the confidentiality of clients and trainees.

Contemporary Variations: Novel Concerns

Informal and Peer Supervision

Aspiring therapists often seek out informal supervision with peers and others to help them process their work, understand their clients better, and find encouragement (Farber & Hazanov, 2014). They do so because such conversations are timely resources for reassurance, validation, and other emotional support. They provide safe places in which to reveal their anxieties, doubts, concerns, shame, and strong reactions with regard to both supervisors and clients. They also can feel free to talk about their lives as students or developing therapists, complications occasioned by their multiplicity of roles, and their ideas and feelings about their vocational journeys. Critics of informal supervision see it as a tempting way for trainees to dilute or avoid expected negative responses by their CFT supervisors and, in so doing, not receive the potential growth experiences that would come from addressing these together. Others (see Coren & Farber, 2019; Farber & Hazanov, 2014) consider informal supervision—if it adheres to ethical guidelines regarding client privacy—to be a valid path to increased clinical skills. They suggest that such consultations might be explicitly integrated into training programs.

Remote (Electronic) Supervision

Remote or electronic professional services are being identified by a number of prefixes, including tele-, distance-, and technology-assisted. For example, tele-health, tele-therapy, distance-therapy, technology-assisted and so forth. Sometimes the prefix is followed by a blank space, sometimes with a hyphen, and sometimes is not separated from the name of the service. However, all of these designations refer to "the scope of CFT practice—diagnosis, evaluation, consultation, intervention and supervision—through synchronous or asynchronous two-way electronic communication including but not limited to remote phone, videoconferencing, email, text, instant messaging, and social media" (Association of Marital and Family Therapy Regulatory Boards (AMFTRB), 2016, p. 8). Unless contained in a quotation, "remote" will be the term used below.

When it comes to supervision, two different circumstances need to be addressed. The first involves those who oversee therapists who are conducting remote services; the second is the provision of supervision through remote conferencing. In either case, there are some basic caveats to be considered.

For example, it is important to recognize from the outset that both remote therapy and remote supervision suffer from the same defect: They often do not meet the privacy and confidentiality requirements set forth in the federal 1996 Health Insurance Portability and Accounting Act (commonly referred to as HIPAA), the intent of which has been to improve the security of any electronic health care transactions.

This being the case, remote formats should be used *mindfully* by all members of a particular training system. Because of situational circumstances and personality characteristics, therapists and their supervisors may feel hurried during a moment, distracted, or, for some other reason, go about things automatically (see Davis, Deblaere, Hook, & Owens, 2020). Because of this tendency, it might prove beneficial for the participants in a training system to engage in anticipatory best practices.

For example, it is important that all participants in a session take a moment to consider the characteristics of their remote formats in anticipation of each session (for examples, see Sahebi, 2020; Wrape & McGinn, 2019). All parties should ascertain that the human spaces they occupy are secure from eavesdropping and are and will remain free of distracting sounds and sights (Brunelli, 2019). Moreover, they should audit what the cameras and microphones might pick up that could be distracting or otherwise deleterious, for example, crying children, barking dogs or, anything else that might be ignored in person, but amplified by a microphone, e.g., keyboard typing. Finally, the participants should be located in front of neutral backgrounds that contain no identifying features or objects of value.

Because it may not be possible to prevent outsiders from invading a meeting that must be private and confidential (Lorenz, 2020), the best defense may be a good offense. Therefore, when employing remote supervision and/or therapies, prudent training system members will make certain that they are running the latest versions of their software. The developers of the most popular of these apps are continually addressing security hazards as they become discovered.

For every remote supervisory session, the participants should designate a host for the meeting. This typically will be the supervisor, and that individual's computer and its videoconferencing software should allow the host to create and monitor "waiting rooms" (Jayarajan, 2020). The use of a waiting room assures that only the intended parties are in the session. The host's computer screen should also be set to "host only." This creates a network that is completely contained within the lead computer (see VMware Workstation 3.2, 2020). Finally, the participants should consider using unique passwords for each session. These passwords would be sent out just before a specific session is to take place and all of the members of the training system must agree not to share their Internet links and codes with outsiders.

More Specifically: Supervising Remote Therapy

In the past two decades, there has been a steady increase in the provision of electronic, remote behavioral health services (AMFTRB, 2016; Cravens Pickens, Morris, & Johnson, 2019; Haberstroh, Barney, Foster, & Duffey, 2014). However, Cravens Pickins and her associates (2020) have uncovered that—despite its exponentially expanding use—few accredited CFT training programs have provided trainees with remote therapy experiences and, where they have, little attention has been given to the form and content of its supervision. This same lack of attention has characterized the professional literature. In the past decade, the occasional presentation of remote therapy has been limited to specific sociocultural contexts and almost universally the description of both the mechanics of the therapies and their outcomes have been descriptive and anecdotal (for example, see the review in Wrape & McGinn, 2019).

If supervisors are to train and oversee the conduct of remote therapies, they need to know what actions are intended to be therapeutic, the different forms that these actions might take, and what outcomes are expected if they are performed with fidelity (see Increasing the Probability of Positive Results, Chapter 9). Moreover, as Caldwell, Bischoff, Derigg-Palumbo, & Liebert (2017) observed, when outcomes of remote interventions have been assessed and reported, they are focused on outcomes descriptive of individuals and not couples, families, and other social units.

In general, beyond certain prescient academic teams (most notably CFTs Blumer, Hertlein, & VandenBosch, 2015, and professional counseling's Trepal, Haberstroh, Duffey, & Evans, 2007), published academic voices of the several CFT disciplines have not indicated a sense of urgency with regard to delineating core competencies in the provision of remote therapies. This contrasts sharply with the well-established CFT Core Competencies (AAMFT, 2004; Nelson et al., 2007; Appendix B) that are the foundation of accredited CFT programs and the MFT National Examination (AMFTRB, 2019).

Therefore, in the absence of focused, explicit, systems-based models, made up of variables with clearly observable behaviors, which can then be informed by empirically based work with regard to the provision of remote therapies, the authors of this text are at a loss to offer anything other than common sense: namely, credentialed and aspiring supervisors should take an appreciative, discovery-inducing, and solution-focused stance informed by what are considered to be common therapeutic factors (e.g., the therapeutic alliance). The vignettes obtained then may lead to testable models that correlate specific competencies with outcomes.

Supervision of therapy that is being done remotely—as well as supervision practiced remotely—can be complicated (see Heinlen, Welfel, Richmond, & Rak, 2003). Let us count the ways:

The therapists being supervised may be using any of several video communicating devices with their clients: smart phones, tablets, laptops, or desktop computers. On these devices, they may be using any one of many videoconferencing applications, e.g., FaceTime, Skype, Zoom, GoToMeeting, and ooVoo, to name just a few. Many of these applications allow group formats for members of a family not in the same room, or for group supervision. At the time of the COVID-19 pandemic, it was not improbable—this subsequently may still be the case—that CFTs could be using electronic equipment to provide sessions to family members located in geographically separate abodes who have been brought together on a remote video conference screen. Those services, in turn, could simultaneously be overseen by supervisors employing their own video connections with the supervisees. Moreover, it was not improbable that therapists, family members, and supervisors may have resided in different states and, indeed, in different countries.

As a general rule the federal and regional requirements governing supervisory work are those of the location in which the client is situated at the time a service is provided. However, supervisors engaged in the manifold forms of technology-assisted service provision, including their own, have the onus of ascertaining that the whole enterprise is secure. Given the complexity of these situations, prudent remote supervisors review training system complexities with appropriate legal personnel (e.g., the Associate Counsel at AAMFT, 2020).

Although there are no widely disseminated competencies for the efficacious provision of remote therapies, several governmental and professional organizations have compiled and promulgated guidelines in pursuit of their respective missions to protect the public welfare. Supervisors who currently oversee the provision of remote therapy by trainees, and aspiring supervisors, should review the caveats in Hughes (2000) and be familiar with the following documents:

- *Guidelines for the Regulation of Remote Therapy Practice* (AMFTRB, 2016).
- *Best Practices in the online practice of couple and family therapy* (Caldwell et al., 2017).
- *Standards for Distance Professional Services* (NBCC, 2016).

Supervising Remotely

Remote supervision refers to the practice of supervision by a licensed supervisor through synchronous or asynchronous two-way electronic communication as described above for the purposes of developing trainee marital and family therapists, evaluating supervisee performance, ensuring rigorous legal and ethical standards within the bounds of licensure, and as a means for improving the profession of marital and family therapy.

Unlike remote therapy, remote supervision has been debated by state regulatory boards for over three decades. Like now, face-to-face supervision has been required by the diverse licensing boards. Aspiring CFTs attempting to acquire their supervised clinical hours in underpopulated and far flung geographic areas argued that this constituted a hardship. They wanted their regulatory boards and professional organizations to allow supervision by telephone. As time passed, technology advanced and informal talk at regional conferences indicated that videoconferencing (e.g., Skype) was being used by some. Further, we believe that remote therapy, as a practice, requires specialized skills, necessitating supervision by someone who is familiar with remote practice. However, despite the practical needs to meet state supervision requirements in outlying regions, state regulatory boards have not noticeably changed their interpretive rules about the form supervision must take (AMFTRB, 2016).

In a personal communication to the authors in April, 2020, the AMFTRB's Executive Director observed that most of the US state regulatory boards had come to allow candidates working on their supervised experience hours to submit *some* hours of remote supervision. Moreover, with the exigencies of the COVID-19 pandemic, virtually all states in the US unofficially accepted remote supervision in various amounts. The director expected this trend to continue after the pandemic, but with the number of remote supervision hours—and their format—varying with the respective regulatory boards. She further observed that published research (e.g., Hertlein, Blumer, & Mihaloliakos, 2014) had indicated that much remote therapy had included unprofessional practices, and that this underscored the importance of the regulatory process.

To date, government regulatory agencies in the US have not set into place their respective standards for remote supervision. In anticipation of this development, the AMFTRB (2016) published a model set of rules:

(A) Therapists must hold supervision to the same standards as all other technology-assisted services. Remote supervision shall be held to the same standards of appropriate practice as those in in-person settings.

(B) Before using technology in supervision, supervisors shall be competent in the use of those technologies. Supervisors must take the necessary precautions to protect the confidentiality of all information transmitted through any electronic means and maintain competence.

(C) The type of communications used for remote supervision shall be appropriate for the types of services being supervised, clients and supervisee needs. Remote supervision is provided in compliance with the supervision requirements of the relevant jurisdiction(s). Therapists must review state board requirements specifically regarding face-to-face contact with supervisee as well as the need for having direct knowledge of all clients served by his or her supervisee.

(D) Supervisors shall: (a) determine that remote supervision is appropriate for supervisees, considering professional, intellectual, emotional, and physical needs; (b) inform supervisees of the potential risks and benefits associated with remote supervision, respectively; (c) ensure the security of their communication medium; and (d) only commence remote supervision after appropriate education, training, or supervised experience using the relevant technology.

(E) Supervisees shall be made aware of the risks and responsibilities associated with remote supervision. Supervisors are to advise supervisees in writing of these risks, and of both the supervisor's and supervisees' responsibilities for minimizing such risks.

(F) Supervisors must be aware of statutes and regulations of relevant jurisdictions regarding sexual interactions with current or former supervisees.

(G) Communications may be synchronous or asynchronous. Technologies may augment traditional in-person supervision, or be used as stand-alone supervision. Supervisors shall be aware of the potential benefits and limitations in their choices of technologies for particular supervisees in particular situations.

(AMFTRB, 2016, p. 18)

The above should be regarded as guidelines. As a practical matter, each state's regulatory boards and professional organizations eventually will promulgate the standards for their jurisdictions. Remote supervisors will be expected to know and to adhere to those definitions and rules while recognizing that rules in place where their therapists and clients are located, respectively, may have precedence, and follow them.

Sahebi (2020) observed that the global pandemic, COVID-19, has increased uncertainty and therefore anxiety throughout entire training systems. Consequently, it is highly probable that there is a growing mistrust of those systems, which previously have been regarded as safeguards of participant safety. Because the supervisory relationship is an essential foundation of clinical training, "supervisors should make every effort to support the working alliance .... Provide warmth, support when requested, empathy about the challenges supervisees may be facing, genuineness including relevant and thoughtful self-disclosure, humor when appropriate, and optimism about learning opportunities that have emerged from training as systemic therapists in the midst of a global pandemic" (p. 94).

A final word about remote supervision: All of the above is concerned with consumer welfare. While acknowledging the importance of these policies, remote supervisors also require explicit knowledge about the theories and behaviors that constitute core competencies in the application of these therapies and core competences in their supervision of them. The widespread provision of distance therapies creates a mandate for behavioral health disciplines to delineate these core competencies, on the one hand, and to conduct efficacy research connecting specific practices to probable outcomes. The latter studies could include comparisons of the results obtained by disparate distance therapies with face-to-face models in diverse sociocultural contexts. Dosage would be an additional independent variable.

Exercises

1. For your personal philosophy of supervision, what are your preferred approaches to supervision and why? Given your context, what approaches are possible? And how will you use those approaches?
2. Some concerns are raised about using therapist reports only for supervision; therapists can (and do) filter their reports through their memories, theories, and other experiences. They may even lie so as to look good to the supervisor. If you use or contemplate using case consultation, what do you think about these concerns and how will you manage them?
3. What are your thoughts about your personal preferences and beliefs about using various electronic technologies in supervision: telephone, transmission of audio or video recordings, use of webcam, etc.? What other possibilities can you think of?
4. What research would you like to see conducted on the modalities of supervision?

6 Approaches to Supervision

Should supervision be hierarchical or collaborative? Directive or curious? Focus on building therapist competence or self of the therapist? In the AAMFT (2014) Approved Supervisor handbook, supervisor candidates are asked to articulate their models of supervision in personal philosophy of supervision papers. In this text, we do not attempt to teach people how to supervise; rather we seek to present multiple ideas about approaches to supervision so that learners can identify, clarify, and articulate their own perspectives and positions. The authors identity with three transcendental goals for CFT educators and trainers: increasing sophistication of family systems scholarship, socialization into the profession of CFT, and cultivation of professional maturity (Lee & Nichols, 2010). To accomplish these ends we tend to be trainee-centered and collaborative rather than focusing supervision on our own therapy or supervision philosophies as the best way for all supervisors to work with all trainees. There are too many variables—trainee, supervisor, client, presenting problem, setting, theoretical approach, and so forth—to suggest that supervision philosophies can be monolithic. Besides that, we are systemic thinkers and believe in equifinality—there is more than one way to learn or supervise competent therapy. Others may have other perspectives.

Our perspectives are similar in that they reside within systemic and developmental frameworks, tend to emphasize trainees' strengths and capabilities, and focus on the processes of supervision and therapy rather than particular supervision content or clinical concerns. This is not to say that we cannot be directive at times, impart information, or suggest tactics based on our own experiences as supervisors and therapists.

We also are similar in that our systemic positions often carry flavors of Bowen Family Systems therapy (Bowen, 1978), particularly in terms of triangles and anxiety; and structural family therapy (e.g., Minuchin, 1974) in terms of thinking that it usually is a good idea for parents to be in charge of their children, therapists to take charge of therapy sessions, and supervisors to structure supervision. We both appreciate solution-focused (e.g., De Jong & Berg, 2013; Thomas, 2013) considerations. However, we primarily are persuaded that effective supervision balances emphasis on trainees' fluency in theory, acquisition of therapeutic skill, and articulation of selves as therapists (see Delphi study by White & Russell, 1995).

We will discuss a variety of supervisory orientations below, following Morgan and Sprenkle's (2007) literature review. The first grouping is how the various

DOI: 10.4324/9781003099833-8

models have historically been presented. The second grouping considers them from an integrative standpoint (e.g., conceptual discussion by Lebow, 1987). The next three groupings are contributed by Morgan and Sprenkle (2007): developmental, social-role, and other approaches.

Major Models of Therapy as Templates

In the early days of couple and family therapy and supervision (see chapters in Liddle, Breunlin, & Schwartz, 1988, and Todd, 2014), supervision was thought to mirror the models of therapy that trainees were learning. Supervisors "taught" trainees how to do therapy in the ways that they, themselves, did therapy and structured their training sessions in the same way. For example, structural therapy supervisors taught concepts of boundaries, roles, rules, hierarchy, enmeshment, and disengagement as well as tactics of mimesis, challenging boundaries, enactment, and inducing disorganization so that families could reorganize in more functional ways. Consequently, they tended to be directive during clinical sessions and to assign homework that would enhance in-session changes. In supervision, these supervisors attended to boundaries in supervision groups or between therapists and their clients, giving clear in-the-moment instructions via bug-in-the-ear devices to trainees as they observed them live during sessions, and being directive in their relationships with trainees.

Bowen therapists believe that therapeutic change is only possible to the extent that therapists are more differentiated than their clients. Therefore, Bowen supervision emphasizes self of the therapist as it emerges in diverse clinical settings. Solution-focused supervisors typically ask trainees to consider what situations look like "when things are going better," effective goal setting for themselves as well as their clients, and ways of appreciating change.

Integrative Approaches

Scanning the professional literature, trade periodicals, offerings at regional and national meetings, and online continuing education indicates that contemporary CFT supervisors are socioculturally diverse and that they are called upon to supervise equally diverse therapists, who work with diverse clients in diverse settings. Therefore, we believe that supervision must be integrative; that is, it must incorporate many approaches into one guiding philosophy of supervision for each supervisor/trainee combination. We recognize that many combinations of theory and interventions are possible and perhaps singularly useful in different times and situations in supervision as in therapy. In short, supervision should incorporate the epistemologies and developmental levels of the supervisor, therapists, and client families. We recognize, however, that many evidence-based approaches (e.g., Emotionally Focused Therapy (Johnson, 2019), Functional Family Therapy (Sexton, 2009), and so forth) require adherence to particular supervision approaches.

However, when integrative supervision was first discussed over three decades ago, Lebow (1987) cautioned CFTs to be alert to incompatible assumptions. There is a difference, observed, between being "integrative" as opposed to "eclectic." Therefore, what is being applied in any one training situation should be a carefully considered product of an overall cohesive, coherent, and theoretically supported theory of supervision. This theory of supervision should address the clinical and professional development of trainees, and the goals and roles of supervisors in light of the needs of their trainees' treatment cases and, indeed, of the training system.

Developmental Approaches

Typically, beginning trainees need more directive and focused supervision whereas advanced trainees, nearly ready for licensure, need less time for learning particular techniques or practices but may benefit from discussing larger issues within a specific therapy approach or about therapy in general (see Stoltenberg & McNeill, 2010 for a broader discussion). Caldwell and Claxton (2010) also present a format for thinking about trainee development. McComb, Diamond, Breunlin, Chambers, & Murray (2018) discovered that trainee cooperation with their structured training and treatment protocol—STIC (see Chapter 4)—declined with veteran trainees. Finally, Shaywanna Harris (2017) encouraged trainers of aspiring supervisors to consider the developmental needs of the entire training system; that is, to address the developmental needs, not only of the trainees, but also of their supervisors. (Marovic and Snyders (2010) provide a systemically informed roadmap of the developmental journey of the evolving CFT supervisor.) Of course, in addition to the above considerations, we want to add the developmental needs of the client subsystem.

Social-Role Approaches

Social-role models focus on what supervisors do within different roles: teacher, consultant, mentor, and so forth. Various models, some quite complex, attempt to match training situations with particular tasks and behaviors. Later in this chapter, Chang discusses his Contextual-Functional Meta-Framework (CFM) approach to supervision, which exemplifies supervisor roles as tailored to specific situations.

Other Approaches: Skills and Feminist-Influenced

There are at least two other influences which, although not in themselves supervision approaches, nonetheless may impact supervisors' ways of thinking and supervising. The first of these is what might be called goal- or skill-oriented influence, which reflects outcome-based education (Nelson & Smock, 2005). It certainly could be said that all good supervisory approaches begin with the end in mind, namely, that which is considered the appropriate end result of a period of supervision between trainee and supervisor. Tomm and Wright (1979) identified three areas of competence in family therapy: conceptual, perceptual, and executive skills. Nelson and Johnson (1999) expanded upon this approach to include evaluative and professional skills. Together, these skills, when mastered, identify one as a competent therapist. The American Association for Marriage and Family

Therapy (AAMFT, 2004; Nelson et al., 2007; Appendix B) called for and supported an ambitious and nearly comprehensive list called Core Competencies for Marriage and Family Therapists (CCs). This compilation has been used in training programs, postgraduate training, and policy work (legislative, licensing, and insurance) to describe what competent family therapists do, and therefore the fundamentals of what must be learned. The list was developed through an inclusive process of consultation with CFT supervisors, CFTs, policy makers, educators, and other important stakeholders such as other mental health organizations and federal boards. General therapeutic competencies, skills, or goal approaches can certainly be used while trainees learn specific therapy approaches and also can be understood within developmental frameworks.

Another vital influence may be feminist-informed supervision. A feminist supervision lens is characterized by an enhanced collaborative and egalitarian relationship between the trainee and the supervisor, and a specific focus on feminist ideas of gender equality, balance of power in relationships, diversity, and so forth (see Degges-Wite, Colon, & Borzumato-Gainey, 2013; Prouty, Thomas, Johnson, & Long, 2007). Clearly, feminist principles can inform nearly any approach to supervision. It is interesting to observe that, in a rare outcome study published in *Feminist Family Therapy* (Green & Dekkers, 2010), CFT trainees self-reported greater satisfaction with their supervision and better learning outcomes, although their supervisors did not.

Common Factors in Supervision

Based on their review of literature underlying the above attempt at categorization, Morgan and Sprenkle (2007) identified common factors in supervision, discussing three dimensions of supervision that they believed cut across all approaches to supervision: (a) emphasis on clinical materials versus professional development; (b) specificity or focus on specific clinical case concerns versus more general therapy concepts, philosophy, or context; and (c) the nature of the supervisory relationship as collaborative versus hierarchical. Morgan and Sprenkle put forth the notion that all supervisory approaches can be identified in terms of a supervisor's place, so to speak, along each of these three dimensions, which help identify supervisors' roles and thus the goals for supervision. They went on to suggest a matrix of supervisory roles based upon the emphasis and specificity dimensions with the supervisory relationship encompassing the whole. These roles include mentor (professional competence and specific situations), coach (clinical competence and specific situations), teacher (clinical competence, general topics, and theoretical or approach-level competencies), and administrator (professional competence and general topics). Relationship aspects fall on a continuum of directive to collaborative. Whether one resonates with Morgan and Sprenkle's ideas or not, their suggested approach to thinking about supervisory models certainly helps to cast the notion of "supervision model" in a different, perhaps broader light than has previously been identified and discussed. That is, we can go beyond concepts and interventions of major models of therapy to a different level of thinking about supervision and the supervisory process: actions that supervisors take depending upon the role they enact in any one situation.

Regardless of how one positions oneself in the Morgan and Sprenkle (2007) matrix of supervisory roles and how that position may change depending upon developmental levels or situational needs of trainees or particular issues being discussed, we believe it is important that we understand how these approaches, factors, and dimensions mesh in our supervision, and especially how they inform the decisions we make and our actions. Therapists who understand their own approaches and cognitive processes in terms of how they make clinical decisions typically are seen as more effective; we believe similarly about supervisors. To the extent that supervisors understand their own philosophies, we believe that moment-to-moment or longer-term decisions of supervision will be better informed, more effective, and more efficient.

In Conclusion, Supervision Maps

Rather than think about "models" of supervision, it may be more beneficial to think about "maps." When using maps, we tend to think about at least two points: Point A (where we are) and Point B (where we hope to end up). In supervision, Point A might be the beginning of a supervisory relationship or an assessment of a trainee's competence relative to a set of desired skills. Point B might be the desired relationship at the end of supervision or evidence of mastery of a set of competencies. Supervisors and trainees may use several maps within supervision much as travelers use road, topographical, or other kinds of maps. We do not want to belabor the metaphor of maps, but we believe it is useful for supervisors, beginning or otherwise, to think about where they want to end up (what an accomplished or competent supervisor looks like), the routes they want to take, the factors that influence those routes, the best kinds of vehicles for those routes, other aspects of the terrain that are not well represented on maps, and so forth. (An illustration of such a developmental map is offered by the late Craig Everett in Lee & Everett, 2004.) Throughout this text so far, we have encouraged readers to consider various aspects of maps and will continue to do so in other chapters, remembering, of course, that the map is not the territory and that, indeed, territory is often fraught with rocks and streams that cannot clearly be depicted on maps.

A contemporary illustration is the CFM supervision model of Jeff Chang. The CFM model is a contextualized, integrated framework for supervision that has been found useful by many readers. It considers both the context of supervision and the roles of the members of the supervisory system as well as the contexts of the members of the system.

A Contemporary Illustration from the Field: The Contextual-Functional Meta-Framework for Supervision (by Jeff Chang)[1]

The *Contextual-Functional Meta-Framework* (CFM; Chang, 2013) is not a model of supervision as such, but rather a meta-framework or heuristic comprised of six components to assist supervisors to conceptualize their work. Each component is captured by an orienting question.

Administrative Context: "To Whom Do I Owe My Allegiance?"

The administrative context defines the parameters of supervision. These could include accreditors; agency mandates; entry-to-practice competency profiles (College of Registered Psychotherapists of Ontario, 2012; Kaslow et al., 2009; Nelson et al., 2007; Northey & Gehart, 2019); legal mandates (e.g., court orders, duty to warn/protect, privacy legislation, etc.), and licensing boards. These could affect documentation and reporting, goals and contracting, number and type of supervision hours, means of supervision, supervisor qualifications, and so forth.

The Supervisory Relationship: "Does Our Supervisory Relationship Support Our Joint Actions?"

In line with a common factors orientation (Duncan, Miller, Wampold, & Hubble, 2010), the supervisory working alliance is central to supervision. Cultural differences between supervisors and supervisees come alive, and if all goes well, are acknowledged and managed, within the supervisory alliance.

Culturally Responsive, Socially Just Approach

Collins (2019) proposed principles of culturally responsive, socially just therapy, defining "culture" broadly to include how one is positioned in terms of ability, ethnicity, gender and gender identity, privilege, and sexual orientation. This includes reflecting on one's cultural positioning and creating an environment for the supervisee to do the same, and interrogating the privileged assumptions about our models of therapy (Doyle & Gosnell, 2019; McDowell, Knudson-Martin, & Bermudez, 2018).

The Supervisory Relationship

As in therapy, the relationship between supervisor and supervisee is likely the most important contributor to outcome. It may be useful to conceptualize the supervisory relationship similarly to solution-focused ideas about relationship (De Jong & Berg, 2013), or the Transtheoretical Model of Change (Di Clemente, 1999). This can help supervisors coordinate their actions with supervisee receptivity. As in therapy, it is beneficial to obtain feedback about the supervisory relationship. Bernard and Goodyear (2009) list several instruments that supervisors can use to track the supervisory relationship.

Supervisory Functions: "When Should I Do What?"

In the CFM, supervision is a life-long endeavor (British Association for Counselling and Psychotherapy, 2018; Goodyear, Wertheimer, Cypers, & Rosemond,

2003), not simply a means to a degree or license. I have identified nine distinct functions, the use of which depends on context and the phase of supervisee development:

- *Clinical educator.* Teaching concepts and theories, focusing on perceptual and conceptual development (Nelson et al., 2007; Tomm & Wright, 1979).
- *Skill development coach.* Modeling and teaching executive skills (Rousmaniere, Goodyear, Miller, & Wampold, 2017; Tomm & Wright, 1979): *discrete generic skills* (e.g., attending, questioning, reflecting, summarizing, information-giving, confronting, structuring), *generic sequences* used across models (e.g., history-taking, soliciting a problem description, conducting a skill-training intervention, or delivering didactic content), or *specific interventions* (e.g., enactments, exception questioning, reframing).
- *Ethics/risk management consultant.* Supporting the application of ethical principles in practice; leading and prompting the supervisee's ethical decision making.
- *Catalyst.* Pointing out and intervening with supervisees' "blind spots," deficiencies, and personal issues that might interfere with their clinical work.
- *Professional gatekeeper.* Monitoring and evaluating supervisees entering the profession.
- *Organizational/administrative supervisor.* Orienting the supervisee to his/her duties and managing performance.
- *Personal supporter.* Creating a warm and accepting context, listening respectfully to events in supervisees' personal lives, staying alert to indications of supervisee impairment, and avoiding a therapeutic role by referring the supervisee to therapy (if necessary).
- *Professional mentor.* Providing advice and support about professional issues and career.
- *Advocate/system change agent.* Advocating for policies, organizational structures, and clinical practices to improve clinical service delivery.

Theory of Change: "Is There a Clash of Ideas, or an Ecology of Ideas?"

In the CFM, "theory of change" refers to the supervisor's and supervisee's theory of client change and their respective models of self-change in the context of theoretical pluralism. The supervisor's task is to promote an *ecology of ideas*, permitting cross-germination, not to promote theoretical uniformity.

Service Delivery System—Isomorphism: "What Are the Relational Patterns Affecting the Supervision Process?"

Supervisors should be aware of how the supervisory relationship and agency dynamics are isomorphic to the therapist–client systemic, and intervene accordingly (Koltz et al., 2012).

Phases of Counsellor Development: "Where Is the Supervisee in the Journey?"

Skovholt and Rønnestad's (1995) study of 125 counselors from lay helpers to doctorally trained therapists with 25+ years' experience, found therapists across six career phases differed along eight dimensions: time period, central task, predominant affect, sources of influence, role and working style, conceptual ideas, learning process, and measures of effectiveness and satisfaction (Rønnestad & Skovholt, 2003; Skovholt &Rønnestad, 1995). Accordingly, supervisors should tailor their approach to supervisees' developmental status.

Exercises

1 What is your preferred approach to therapy? Is it a singular approach, an integrated approach, or perhaps an evidence-based approach?
2 How does your preferred approach to therapy impact your approach to or philosophy of supervision?
3 As you read through the different approaches laid out in this chapter, how do these ideas impact your philosophy of supervision? What do you recognize as consonant with your approach and what is different or even disconsonant?
4 Do you resonate with Morgan and Sprenkle's (2007) Common Factors approach to supervision? How do you think about the different roles that they identified?
5 If the Morgan and Sprenkle approach does not fit with yours, what makes more sense in terms of supervisor roles?
6 How does Chang's approach affect your thinking about supervision? Again, what resonates and what does not?

Note

1 We thank Dr. Jeff Chang, Associate Professor at Athabasca University, for his contributions to this text.

7 Effective Supervision According to the Literature

There are two basic questions to be asked by every supervisor with regard to the content and goals of supervision: How do we know these are the important factors to be researching? How do we know that this content and these goals are being trained?

The ideal would be for this chapter to compile the empirical supervisory literature, that is, supervisory models, concepts, and processes that have been demonstrated to be effective for diverse supervisors and trainees, in diverse training systems, with diverse training goals and issues. Unhappily, no such chapter is possible at this time. Empirically based family therapy models are still developing (see, for example, Chapter 9) and little attention has been given to the executive, micro-, and metaskills that are expected to underlie successful performance of any supervisory intervention model. Therefore, it is not surprising that there is little or no scientific validation of supervision models. Indeed, given the complexities and nuances suggested by a four-plus level model of a training system (supervisory consultant and/or setting, supervisors, trainees, and clients; see Lee & Everett, 2004), such a program of research appears overwhelming. The second author once attempted to determine common skills thought by CFT supervisors to be basic competencies of CFT supervision. After doing a pilot test on several supervisors and getting as many different ideas as respondents, she gave up.

An Evolutionary Look at Best Practices in Supervision: From Opinion to Empiricism

Opinion (Before 1990)

Early on, supervisory goals and change processes were specified by the major CFT theories employed (Kniskern & Gurman, 1988). To some extent they still are (see specific chapters in Lee & Everett, 2004; Lee & Nichols, 2010; Liddle, Breunlin, & Schwartz, 1988; Todd & Storm, 2014). Alleged evidence for supervisory efficacy was both face validity (effective supervision parallels the goals and change processes of the various therapy models) and anecdotal. Such conceptualizations also were impersonal and pre-integrative (see Lebow, 1997a, 1997b).

DOI: 10.4324/9781003099833-9

Generic Family Therapy Skills

In 1988, the dominance of "what the major theories tell us to do" began to fade. In addition to the goals and processes called for by major treatment models, Liddle and his associates (1988) paid attention to what the reader might consider generic family therapy skills. That is, in their classic supervision text, they called for systematic evaluation of training programs based on "an (empirically determined) increase in trainees' conceptual, perceptual, and technical or executive skills" (p. 369). Conceptual skills were those that related to therapists' ability to formulate problems systemically, and to understand the way rules govern family behavior and make family interaction predictable. Perceptual skills were those skills that related to therapists' ability to evaluate a particular family within the therapists' conceptual frameworks. Executive and technical skills referred to therapists' ability to act in family sessions in ways that were consistent with the goals of the training program, systemic formulations, perceptions of the family's dynamics, and increasing skills according to chosen therapy approaches (see also Tomm & Wright, 1979 and AAMFT, 2004). Liddle and his associates then reviewed empirical studies of therapist factors (e.g., structuring and relational skills) that were later discovered to be associated with family therapy outcomes. Presaging contemporary concerns with the working alliance, and meta- and microskills, they recommended research to see if such skills could be taught and nurtured:

- Knowledge of the substantive materials on which family therapy is based and the ability to integrate such material with the assessment and treatment of families;
- To think and intervene systemically while remembering that systems contain individuals;
- To "stay in the room" with a family physically, emotionally, and intellectually (joining, managing resistance, and so on);
- To attend adequately to the functioning and manifestation of the dynamics of the family system and subsystems;
- To adequately assess the strengths and problems manifested by a family;
- To be able to describe the structure and the processes of family systems and subsystems;
- To plan and implement treatment plans consistent with the initial and ongoing assessment of family strengths and problems;
- To continue assessing adequately and flexibly change strategies as indicated;
- To act ethically and within legal constraints of therapy.

Others added to this list of generic family therapy skills to be taught and cultivated through supervision, for example Figley & Nelson (1989) and Nichols (1988). Also, in 1988, Liddle and colleagues were the first to recommend attention to contextual issues in family therapy supervision and training. They specifically cited gender-linked understanding of hierarchy, power, and roles as well as family life cycle and cross-cultural issues.

Professionalism

Concurrent to changes enhanced through the work of Liddle and his colleagues (1988), Figley and Nelson (1989), and Nichols (1988), voices were raised in support of another primary goal of supervision: professionalism. Beyond supervising CFT theories and applications, supervisors were also to concern themselves with the identity of their trainees within the profession of family therapy (see Nichols, 1988; Nichols & Everett, 1986; Liddle, 1988). This included increasing identification with the profession, "professional self-confidence," and a solid grounding in ethics, law, and standards of practice from a family therapy orientation. Ironically, in reference to what perhaps is, even now, inchoate, trainees were to be familiar with and respect both family science and empirical research in family therapy. Karam and Sprenkle (2010) later suggested that rather than training students in the scientist–practitioner model, which encourages students to learn the rudiments of research and become applied researchers, it might be more practicable and useful for master's-level students to become "research-informed" practitioners. That is, students would become consumers of research and sufficiently conversant with research methodology to critique the research that is reported in professional journals.

The Decade of Delphi Studies (1990–2000)

Delphi studies (see explication by Stone Fish & Busby, 2005) are a systematic way to establish consensus among experts in a topic or field in which there are no existent empirical data. In the absence of such data, for example, practices and outcomes, expert participants "respond" to each other in a series of surveys that establish their combined opinions about a topic. In the present case, there have been several explorations to ascertain what supervision experts agree are the essential goals of supervision and what trainees consider best and worst supervisory practices. Readers should go to the primary sources; the information is rich and nuanced beyond the highlights offered here. There have been two foci of these national Delphi studies that are pertinent to our work: content of training and supervisory processes.

Content of Training

Experts first sought consensus with regard to what concepts and techniques were the content across the major models of CFT (Figley & Nelson, 1989, 1990; Nelson & Figley, 1990; Nelson, Heilbrun, & Figley, 1993), and the amount of overlap among these models (Lee, Emerson, & Kochka, 1999; Midori Hanna, 2019). At about the same time, professional and economic forces led to the development of a National Examination Program in Marriage and Family Therapy (summarized in Lee & Sturkie, 1997, and updated periodically at www.amftrb.org). This examination required a national delineation study to arrive at a basic consensus of what those aspiring to the practice of family therapy should know and be able to do. A panel of experts, representative of practice settings—universities, institutes, and private offices—described the practice of family therapy in terms of the major areas of responsibility (practice domains), the specific work-related tasks associated with each domain, and the knowledge and skills necessary to perform those tasks. This content later was affirmed by a national vote among practicing couple and family therapists. Because the practice of family therapy has changed over time, these studies were repeated in 1998, 2004, and 2012. Given their important role in the family therapy credentialing process, supervisors need to remain cognizant of this national examination and its specifications and can do so by regularly reviewing the website of the Association of Marital and Family Therapy Regulatory Boards (amftrb.org).

In the early 2000s, a closely related initiative involved the development of what would be called the Core Competencies in Marriage and Family Therapy, or CCs (AAMFT, 2004; Nelson et al., 2007; these competencies are introduced in Chapter 4, detailed in Chapter 8, and provided in Appendix B.) The developers took as their goal to ascertain the basic floor of knowledge that practicing family therapists should be expected to know, discern, and do in their clinical work when they begin practicing therapy independent of supervision. Moreover, in 2005, the COAMFTE shifted its standards to an outcomes-based format. Therefore, supervisors in both educational settings and postgraduate training need to stay abreast of those standards. Finally, supervisors should be advised that the CCs and COAMFTE accreditation standards include the capacity of family therapists to interface adequately with diverse health care settings and professionals.

Supervisory Processes

White and Russell (1995) asked a national sample of AAMFT Approved Supervisors to arrive at a consensus about the most important characteristics of effective family therapy supervision. An initial list of 771 items was eventually reduced to three common beliefs:

1 Interactions with trainees are to be characterized by clear expectations with regard to procedures, methods, and performance evaluation;
2 There must be a solid working alliance (that is, shared goals and enough of a relationship to support work on those goals);
3 The supervisors' attention should be distributed across details of case management, theory and skills development, and the self of the therapist.

The Advent of Surveys, Quantitative Analyses, and Qualitative Studies

By the year 2000, Delphi surveys were replaced with semi-structured and closed-end national surveys of supervisees, and the quantitative and qualitative analysis of these data. For example, a national sample of 160 CFT supervisees were asked about their best and worst supervisory experiences on a semistructured survey instrument (Anderson, Schlossberg, & Rigazio-DiGilio, 2000). Their positive memories involved four dimensions of supervisor behavior. Supervision was a safe place in which there was:

- A sense of openness in the supervisory environment; that is, supervisors who welcomed mistakes, were open to feedback, and explored new ideas;
- A focus on strengths while communicating respect, encouragement, and support;
- Encouragement of personal growth issues and a willingness to confront blind spots and resistances;
- Conceptual and technical guidance and direction; supervisors' offering useful conceptual frameworks and practical skills.

In contrast, the sample of therapists agreed that their worst experiences were with closed, rigid, critical, invasive, and/or vulgar supervisors.

These findings were replicated by Drake Wallace, Wilcoxon, & Satcher (2010) in a factor analytic study of responses provided by a national sample of 278 experienced American Counseling Association counselors. This sample tied their satisfaction to an additional central concern: the relative presence or absence of clear, mutual expectations. Concurrently, another national survey of 42 CFT supervisees (Green & Dekkers, 2010) demonstrated that feminist supervision principles—attention to power and diversity issues—were statistically correlated with the extent to which these trainees were satisfied with their supervisory experiences. Congruent thematic analyses of surveys conducted by Okafor, Stevenson Wojciak, & Helfrich (2014) and by Piercy and his associates (2016) also uncovered valuable nuances in the supervisor–supervisee training subsystem, as does the interviewing of lesbian, gay, and bisexual supervisees reported by O'Brian and Rigazio-Digilio (2016).

Contemporary Research Initiatives

Currently, there are three major research initiatives in family therapy that have implications for its supervisors. The first is the empirical validation of specific kinds of family therapy. If a therapist extends one of these treatments to a clinical situation, that person presumably must conform to what has been scientifically shown to produce the desired results. This requirement for treatment fidelity across settings has led to manualized treatments; that is, auditable specification both of who should be treated and the lock-step requirements for the intervention. An excellent example of a manualized intervention is Multisystemic Therapy (Henggler & Sheidow, 2012). Supervision of empirically supported or manualized treatments is discussed in Chapter 13. A federally used rating system and examples of manualized treatments ranging from "well-supported, efficacious treatment" to "treatments eliciting concern" is available (Saunders, Berliner, & Hanson, 2004).

The second major research initiative is the exploration of generic factors that are thought to be common to all methods of psychotherapy, and therefore may inform the common finding that many therapies appear to be equal in their ability to facilitate change. There has been considerable discussion of what those common factors might be, leading to several conceptual models. One such model (Imel & Wampold, 2008) was derived psychometrically and presumably uncovered two dimensions (thinking and feeling) and three clusters (bonds, information, and roles). The researchers suggested that 30% to 70% of therapy outcome may result from these common factors. For further discussion of common factors and supervision, see Chapters 2 and 6.

Sprenkle and his associates (2009) suggested that the alleged existence of such common factors does not obviate the various major models of family therapy. There may be an interaction: Various therapeutic models may empower diverse clinical situations because of how—in those situations—they intensify the so-called common therapeutic factors. Prudent supervisors keep their eyes on both interventions and common factors such as therapeutic alliance. Nevertheless, just as Sprenkle (2005) observed that "there is not a scintilla of evidence supporting one major MFT theory over another," the same can be said of "common factors." Although generic therapeutic factors sound reasonable, there is no empirically determined evidence for them. They remain popular assumptions and have become the vehicle of choice for CFT training in many places.

A related area of inquiry actually began with Bordin in 1979. It has been alternately termed the "therapeutic" or "working" alliance. Bordin postulated that the efficacy of psychotherapy benefited to the extent that clients and therapists agreed to accept each other and an emerging emotional bond between them as well as goals, theory, and techniques. Subsequently, these concepts were developed into self-reports and rating scales to be applied to clients, therapists, and their interactions. Two comprehensive historical reviews of the literature are offered by Shelef and Diamond (2008) and Knerr and his associates (2011). Overall, it is possible that ratings of recorded sessions by trained observers may have the most predictive validity of what happens in therapy vis-à-vis the therapeutic alliance. In fact, the popular Vanderbilt Scale of Therapeutic Alliance—Revised (Shelef & Diamond) has been psychometrically reduced to five easy-to-observe items while doing family therapy. Sessions indicative of a working alliance are characterized by understanding and support, acceptance of the method employed, trust and nondefensiveness, common viewpoints, and common goals and tasks. These same observations may indicate effective working alliances among trainees and supervisors as well as therapists and clients.

Upon reflection, several observations appear to be important and several of them are valuable opportunities for research by supervisors and their trainees about supervision as well as therapy:

- The ability of the items that predict outcomes of various forms of therapy used with various clients is less a research question than an entire program of systematic research. "What characteristics of the therapeutic interaction, if any, are likely to be most associated with successful outcomes, with what groups of clients, using what forms of therapy?"
- The working alliance does not focus on the characteristics of either clients or therapists; it is transactional. Long ago, Marziali, Mamar, and Krupnick (1981) concluded that therapist and client interactions contribute to the attitudinal-affective climate of the therapy and cannot be ignored when evaluating outcomes. More recently, Knerr and his associates (2011) looked at working alliance formation as a function of CFT client traits and investigated how couples interacted in

its formation. Although Marziali and colleagues may have missed some factors in a complex process, Knerr's research team clearly understood the complexity of the processes involved. It is hopeful that their sophisticated multivariate analyses will soon include the role of therapists and settings in cultivating openness and enthusiasm in their clientele.

- If a working alliance can be defined by five observable interactional characteristics, then it might be an excellent vehicle for training in important therapeutic metaskills. These possibly could be tied to supervision or even therapy outcomes.
- If a working alliance can be defined and observed in clinical situations, and seen to be of value, it might usefully be extended to the supervisory system, that is, the observable interactions between supervisors and trainees.

Exercises

1. What are your ideas about how little research there is in CFT supervision?
2. If you were to design a supervision study, one question might be about which supervision activities most predict positive outcomes. This would require (a) some idea of positive outcomes and how to measure them, and (b) which activities to measure and how you would measure them. What are some ideas about this?
3. What other research questions can you think of that would be useful for studying CFT supervision?

8 Supervision Based on Core Competencies

In Chapter 6, we observed that supervisors historically conceptualized their philosophies of supervision in terms of their preferred models of therapy and taught those models to trainees. Rarely would therapy training be understood as including the supervisor and larger training system or supervisory processes, and even more rarely as isomorphic to clinical and other processes in that training system. More recently, we have observed supervisors of specific approaches applying ideas from those approaches to the therapist/client system as well as their supervisory process. That is, a supervisor using a structural approach would monitor boundaries in the therapist/client system as well as the supervisor/trainee system. However, a current trend is to create overarching models applied to diverse approaches to supervision. For example, in Chapter 6 we described Morgan and Sprenkle's (2007) invitation to use common factors in supervision and the meta-framework approach by Chang (Chapter 7).

In addition to their proposed common factors and to supervisory approaches that teach specific therapy approaches, Morgan and Sprenkle (2007) reviewed supervisory approaches that focused on what trainees need to learn. This so-called "outcome-based" education (OBE) approach has become more and more popular in US education (see Nelson & Smock, 2005, for discussion related to CFT education and some challenges; Nelson et al., 2007) and led to the development of the AAMFT Core Competencies (Appendix B). Outcome-based education necessitates that instructors focus on desired end results instead of specifying educational inputs and a particular number of supervised hours of clinical practice. Outcome-based approaches are predicated on the notion that getting to the destination is far more important than the particular road taken. In the case of CFT, regulators have the duty of quality control in order to protect both the consuming public and the profession itself. Therefore, CFT educators, trainers, and their trainees need to be able to demonstrate that the end product of their interactions consists of fundamental lore and competencies.

For example, couple and family therapists must be able to comfortably interview multiple people at the same time, and to manage dynamics in these settings so that therapists reach the ultimate goal of helping clients reach their goals. It matters less whether they learn these skills through role play, in-room observation, practice interviewing with nonclinical "clients," live supervision, or a mix of these methods

DOI: 10.4324/9781003099833-10

and others. Again, the purpose is the end result, and not a particular number of hours in a classroom or practicum setting.

In CFT, we see things through a systemic paradigm: We focus on patterns of interaction among people in a system. Trainees must learn to appreciate their own interaction tendencies in diverse contexts and systems, as well as those between them and their clients and between their clients and significant others. Trainees must also be able to engage clients within systems. Therefore, their training also includes a focus on microskills, for example, their abilities to listen, reflect, manage conflictual situations, and so forth, all among multiple people in a therapy room. Many or most schools of CFT also help trainees focus on specific skills related to particular approaches to therapy, whether classical approaches or evidence-based and integrative approaches (Lee & Nichols, 2010).

When working with postgraduate trainees, supervisors often focus on their own approaches to therapy or those selected by trainees. They attend to sophisticated skills such as conceptualizing a system and its multiple levels and contexts, interacting with other professionals, or selecting interventions based on philosophy and experience rather than textbook or supervisor recipes (e.g., J. T. Thomas, 2010).

The Need for a Standard

At both beginning and advanced levels of training, supervisors are obliged to pay attention to actual behaviors and evaluate therapists' competence against some sort of standard. Therefore, in 2003, the American Association for Marriage and Family Therapy (AAMFT) formed a task force with a steering committee to develop a list of skills or core competencies that could reasonably be expected of CFTs if they were to practice therapy without supervision. Through a multi-step process (see AAMFT, 2004; Nelson et al., 2007), the task force developed a format and list of competencies specifically for couple and family therapists.

The steering committee chose a format of CFT domains that reflected the typical progression through therapy, namely, from screening clients through evaluating therapy progress. Within each domain, subdomains were selected based on prior conceptualizations such as Tomm and Wright's (1979) triad of conceptual, perceptual, and executive skills. To these domains of skills were added evaluative and professional skills based on the data of the Basic Family Therapy Skills project (e.g., Figley & Nelson, 1989; Nelson & Johnson, 1999). Each subdomain includes a number of skills or competencies, mastery of which is considered essential for the independent practice of CFT at the time of typical licensure (presumed to be two years after acquisition of a terminal CFT degree). Common sense, the National Licensure Examination Program (Association of Marital and Family Therapy Regulatory Boards, 2020), and contemporary CFT program accreditation standards (COAMFTE, 2017) suggest that CFT supervisors focus their assessments of trainee capabilities on these fundamental outcome standards or something similar.

Core Competencies in CFT

The list of CCs (AAMFT, 2004; Nelson et al., 2007) appears daunting at first for many supervisors and therapists. It is lengthy, complex, and may seem impossible to meet. However, after spending some time with the format and items, most therapists and supervisors realize that the list is, quite simply, what we do: the skills, attributes, and behaviors that make us couple and family therapists. We master these competencies in a developmental manner and, as supervisors and licensed clinicians, we are better at most of them than we thought we were. Further, as systemic therapists, we see patterns: an emerging picture of areas of competence and areas that might benefit from attention. In this fashion, the list itself, or some form of it, can easily be used both to screen new trainees for areas requiring attention, developing a supervision plan, and to evaluate them toward specified goals at specified times.

Because the list is not meant to be mastered at the time of graduation from a CFT master's program, supervisors of postgraduate trainees can use the list to determine priorities in training. In collaboration with trainees, supervisors can set agreed-upon goals with means for evaluating trainees on those goals. To date, little research has been done on what supervisors as a group believe are the most important goals. Nelson and Graves (2011) surveyed supervisors of postgraduate trainees and found some interesting patterns about what that group thought was most important for trainees to bring with them to advanced training. The authors learned that supervisors have high standards for their trainees and need them to come to postgraduate training with high levels of skill and competence. At the same time, they recognize their responsibilities for taking new postgraduates through a process of becoming competent therapists. Further, supervisors may be able to get some idea from the Basic Family Therapy Skills project, especially Figley and Nelson (1989), which lays out the results of surveys regarding what supervisors thought was most important for beginning therapists. Also, supervisors can create training plans by combining consensus across core competencies needing to be mastered with their own philosophies.

Subdomains within CFT Core Competencies

In the remainder of this chapter, we examine the contents of the CCs by exploring each of the five task domains' constituent subdomains.

Conceptual Competencies

Conceptual skills are the kinds of things that often are learned from books, lectures, and discussions about CFT. Although there are many skills common to all mental health professions (Lee, Emerson, & Kochka, 1999; Midori Hanna 2019), and also many skills unique to particular approaches to CFT, the CC conceptual competencies focus on generic CFT cognitive skills. Also, many of the CCs apply to other mental health fields and others might be what CFTs would consider as "value-added." That is, a particular skill might be enhanced when seen through a systemic lens.

System Concepts

At the top of the list of important conceptual skills are those related to system thinking: not "systems thinking" or "systems theory," but system *thinking*—the ability to think about the world and all that is in it from a paradigm that says all things are recursively connected in some fashion. Therefore, changes in one part of a system effect changes in all other parts, including relationships among the parts (von Bertalanffy, 1968). This is particularly true in human interaction. As interactional or relational therapists, we understand that what goes on inside people's heads is important to their feelings and behaviors. We also believe that behaviors are important to thinking and feelings, and feelings are important to thinking and behaviors. They are all caught up together and influence each other in systemic and systematic ways that remain mysteries to us. In addition, what goes on with individuals also interacts with other individuals within a context of systems, subsystems, and relationships among the various parts of the context. This is the concept encompassed in the notion of *wholeness*: The parts are important, but adding them up (the sum) produces a different logical level of understanding. The *whole* is *different* from the *sum of the parts*.

However, as Bateson (1972) and the folks at the Mental Research Institute (e.g., Watzlawick, Bavelas, & Jackson, 1967) taught, where we focus our first attention (a concept called *punctuation*) says more about us as observers than about what actually happens. When we add another person to the mix, we have a conglomerate of thinking, feeling, behaving, and relating to each other's thinking, feeling, and behaving in ways that lead to meanings about those thoughts, feelings, behaviors, and relationships. Individuals then construct meaning about everything together. The worldview of system thinking as a paradigm is centered on the concept of wholeness: the wide perspective that each part and its relationship to all other parts, including relationships and meanings, make up a complex mix. From this epistemological point of view, a number of system concepts are important in CFT that are distinct from individual therapy. It is important for supervisors to be mindful of these concepts in their work with supervision and training systems as well as to ensure that their trainees develop systemic understanding of systems. There are a number of resources for reviewing system concepts and helping trainees work from a system paradigm. The classic introduction to structural family therapy—*Family Therapy Techniques* (Minuchin & Fishman, 1981)—with its many illustrations, immediately and compellingly shifts a trainee's focus from the individual to behavior as a function of family dynamics. In the past few decades, the majority of CFT introductory texts are centered around the family system and take into consideration the larger ecosystems of which it is a transacting unit (for example, Becvar & Becvar, 2012, 2017, and the many good illustrations in Shajani & Snell, 2019).

Patterns. First, the relationships among the parts become the focus of relational therapists. Yes, the parts themselves are important, but it is easy to get caught in blame-games as therapists when we focus on the parts. Therefore, we strive to describe patterns of interaction (e.g., Bateson, 1972; Green, 2011; Watzlawick et al., 1967) in their social contexts (Minuchin & Fishman, 1981). We then target these patterns (rather than focusing on individuals) for interventions to interrupt them. This applies to patterns of interaction between therapists and clients; supervisors and trainees; and trainees, supervisors, and training systems.

Circular Causality. Second, we focus on circular rather than linear thinking. We do not focus on the causes of the troubles that are put before us, but on patterns of interaction. The outcome of an interaction becomes information that is fed back into the system, and thereby affects meanings and subsequent behaviors, thoughts, feelings, and other interactions. A does not cause B; rather, it influences B, but so do a number of other things that influence A and B. The response of B becomes new information that is fed back into the system and further influences the pattern.

Other System Concepts. We talk about *morphogenesis*—the tendency for a human system to grow and change—and *morphostasis*—the tendency for human systems to maintain stability. We talk about *open* and *closed* systems, *boundaries, process* versus *content*, and so on. We look at *complementarity*, *recursion*, and *isomorphism* as concepts that help us understand patterns of interaction and how they are repeated in different areas of people's lives and across subsystems and systems. Almost any good textbook on CFT will provide a decent discussion of basic system concepts, and we believe it is vital that relational supervisors work with their trainees to understand these concepts in families and in therapy. Note, however, that various authors put forth slightly different meanings for some of the concepts.

Furthermore, because of isomorphism, the notion that patterns of interaction tend to be similar across subsystems, we believe that it is important for relational therapists to apply their understanding of these ideas to families, to therapy, and to supervision. We often have noticed that when chaotic interactions in families are allowed to dictate chaotic interactions in therapy, it is easy for supervision also to become chaotic. Similarly, when supervisors help therapists remain calm and think through the dynamics and patterns of what is happening in therapy and in client families, it is easier for those dynamics and patterns to occur in the therapy and family systems. The alternative is for therapists to be inducted into the system in such a way that they cannot see themselves as part of the interactions and thus are unable to interrupt the patterns in helpful ways.

We encourage supervisors to review system concepts for themselves and with their trainees as ways to enhance the learning of other competencies in family therapy.

Couple and Family Therapy Conceptualization

Although many couple and family therapy supervisors practice particular approaches to therapy, we believe it is helpful for supervisors to encourage therapists to read widely and to understand many paradigms, theories, models, and approaches. We find interesting discussions and debates in nearly all journals and texts related to family therapy. These sharpen our thinking and challenge our practices. By understanding different approaches and the integration of many approaches, therapists become better at thinking critically and evaluating how different ideas fit into (or not) their own approaches.

Understanding many approaches not only helps trainees prepare for licensing examinations, it helps with conversing with other professionals, ideas for stuck times in therapy, and challenging one's own work so that it does not become stagnant. Trainees leave most graduate programs with rather narrow knowledge about a variety of approaches. Reading unfamiliar texts and attending workshops on other approaches after graduating serves to improve their abilities to conduct and evaluate therapy. Becoming theoretically multilingual makes it possible for couple and family therapists to co-edit common understanding with both supervisors and clients, and facilitates integrative approaches to supervision and clinical interventions (see below and Lee & Everett, 2004). Learning about many therapy approaches also helps trainees discover more about what does and does not fit for them and their work.

Competency in Assessment, Diagnosis, and Evaluation

This area of competency includes the ability to use the language of CFT and other orientations to adequately recognize (see perceptual competencies, below), assess, and communicate within and across clinical spheres of practice. It addresses the need for a fundamental conceptual base and recognition of the limits of standardized forms of assessment and diagnosis.

Conceptual base. Couple and family therapists should be trained to understand the nomenclature and cultures of many approaches to therapy so that they can be conversant with other professionals, particularly those who practice from a linear or medical approach rather than a circular view of causality. Science and mental health theory do not always agree and many relational therapists also understand that some phenomena are biologically or medically based or influenced. Until science can definitively distinguish cause and effect among biology, context, and behavior or emotions, debates will continue. Regardless, relational therapists and supervisors will be interested in how all of these factors influence each other and manifest that influence. Conceptual bases include system thinking, cybernetic approaches, attachment theory, and brain science, among others. Others use a dialectic approach wherein two disparate epistemologies are considered, for example, postmodern and empirically based practice (e.g., Jacobs, Kissil, Scott, & Davey, 2010).

Therefore, some therapists and supervisors will be more interested than others in DSM diagnoses and relationships among medications, behaviors or symptoms, human interactional dynamics, and perhaps neuroscience. Capacity to think in this way also may be mandated by the institutional context of the intervention. Along with individual symptom assessments and diagnoses, relational therapists are interested in the way different people in client systems think and behave in interaction with those assessments and diagnoses as well as other contextual factors that impact multiple levels of the system. Relational therapists also are interested in the interactional dynamics among the people who are part of such client systems, including family members, coworkers, and other professionals. Depending upon a particular therapist's or supervisor's perspective on these issues, the nomenclature related to individual and system therapies can help in determining how to talk to other people including clients, family members, physicians, and so forth. This kind of collaborative talk can also help determine treatment plans.

Standardized assessment and diagnostic procedures. Couple and family assessment inventories can help trainees recognize a client system's dynamics. Not all have been found to be scientifically valid, but some have proven to be quite robust. Examples are the *Revised Dyadic Adjustment Scale* (Busby, Crane, Larson, & Christensen,1995), *Marital Satisfaction Inventory – Revised* (Snyder & Aikman, 1999), and the *Systemic Therapy Inventory of Change* (Pinsof & Chambers, 2009). In addition, other scales can help the members of training systems (supervisors, therapists, and clients) assess the kind and level of improvement being made toward particular goals of therapy. Knowledge about devices for evaluating therapists such as the *Basic Skills Evaluation Device* (Nelson & Johnson, 1999), the *Family Therapy Skills Checklist* (Briggs, Fournier, & Hendrix, 1999), or the CC list itself (AAMFT, 2004; Nelson et al., 2007) can help therapists evaluate both therapy and themselves. In addition, if the training system of which you are a part is shaped by a postmodern, social constructivist epistemology, evaluation forms with demonstrated trustworthiness have long been available (Flemons, Green, & Rambo, 1996; Glenn & Serovich, 1994).

Northey and Gehart (2019) condensed the Core Competencies into 16 categories, mapping the original Core Competencies, and revising them in a way they believe will better match the AMFTRB domains used for the MFT National Examination and better match curriculum requirements for COAMFTE-accredited program curricula.

Regardless of the kind of assessment or evaluation devices used, relational therapists use them in conjunction with first-hand interviewing and observing client and therapy dynamics. This first-hand knowledge and assessment often cannot be captured in paper-and-pencil tests, and it is important that therapists gain clear understandings of the purposes, conduct, and evaluation of their own experiences as actual knowledge or evidence when moving through different phases of therapy, guided by supervisors.

The role of the supervisor in the area of knowledge competencies in this domain often is quite clear: teaching and referring to respected literature. The supervisor's role in this area is important, but should be limited to assessing the trainee's knowledge in certain areas and directing them so that they can learn the material themselves and bring it back to supervision for discussion about how it impacts or informs their therapy.

Ethical and Legal Imperatives

Couple and family therapists practice under a different paradigm than individual therapists who focus on the thoughts, feelings, and behaviors of individuals.

Instead, they focus on patterns in relationships. The "client" in CFT is the couple or family as a whole—the patterned relationship dynamics, and not only the individuals within the client system. Accordingly, we have different ethical standards to uphold. For example, CFTs must obtain written permission (authorization) from everyone who has been in therapy in a clinical case in order to release information to a third party, even if only one individual wants the information released, and there is an individual who attended only one session. Even when seeing individuals in therapy, systemic or relational therapists keep the significant others of the treatment systems in mind. In so doing they discern patterns of interaction and relationships as well as thinking, feeling, and behavioral systems. Chapters 11 and 12 cover CFT ethical and best practice standards in more detail. Suffice it here to say that ethical and legal knowledge is very important in relational therapy and can be complex and even complicated. Often there are twists and turns that seem incompatible.

Perceptual Competencies

Perceptual competencies are those that tie conceptual competencies to actual therapy data. For example, a trainee may be quite adept at book knowledge yet must be able to understand concepts within the context of real rather than hypothetical client systems. It is an interesting academic exercise to understand how to read relational maps from structural family therapy (Minuchin, 1974). Doing this can lead to many discussions and ideas. However, it is a very different exercise to learn how to apply family dynamics to those maps and how to trace both the desired and actual changes in clinical family interactions. For example, one of our favorite questions when trainees discuss structural maps, couple sequences, or family genograms is, "What tells you that this is so," meaning, "What are the perceived data that lead to this idea?" One trainee mentioned a client who had a "gleam" in her eye during an interaction with her husband. The student conceptually believed that the client was teasing the husband because she perceived this "gleam" as evidence of "fun." It was not until a third party pointed out that the husband had looked away and frowned that the trainee re-examined her hypothesis, which had become a fact in her mind. The third party thought the "gleam" might be moistened eyes accompanied by a forced smile, interpreting it as disappointment or hurt in the interaction with the husband. She had used data from the relational dynamic—the husband's response—rather than the wife only. There are other possibilities as well. The point is that concepts inform what we see (perceptions) and the meanings we make from our observations.

Interactions with others, conversations, and contexts affect perceptions. We believe that it is important for supervisors to help trainees hold their so-called knowledge tentatively. Prudence dictates a critical eye toward how one's view may or may not be useful for a situation (or even valid). For example, understanding expert opinions on eating disorders (a complex phenomenon involving body chemistry, society's ideas about bodies, and relational dynamics) freed one client family to explore options based on a new understanding of the phenomenon rather than the one they had been operating under (namely, their daughter was trying to hurt them). In contrast, another client family found it alienating and devaluing of their opinions.

Some therapists and clients believe a particular form of therapy is preferred because it has been deemed "best practices," "evidence-based," or endorsed by a TV personality. For others who have been through several such treatments, these ideas may hold no sway. The therapist in such a situation will do best by working from a different approach. Therapists must weigh different ideas when determining the best courses of action or interventions for specific situations. In this way, knowledge or conceptual competency meet observations and become a different kind of "knowledge," that is, one that applies uniquely to a particular situation.

The role of the supervisor with regard to perceptual competency is to continually evaluate the trainee's progress in connecting knowledge with therapy information. This can be done through observations of the trainee's therapy, or observations of what trainees say when they are watching colleagues' therapy or participating in group supervision. They also can include observations of video recordings, discussions around role plays, and discussions about the trainee's observations in general.

We have found that it often is easy for supervisors to tell therapists what they are doing that is either good or that needs improvement. However, they often do not connect these behaviors (see next section on executive skills) with knowledge from books and articles and what is happening in the therapy room. More than once, a trainee has described grand patterns of sequences, hypotheses about interactional dynamics, and/or the perspectives of this or that therapy or theory approach. It often is more difficult to ask or observe how the therapist connects concepts and hypotheses with what is actually happening. Sometimes, therapists have tunnel vision. That is, they are missing things because they are focused on their own perspective of events rather than the family's, or they are tracking information that may not fit the concepts or hypotheses that require consideration. We tend to see what we are looking for and this is true for therapists and supervisors as well.

Executive Competencies

Executive competencies are those that we tend to think of as the "doing" of therapy. They constitute the biggest share of most of the therapy competency domains. We might think of them as interventions. However, they go beyond interventions. Executive competencies include making sure that clients understand the "informed" part of Informed Consent, administering assessment devices or other paperwork as appropriate, filling out and filing paperwork as required and appropriate, assessing through interview questions, and so forth.

Executive skills also include interventions as prescribed by singular approaches. However, when trainees are learning integrated models, executive skills include those that assist in integrating different philosophies, assumptions, concepts, interventions, and evaluative methods from different approaches. It often is easy for supervisors to do therapy through their trainees and simply tell trainees what they should be doing rather than leading them in an exercise of decision-making about what to do. Supervisory roles and skills are different in outcome-based contexts where the focus is on what trainees learn rather than what supervisors tell trainees to do. Throughout the process, however, the role of supervisors is to teach and coach; the role of therapist resides with the clients. This leads to the dictum: "Supervisors do not do the therapy; trainees do."

Supervisors often ask trainees what they want from particular supervisory sessions or their learning goals for a particular session with clients. Supervisors stay trainee-centered better when they focus on trainees' goals rather than clinical content. At the same time, the supervisor needs to know how the therapist's knowledge and perceptions fit into a therapy approach that leads clearly through a decision tree toward specific interventions and desired outcomes.

To help trainees improve particular in-session skills, supervisors often take on the role of coach. In Morgan and Sprenkle's (2007) view, this is focusing on particular skills with particular clients. On the other hand, supervisors may also use these moments in supervision to teach certain skills to improve therapists' performance in general with an idea toward coaching as a next step.

Evaluative Competencies

There are many ways to conceptualize evaluation. In the context of the CCs, there are two: evaluation of therapy and evaluation of self as a therapist. We are aware that these areas overlap. For example, skill at evaluating therapy progress requires skill in assessing one's own therapy behavior. Across the different domains of the CCs, evaluation skills point toward the ability of therapists to objectively and subjectively assess progress in therapy as well as their own progress as competent therapists: what they do well and what they need to work on.

As supervisors, our roles may include and overlap with all of Morgan and Sprenkle's (2007) categories. As teachers, we may help trainees learn about assessments in general and how to administer and interpret paper assessments as well as information derived from interviewing and observing clients and their systems. We then may coach trainees in the different skills needed at each step, and step back as they gain experience and expertise. We may serve as mentors to help them situate such ideas within their own philosophies of therapy and, as administrators, we may review their work for completeness and accuracy.

Learning to evaluate oneself as a therapist requires a different set of skills, many of which require stepping back and viewing oneself from outside the therapy or supervisory system, or even outside oneself. This requires a critical eye and an ability to critique one's own work. Because doing so is often subjective, trainees can use evaluation instruments for self-evaluation as well as their supervisors' evaluation of the trainees' progress. Gehart (2010) provides many ideas for helping therapists evaluate themselves across the CCs. Nelson and Johnson's (1999) Basic Skills Evaluation Device, although designed and tested for therapists who are just beginning to do therapy, can also be used to help therapists evaluate themselves at many different developmental stages. As supervision progresses, we would hope that trainees' evaluations of themselves and their supervisors' evaluations of them would come together. Therapists also might ask clients for feedback (e.g., "Are we on the right track?" "Is this working for you?"), or use other assessment devices to evaluate the accuracy of their self-assessments. The Session Rating Scale and Outcome Rating Scale (see Duncan, Miller, & Sparks, 2004) are good tools for obtaining feedback from clients that can be used to evaluate both therapy and therapists, including the therapeutic alliance (see also Sparks, Kisler, Adams, & Blumen, 2011, regarding using client feedback to guide therapy).

In this realm of self-evaluation, we believe that supervisors perform roles as coaches, helping therapists improve their abilities to judge their own ideas and behaviors against the therapy approaches they prefer. Supervisors also estimate trainees' conceptual, perceptual, and executive skills and we would hope that clients' outcomes correlate with these evaluations.

Jay Lebow (1996, 2006) described a process he engaged in to evaluate his therapy outcomes as well as his abilities over time to help clients reach their goals. He did this by examining his progress notes and gauging client outcomes for each case. By looking at his notes over time, he noted what worked best for him for certain kinds of cases (e.g., teen troubles). He then adjusted his therapy accordingly. Using this method (practice-based evidence), a therapist becomes a researcher of his or her own therapy and can substantially improve evaluation skills over time for both therapy outcomes and skills as a therapist.

Therapists also sometimes get stuck in therapy for reasons other than lack of perceptual or executive skill. For example, their own "stuff" may impact therapy in negative ways (a clue may be that they over- or under-react.) Current personal stresses such as divorce or caring for elderly parents, family of origin factors such as family dynamics around alcohol use, and a myriad of other personal factors impact therapists' objectivity. Therapists must be able to recognize and evaluate these factors effectively and supervisors should be both alert for these issues and capable of helping their trainees with their management of them (Aponte et al., 2009). Failure to do so can lead to compromised judgment and impairment.

Professional Competencies

In many ways, some of the most enjoyable times in supervision—other than celebrating well-executed interventions and client change—are watching new or newer therapists grow in skill, confidence, and professionalism. Professional competencies include a diverse set of behaviors: wearing clothes appropriate to therapy settings, learning the difference between appropriate and inappropriate touch, managing one's own feelings, interacting appropriately with other professionals, keeping skills sharp by reading, attending conferences and workshops, and discussing cases with colleagues while being received into the ranks of our field. Professional behavior also includes keeping abreast of new knowledge and requirements in the field and assisting with broader activities such as being active in professional organizations or helping with legislative activities that benefit families and therapists.

Although this subdomain of the CCs has the fewest items associated with it, we have noticed that therapists who do well in this area often are those who do well in other areas. We each have had students in our ethics courses raise their hands while we were discussing scope of practice and comment on the fact that, by ethics code and law, we are not supposed to use skills that we have not yet developed. We had the trainees discuss this apparent conundrum by considering the differences between using interventions for which one has not yet been trained as opposed to practicing in a context of supervision.

A CFT graduate student was asked what she would consider to be the best way to practice ethically and she replied, "to practice well." In her response she came across as more collegial than some licensed folks we have known. She understood that professional therapists—those who practice ethically and responsibly—are the ones who attend to the outcomes of their therapy as well as their own progress as competent therapists, or how accurately they followed a written code. We believe that supervisors can help provide contexts for this kind of growth. However, it requires second-order change that we can, at best, stand back with fingers crossed and celebrate when it happens.

Impaired Participants in Supervisory Systems

There is one other area we would like to discuss before concluding this chapter: the ability to evaluate one's self in terms of impairment or judgment (e.g., F. N. Thomas, 2010). All mental health ethics codes and many state/provincial laws that regulate the practice of therapy require that therapists take steps to protect themselves and thus their clients from impaired judgment. There are many kinds of therapist impairment. However, to date, most literature on impaired therapists relates to inappropriate sexual behavior or substance misuse/abuse. That said, the literature on therapist self-care covers topics such as fatigue, illness, grief, life circumstance, family of origin triggers, and inability to manage boundaries (F. N. Thomas, 2010; J. T. Thomas, 2010). For many of these concerns, therapists may be too close to judge themselves well. Often, family members or other therapists may see symptoms of impairment before the therapists do.

In the supervisory context, of course, supervisors must keep always keep watchful eyes to evaluate therapists' ability to make sound judgments (F. N. Thomas, 2010; J. T. Thomas, 2010). It also is our responsibility as supervisors to help our training therapists learn signs of impaired judgment and act accordingly. More is said in the chapters on ethics (Chapter 12) and self of the therapist (Chapter 13) in this text. However, it is clear to all of us that the same proscriptions and prescriptions that apply to therapists and our trainees also apply to us as supervisors. We too need to appreciate the extent of our reactions to trainees, case situations, and institutional structures. We need to keep our knowledge current and to stay informed about the "best practices" of CFT. In this regard, we are saddened to see that there is a tendency for supervisors and therapists to diminish their professional reading and organizational participation once "out in the field" (Lee, Nichols, Nichols, & Odom, 2004). Likewise, there has been a substantial decrease in the number of therapists and supervisors who have undergone their own therapy (Lee et al., 2004).

Managing impaired training systems is often a challenge for supervisors. Whether supervisors are part of the training programs or agencies in which their trainees are learning therapy, supervisors may sometimes be called upon to advocate for their trainees on the one hand, or clearly explain rules to their trainees. Changing extra-level systems (e.g., administrators) can be daunting but sometimes must be attempted and, at other times, accepted and worked around. It is incumbent on supervisors to remember principles of isomorphism and to be on the lookout for how they may be contributing to training system impairment. Consultation with trusted colleagues can be invaluable at these times.

Exercises

1 Choose a domain and subdomain of the core competencies. (a) How might you assess a trainee for competence in this area? (b) How might you help a trainee improve competence in this area?
2 What kind of a process might you use for evaluating trainees' progress?
3 If the CCs do not work for you in terms of setting goals and evaluating trainees' development as therapists, what else might you use?
4 Choose a CFT concept. Think about actual clinical data connected to that concept. How do the two together look different from each separately (wholeness and relationship)?
5 What can you do to help you stay trainee-focused rather than doing therapy through the therapist?

9 Supervising Manual-Based Models

In the past two decades, mental health disciplines have privileged therapeutic approaches with empirically demonstrated efficacy (Craighead, Craighead, & Miklowitz, 2008). This is not to say that other interventions are not effective, but that they have not been demonstrated so in a systematic way, involving randomized, rigorously constructed clinical trials using treatment manuals (Wampold, Ollendick, & King, 2006; see also Sexton et al., 2011 for discussions of guidelines for classifying evidence-based treatments in CFT) and employing adequate control groups and attention to method biases (Podsakoff, MacKenzie, Lee, & Podsakoff, 2003). Family therapy researchers have attempted to meet some of these challenges and their work has been reviewed in special issues of the *Journal of Marital and Family Therapy* (October 1995, and January 2012). These treatments historically have been grouped under several names: "empirically validated treatments/therapies," "empirically supported treatments/therapies," "evidence-based treatments," and "manual-based treatment/therapies." In this chapter, all of these will be considered "manualized interventions" in that all of them presuppose a detailed user's manual that states how the intervention must be done.

The overall viability of manualized interventions has been hotly discussed (Beutler, 2000; Marsiglia & Booth, 2015; Reed, Kihlstrom, & Messer, 2006; Rubin & Parrish, 2007; Spring et al., 2005). Nonetheless, political and economic forces ensure that many contemporary and future family therapy supervisors will be supervising "manualized" interventions. Once a credible review board decides that an intervention is an efficacious and cost-effective treatment for a specific mental health issue in a specific population, a strong argument can be made for others to do the same thing in order to get comparable positive results. For others to "do the same thing" presupposes that the actual approach has been thoroughly described in an intervention manual and taught to other clinicians thoroughly, so that, if the client population is the same, comparable results can be expected (examples include Kim, Smock, Trepper, McCollum, & Franklin, 2010; Wiebe & Johnson, 2016). Therefore, conversations around these assumptions typically involve concerns about the comprehensiveness of the treatment manual, treatment fidelity, therapist allegiance, and appropriate client population.

At the core of evidence-supported interventions is the requirement that once a regimen is established, it will be repeated in additional settings in exactly the same

DOI: 10.4324/9781003099833-11

way; otherwise, one would not obtain the same results. Therefore, the proponents of a given approach must find a way, not only to teach and train the crucial parts of an approach, but also to audit its performance in the field with diverse clients in diverse settings (Marsiglia & Booth, 2015). The interface, of course, between developer and clinician is the clinical supervisor. In order to adequately supervise a manualized treatment, supervisors must be trained in its procedures, and their performance and that of their trainees must be consistently and adequately monitored and audited. That is why intervention developers (e.g., Deblinger & Heflin, 1996) require those who wish to use their programs to become certified in its use and to participate in *strict oversight with continual correction*. Many contemporary technique certification programs do not meet the latter requirement.

Various review panels have compiled family interventions offered in the professional literature and have rated them in terms of their documented efficacy for given problems in given client samples. A typical example is the Urban Institute's juried compilation of intervention for families with adolescents at risk for homelessness (Pergamit, Gelatt, Stratford, Beckwith, & Martin, 2016; see also Craven & Lee, 2006, and Saunders, Berliner, & Hanson, 2004). Each such formal list of recommendations is the product of systematic reviews (Uman, 2011) made of interventions described in the professional literature. The results of several studies employing each intervention are then synthesized (e.g., Craven & Lee, 2006; Saunders et al., 2004). Subsequent ratings take into account not just the benefits to be expected from an intervention program, but existing infrastructure (manuals, training programs, provisions for oversight) and quality and amount of the efficacy research. The ratings typically range from "1" (well-supported, efficacious treatment) to "6" (a treatment largely lacking empirical support and that merits clinical concern).

Supervisors who have been trained in the model and have great confidence in it (allegiance), which is recognized as a necessary component for positive clinical outcomes, will have little difficulty. Examples of supervision for such models include Emotionally Focused Therapy (EFT; Johnson, 2008), Multisystemic Therapy (Henggler & Schaeffer, 2010), and Functional Family Therapy (e.g., Sexton, 2009).

> The founder and disseminators of EFT (e.g., Johnson, 2003) have emphasized the scientist-practitioner orientation of this approach and recent literature is rich with examinations of both EFT treatment (see reviews in Denton, Burleson, Clark, Rodriguez, & Hobbs, 2000, and Wiebe & Johnson, 2016) and supervision (e.g., Inouye, Madsen, Palmer-Olsen, Faller, & Best, 2017; Palmer-Olsen, Gold, & Woolley, 2011). However, none meet the rigorous requirements of randomized clinical trials. Several are qualitative. And although several of the quantitative treatment investigations employ control groups, they do not involve large samples or random assignment to groups.

It may be difficult to supervise models that have been "transported" from clinical trials, with their clearly defined clinical populations and great oversight, to the "real" world of mental health agency therapy where things are typically messier, therapists not as well trained in the approach or as keen on it, and the population more diverse on many factors (see Addis, Wade, & Hatgis, 1999; Marsiglia & Booth, 2015; Westen, Novotny, & Thompson-Brenner, 2004).

The Challenge of Executive-, Meta-, and Microskills

Some critics of the trend toward manualized treatment decry what they foresee as "cookie cutter" approaches to mental health. However, even very detailed manuals, accompanied by rigorous training and clinical oversight do not necessarily bring the constancy that is assumed by those who conduct clinical outcomes research. Clients seldom exhibit symptoms as singularly as defined in the random trial phase of research. Also, important concerns have been raised about the validity of definitions and behaviors obtained in one subculture when they are transported to another. For example, the connotations of words and behavior in rural areas in the Deep South may not be the same as those in inner-city Chicago. Moreover, supervisors and trainees are different in kind, amount, and nuanced flexibility with regard to their executive-, micro-, and metaskills as well as their general philosophies about clinical concerns, clients, and how best to help those clients. Yet, these supervisors and therapists, although not using manualized treatments, are effective at helping clients overcome their clinical concerns (Messer, 2004; Spring et al., 2005; Westen et al., 2004). Indeed, the relative presence of these skills in unique combinations of supervisors, therapists, and clients are at the core of what Beutler and Harwood (2000) call "prescriptive psychotherapy." They hypothesized that these skills are the ultimate change agents in therapeutic interventions and will be found to outweigh both clinical theory and diagnosis in facilitating client change. Therefore, prudent supervisors will be alert to the development of such skills apart from what clinical theory or protocol is employed.

Executive skills are those behaviors involved in the administration of an interview or intervention. These include time management, where attention is focused, the intervention itself and how it is delivered, what processing is done, and how problems are solved within the research-based approach.

Microskills comprise the cornerstone of effective therapy or supervision, most especially, effective communication: attending, questioning, clarifying, affirming, encouraging, summarizing, reframing, and so on. Falender and Shafranske (2004) observed that a rarely mentioned but vitally important microskill is awareness by supervisors of what they do not know in a situation. After all, the data of supervision often are hearsay (progress notes, verbal and written summaries, and informal consultations) and even that which is available live or on video is filtered through both trainee and supervisor perceptual lenses. What is important to the current discussion is that such characteristics of supervision are neither mentioned nor taught in intervention manuals. However, they may be vital to effective interventions and can be modeled and coached through good supervision. For example, microcounseling (Daniels, Rigazio-Digilio, & Ivey, 1997) is a technique for teaching microskills to beginning therapists. Daniels and colleagues have organized skills into a hierarchical sequence and teach one skill at a time.

In a similar vein, also not a part of intervention manuals, but coachable, are metaskills. Metaskills are the unique feeling qualities and attitudes said to characterize effective therapists and supervisors, and that facilitate their work: "deep spiritual attitudes and beliefs manifest in therapy and in every daily life" (Mindell, 2001, p. 15).This is not as nebulous as at first it may seem. For example, two easily recognized metaskills are excitement about one's own experience and the tendency to keep at and follow something until comprehension dawns from blindness or mystery. One very important metaskill for positive results of any approach is the belief on the part of the therapist that the approach is appropriate and will be effective. Supervisors of such approaches often must instill this belief.

Guidelines for Ethical Practice

Supervision of manualized interventions presents a special problem in supervision: Manualized treatments are meant to be carried out as written and often do not attend to within-diagnostic group differences, including the presence of comorbidity. That is, both anxiety and depression may be present, or substance use, or tendencies toward obsessions or compulsions, and so on. Moreover, they also do not recognize the importance of the executive, meta-, and microskills involved in successfully addressing complex clinical cases in diverse treatment and cultural settings. In fact, these caveats were raised when manualized interventions were first being published (see Henry, Strupp, Butler, Schacht, & Binder, 1993). From the beginning, there was some evidence that training in manualized interventions might dampen the development or demonstration of these vital healing skills. In addition, intervention manuals often are experienced by clinicians as inflexible and dictated by theories sometimes unfamiliar to the practicing clinician (Caspar cited by Beutler, 2000). Caught between contemporary pressures to employ manualized treatments, the lack of adequate training and supervision in the field (as opposed to clinical trials), and ethical concerns about the welfare of clients, therapists, and the larger community, what are trainers and supervisors to do?

Supervisors need to be aware of false confidence on the parts of themselves, manualized program developers, trainees, and clients. However, they also need to be aware of cynicism on their part that may prove a barrier to training and effective intervention. Supervisors need to attend to the climate of "healing" that may be involved in therapeutic change. In short, supervisors need to develop executive, meta-, and microskills in themselves, their trainees, and the clinical setting. If supervisors demonstrate these characteristics and a genuine belief in the treatments they are supervising, supervision and treatment can go well.

In a prudent and balanced way, supervisors need to be led by their professional acumen where there appears to be a conflict with the apparent rigidity of a manualized intervention and ethical clinical treatment. Consultation with the model developers and external sources may be necessary. Insights and concerns should be part of a circular communication and feedback system throughout the supervisory system, and it must include the manualized program developers/administrators. Experiences "out in the field" are necessary for a manualized program's evolving sophistication; that is, the recognition of signs of mismatch and decisions about what and how to change, given a specified clinical context.

Increasing the Probability of Positive Results

From early on, many supervisors and therapists have had grave misgivings about manual-based interventions (Addis et al., 1999). Common concerns have involved the apparent lack of attention to therapist variables or the therapeutic relationship, unmet client needs, competence and job satisfaction, treatment credibility, restriction of clinical innovation, and the feasibility of manual-based interventions, given the diversities inherent in contemporary clinical practice. Such meaningful concerns notwithstanding, it is likely that most supervisors will find themselves expected to supervise manual-based interventions, especially if they supervise therapists through academic and research institutions, large-scale service centers, and community clinics that have adopted specific evidence-based approaches. Clinical trials may be an important part of these institutions' missions.

Whatever caveats clinicians and their supervisors may hold, the probability of success of manualized interventions with clients can be expected to be increased to the extent that:

1 Supervisors are certified to teach and train the manualized intervention in question.
2 There is a well-constructed intervention manual embodied in an administrative system that provides adequate training in the approach, close auditing of its application, and correction mechanisms that maximize treatment fidelity. This process requires continual and consistent interplay between those applying the intervention and program training staff, managed through supervisors. It also requires an administrative buy-in to the approach.
3 Trained therapists who hold allegiance to the approach.
4 Consistent attention is given to the development of executive, meta-, and microskills. Supervisors and trainees need to recognize cues that signal a need for flexibility and when to shift what is being done, as well as what the approach suggests about such shifts. Skills need to be conducive to healing and change. Self-observation, modeling, shaping, and positive social reinforcement are important training tools for such vital skills.
5 There is constant alertness for mismatch of manualized instructions with the contextual factors where they currently are being applied; that is, there needs to be some mechanism for taking clients out of the approach when necessary. Perceived obstacles to the use of manualized interventions in complicated settings, compounded by a lack of empirically based guidelines stating what should be done and under what circumstances, may result in field modifications of what the program originators intended (Ruscio & Holohan, 2006).

This alertness to modifications in the program, like treatment fidelity, requires continual and consistent interplay between those applying the intervention and program training staff. Supervisors are the interface between both systems and may ask the developers to provide booster trainings.

6 Supervisors hold themselves to ethical guidelines for practice with manualized interventions.

The bottom line for supervising manualized approaches is that therapists and supervisors must believe in the approach and have good relationships with the developers so that problems can be managed without detriment to clients or to the research. In clinical trials with closely controlled manuals and supervision, this is not too difficult. However, for therapists and supervisors who are working in transported situations, that is, without such close controls, the situation is more complicated and requires close collaboration with the developers of the approach.

Exercises

1 What are your personal beliefs about different levels of manualized treatments? (a) Related to controlled research? (b) Carried out in agencies that cannot control many variables?
2 Suppose you are a supervisor in an agency where administrators have decided to use a "Best Practices" approach about which you are skeptical. How do you think you can engage people at different levels in the system in a way that does not encourage collusions and negative triangles, yet addresses your concerns?
3 One of our ethical imperatives is to further the field of CFT, which includes participating in or encouraging research. What can you do in your setting?

Part 3

Contextual Considerations

An Overview

DOI: 10.4324/9781003099833-12

10 Contextual Aspects of Supervision

Setting, Culture, and Self

As relational, systemic therapists, we know that context influences people's actions, thoughts, emotions, and interactions. We are not islands, but selves in context. Each member of the training system perceives, thinks, feels, and acts differently with regard to all others depending on the professional context as well as a myriad of other factors. The personal and professional backgrounds of therapists and supervisors, characteristics of the training setting, and general factors of culture all combine in the mix of therapy and training. Context also includes the explicit and implicit purposes for which an interaction is taking place; for example, case conceptualization, and live or video observation may focus on client data or self-of-the-therapist issues, group interaction, and so forth, each having different goals within and experienced differently by varying members of the training system and others.

The complexity of these multiple realities is compounded by the influence of each party's epistemology and language, meanings taken from subcultural memberships and experiences in the past and present, lessons taken from past and present experiences, and supervisory needs and wants, each a product of prior experiences. Prior training and experiences likely have a great influence on perceptions that each person in the system brings to bear. We tend to see things through the lenses we develop, and therapists are particularly good at using these lenses, which often determine meanings and thus actions we take.

In this chapter, we explore different aspects of the training context to which we believe supervisors should attend. These diverse properties are not "issues" that somehow need resolving as they often have been referred to in the past (as in, "gender issues," or "family of origin issues"); rather, they are part and parcel of the systemic atmosphere and permeate all aspects of the training system including the good, the bad, and the ugly.

Overview

An understanding of context is important when examining patterns of behavior in client systems such as couples and families, or larger systems such as supervision and community. Similarly, it is important to understand a trainee's identity and position or social location relative to race, gender identity, sexuality, and so forth, which affect their perspectives or worldviews. These worldviews influence their understanding of

DOI: 10.4324/9781003099833-13

therapy, their clients, and the decisions they make. Relational supervisors are keenly aware of the impact and potential difficulties and resources of contextual factors in their trainees' lives, including, perhaps, changing from an individual to a relational paradigm of clinical matters. An expanded view of clinical behavior that includes multiple features of context and the relationships among those features assists relational supervisors in their roles and behaviors with trainees.

In addition to attending to factors in trainees' contexts that impact and are impacted by clinical work and training, relational supervisors understand themselves as part of the supervisory context. This requires an awareness and understanding on supervisors' parts of their own contexts and how aspects of those contexts recursively impact and are impacted by supervision and self. Chapter 13, on selves of the therapist and of the supervisor, expands upon this complex and important dynamic.

This chapter focuses on elements of trainees' contexts that impact their clinical work, supervision, and selves as therapists and trainees, and therefore should be focused upon in supervision. Various authors propose different ways of viewing and doing this and relational supervisors find ways that fit their own philosophies of supervision. (See, for example, the *Therapist Personal Agency* model; Mutchler & Anderson, 2010.) Among these contextual factors are the trainee's developmental stage as a therapist and state as a trainee (student, postgraduate trainee, MFT, and non-MFT); setting (graduate academic program, practicum agencies, and postgraduate settings); and factors such as class, religion, ethnicity, race, country of origin, age, size, sexual orientation, gender identity, ability, indigenous identity/perspective, society's view; and the intersectionality of these factors. These factors also are critical to the training system because they affect power, privilege, and goals at every level. This chapter does not delve into detail about each area but presents an overall view of how relational supervisors can both focus on and use contextual factors, and offers some thoughts about supervisory tasks and practices.

Historical Context

Early in our careers as family therapists and family therapy educators, the women's movement in family therapy boomed after Hare-Mustin's 1978 article on feminism and family therapy was published. This classic article ushered in an expanded way of thinking about family dynamics that included how social context influenced those dynamics. Soon thereafter, Monica McGoldrick and Joe Giordano (1982) published *Ethnicity and Family Therapy*, the first of five major books (McGoldrick, Anderson, & Walsh, 1989; McGoldrick, Giordano, & Garcia-Preto, 2005; McGoldrick & Hardy, 2008, 2019) that have influenced CFT mightily.

McGoldrick and Giordano's (1982) text is considered to be seminal in family therapy education. It encouraged family therapists to look beyond structural hierarchies and boundaries within families, and beyond interactional patterns of communication and relating among family members. Clinicians were encouraged to recognize and consider broader contexts that influence individuals and families. For example, an ecosystemic (see Bronfenbrenner, 1979) expansion of Bowen's (1978) ideas about family intergenerational influences included contextual factors of race, ethnicity, gender, and so forth. McGoldrick and Giordano's book was not intended to be a "bible" of "what people of different ethnicities are like." Rather, they were clear in their introduction that the book was intended to provide a starting point for therapists to understand factors of their own ethnic identities as well as those of their clients and how those intersect in therapy.

However, many people ignored that introduction and used the various chapters to stereotype people of different ethnicities (e.g., the African American Family, the Mexican family, and so on). Later editions of the book included language in chapters that helped to dispel their use as stereotypes and, over time, we have learned to be more "culturally humble" (Hook, Davis, Owen, Worthington, & Utsey, 2013; Tervalon & Murray-Garcia, 1998), that is, respectfully curious about our clients' lives, and continually engaging ourselves in self-reflection and self-critique so as to reduce assumptions and inappropriate and unnecessary power imbalances in therapy.

Today, competent relational supervisors understand the complexities, interrelationships, and isomorphic dynamics of different aspects of clients' and trainees' lives including their contexts. In many ways, this has made therapy and supervision more complex and it often seems difficult to keep all the contextual plates spinning on their sticks without dropping some. Indeed, it is nearly impossible to do so without an informative paradigm that gives race, ethnicity, gender, sexual orientation, class, age, and a myriad of other factors at least as much importance as generation and relational patterns of interaction. Indeed, we have come to understand these things as part and parcel of patterns of interaction because they influence both actions and the meanings of those patterns for individuals and systems. This paradigm often requires a fundamental shift in worldview, similar to the shift when one sees things systemically instead of linearly. Systemic therapists understand cultural competence, awareness, sensitivity, humility, respect, and responsiveness as encircling the ecosystemic map of individuals and families at another level, permeating all.

The field of marriage and family therapy not only has embraced the notion of cultural competence as fluid rather than an "issue" (Tervalon & Murray-Garcia, 1998) but also talks about cultural humility (Hook et al., 2013), which is a self-reflective, curious, and respectful stance. It is not difficult to understand context as a vital, isomorphic component of relational supervision and training. This component or stance places supervisors on a journey with trainees, constantly altering our understanding of ourselves, our trainees, clients, and training systems, each recursively influencing the others. It also requires that supervisors strive to make supervision a safe place for the journey. We challenge our own assumptions, include trainees and others in the development of contracts, discuss differences openly, and use strength-based views in supervision (Charlés & Nelson, 2019).

Settings

It may seem strange that we would consider a training setting to be a vital part of "context," which often is thought of as the same as "culture." However, all settings are "context" and each has its own culture of values, practices, rules, and structure.

This includes who makes the rules, who can change them, and how a particular person might go about changing them. Settings can be empowering or oppressive, ossifying or creativity-inducing. Regardless, it is important for trainees and relational supervisors to understand aspects of the settings within which training takes place. Nowadays, training occurs in a great many diverse settings, for example, graduate program clinics, university clinics, public and private agencies, private practices, medical institutions, and schools. Each provides its own culture as well as overt and covert rules. We cannot cover all possibilities in this text; however, we will attempt to provide some general ideas.

Graduate Programs

The first training setting that most of our trainees encounter is their graduate programs. These programs are not monolithic or uniform. Each has its own "flavor," often as part of its own larger context. Graduate programs are housed in different kinds of institutions and in different kinds of departments. They may be accredited by the Council for Accreditation for Counseling and Related Educational Programs, the Commission on Accreditation for Marriage and Family Therapy Education (COAMFTE), or some other entity. Relational therapists may be trained in social work, psychology, CFT, or other clinical programs. Departments that house CFT programs include those with titles similar to Family Studies and Human Development, Education, Counseling, Religion, or something else. These graduate programs, in turn, are situated in even larger contexts. They may be housed in public or private universities, religiously oriented or secular, and in urban and rural regions in the United States or in other countries. Programs may train students at the master's, doctoral, or some other level.

Within graduate programs that teach CFT, diverse cultures can be discerned. Each of us (Lee and Nelson) has worked in universities with high expectations for scholarly productivity on the part of faculty and securing of external funding. In this larger context, we might not have been as easily accessible as students or we ourselves might have liked. In contrast, Nelson also once worked in a laid-back master's program that contrasted with other, more formal programs. Students were encouraged to call professors by their first names and to visit their offices often. Supervising in or for different programs requires understanding the written, spoken, and unspoken rules of those programs, just as we know we must understand the rules, roles, and boundaries of the families with which we work. In some programs, all supervision is done by full time faculty. In other programs, outside supervisors are important and valued, yet have little influence on the program. In still others, outside supervisors are considered part of the "family" and are invited to participate in many aspects of the educational program and setting.

Faculty must balance teaching, supervising, administrative, and other role requirements. However, just as we must, as clinicians, put our clients first, we must have similar values with trainees in order to be ethical relational supervisors. This means we must be clear about our accessibility and availability, about the protocols for students to follow during crises, and about our limits both personally and professionally. We also must be clear about multiple relationships when we are teachers, clinical supervisors, or assistantship supervisors. Each role has potential for exploiting students and we must take precautions to avoid exploitation (see Chapter 11 and the AAMFT Code of Ethics, 2015a).

As outside supervisors, we must be certain that we understand the expectations and roles that we serve within the graduate program. Are we independent, expected to take care of all concerns within our own supervisory system? Or are we expected to stay in close contact with the program, working closely when there are concerns related to our trainees' clinical and supervisory work? What constitutes a level of concern that would trigger a call to the trainee's supervisor or program? What multiple relationships with the program or the students might require awareness and vigilance so as not to exploit our relationships with trainees?

Outside supervisors must be careful in potentially destructive triangles with graduate programs and students. We advise keeping frequent and clear communication with faculty in the program, including an introductory meeting and consultation when needed. Ungar and Costanzo (2007) reported several factors that are important to working relationships between programs, agencies, and outside supervisors. These include awareness of the politics of the clinical leadership, boundaries between the setting and the supervisor, ensuring appropriate informed consent from clients, access to clinical data through client charts, recordings, or live observation, and attention to clear information about the logistics of supervision such as place, time, and fees. We would add that close communication among all parties is essential to a quality learning environment for trainees.

Faculty and outside supervisors also need to keep in mind the trainees' contexts, which may include classroom and on-site clinics as well as larger contextual obligations such as teaching and research assistantships. They also have personal lives and families that are both nurturing and demanding (see Lee, Eppler, Kendal, & Latta, 2001). However, despite being sensitive to all of this complexity and its attendant obligations, supervisors must be clear with students about their responsibilities to clients and supervision. The authors have not found it unusual for trainees to collude with clients around examination time, when major papers are due, and holidays. Trainees uncritically—if not enthusiastically—allow clients to cancel sessions and may cancel supervision sessions themselves or come unprepared. Supervisors must be clear about how much and for what reasons they are willing to allow flexibility.

Prudent relational supervisors not only model balanced and appropriate boundaries, they also develop contracts (see Chapters 3 and 14) with programs as well as students and agencies so that everyone is clear about roles, rules, and accepted practices. This includes policies and procedures for times when difficulties arise.

Postgraduate Training

Postgraduate training programs may be more diverse than graduate programs. Different fields in which marriage and family therapists are trained certainly influence training in different ways. Jurisdictional laws and rules such as licensure strongly affect training contexts. Trainees and supervisors must work within these laws and rules. In some US states, trainees may not practice on their own and must be employed by agencies until they are licensed for independent (of supervision) practice. Also, in some jurisdictions, the rules about the qualifications of supervisors are relaxed and in others, quite strict. These rules often are contextualized in the jurisdiction's laws about mental health professionals in general. For example, in many US states, supervision may be done by any person who has been licensed in any mental health field for at least two years. In others, supervisors must be licensed CFTs with specific supervision training.

Apart from state regulatory laws, the AAMFT has rigorous standards that its Approved Supervisors must meet. To be designated Approved Supervisors, candidates must complete coursework and be mentored (obtain supervision of their supervision) by experienced Approved Supervisors. Courses are taught in a variety of ways, most specifically in doctoral programs (where the course emphasizes the study of supervision in addition to the development of basic supervision competencies), in 30-hour courses approved by AAMFT, or by a combination of an interactive workshop plus study in a 15-hour didactic course. Courses may be offered in single sittings, in modules over time, or electronically (see AAMFT, 2014).

Postgraduate trainees are referred to and licensed or legitimized through a variety of titles, including intern, licensed associate, or others. Typically, such trainees must complete their graduate studies before they can obtain this kind of license or permission to practice outside of a graduate program. Coursework and basic clinical experience required by law often are modeled after the AAMFT standards for Clinical Fellow membership in AAMFT or COAMFTE accreditation. Some trainees must take a national examination early in their postgraduate training and others may take the exam later. They typically are required to practice for a minimum number of years and for a minimum number of clinical and supervisory hours, some of which usually must include couples and families as well as children and individual adults. Clinical hours are typically face-to-face therapy as opposed to other training activities such as paperwork, consultations, staffing, and supervision. In some places, they may be conducted via electronic means such as the Internet as long as they follow the AAMFT Code of Ethics (2015a) and HIPAA guidelines (US Department of Health and Human Services, 1996) for confidentiality and security.

Some jurisdictions require supervisors to be employees of the training agency and others allow supervisors to contract independently with agencies or trainees. Nearly all laws require freedom from constraints that could negatively impact the supervisor's independent judgment regarding the qualifications of the trainee to practice therapy. For example, Florida (State of Florida, 2018) does not allow supervision to be by a spouse or other family member. These laws and rules are designed to protect the public, not promote or inhibit clinical practice.

As the reader can see, different constraints and choices can greatly affect what happens in supervision and how the parties see themselves and their responsibilities in their respective roles. For example, in jurisdictions that have strict rules about scope of practice or settings, supervisors often have more constrained responsibilities for oversight. At least one state specifically requires that all trainee cases be reviewed "periodically" (unhappily, without defining what that means).

For trainees and supervisors who believe trainees are capable of choosing cases to present for supervision on their own, this may feel constraining. The supervisor in such a situation, who thinks the rule is unnecessarily strict, may join in an overt or covert collusion with the trainee to circumvent the rule, jeopardizing ethical practice. We encourage readers to examine the laws and interpretive rules of their own jurisdictions carefully and frequently, identify those that are negative, neutral, or positive to their own philosophies of supervision, and develop strategies with colleagues or mentors to prevent negative impact on trainees, supervision, the training system, or clinical work.

Agencies and Private Practice

In addition to the atmosphere or culture that is in many ways defined by jurisdictional requirements, the physical settings for training also carry unique expectations and dynamics. Often, one of the first things an employee of any setting needs to learn is how things work: who is in charge of what, what the rules are, consequences for breaking rules, who can formally or informally change rules, what the policies and procedures are and how strictly they are enforced, and so on. For example, in some agencies, clinicians are available for quick consultations with trainees and treat trainees with respect as colleagues. In other agencies, clinicians are perceived as busy, independent, and hierarchically above trainees and therefore not interested in the opinions or observations of the trainees. Trainees can do well in either kind of setting. But what is key is understanding the atmosphere and system dynamics of the setting.

Relational supervision in such settings may focus in part on the dynamics of the workplace. In such places, supervisors may take on multiple roles such as administrative supervisors, clinical supervisors, case managers, or mentors, thereby helping the trainee navigate the training system. It often is advantageous for such supervisors to work from within the agency because they better understand the culture and atmosphere of the setting. In other instances, supervision from persons outside the agency may be more objective and can help trainees see the agency as a whole, that is, as a system, and their parts in it a little more clearly. Regardless of the setting or the supervisor's relationship with the setting, it is helpful for supervisors to understand the contextual factors that impact themselves, their trainees, and supervision.

"Culture"

In this chapter we define *culture* as all the things in a particular context that impact the way one sees oneself, that is, one's identity in that context, whether as part of the dominant group or at the margins or outside of the group. Those at the center often have the floor and it is difficult for those at the margins to be heard or understood. In a "melting pot" metaphor, those at the margins blend in or assimilate and become part of the larger group. The problem with this metaphor is that it then discounts, negates, and oppresses those at the margins. Witness the need for gay youth to pretend they are not gay in order to be safe in schools and sometimes in their own homes. A "cultural stew" metaphor allows those gay youth to contribute and belong to the group while maintaining their own unique characteristics and identities. Groups that embrace this metaphor celebrate differences as contributing to the whole.

Culture also can be thought of as atmosphere, that is, something that helps define what is considered to be important and expected, as in an office culture or medical culture. This atmosphere typically is passed through group interaction such as the entity or family, training system, or community. It includes both internal (e.g., bias, beliefs about self and other) and external or institutional (e.g., social policies, systemic bias) ideas, values, and philosophies. Thus, one learns one's "place" in the larger society or family and easily questions those who would move out of their appropriate "places" or roles. All the time, however, these places and identities are shifting and changing in fluid and dynamic rather than characterological ways that relational therapists and supervisors seek to respect rather than attempting to find the "real" person or identity. Doing so helps to understand and work with the impacts that various locations, cultures, beliefs, and so on affect feedback in supervisory and training systems.

Relational interventions increasingly involve culturally diverse supervisors with culturally diverse trainees with culturally diverse client families in culturally diverse training systems. By way of illustration, one of the authors (Lee) supervised a second-generation Latina from a major urban area who was supervising a Midwestern Chippewa in his therapy with a mother and son in their home on a Southwest Navajo reservation. Amanor-Boadu and Baptist (2008) observed that ever more frequently, international individuals are supervisors, trainees, and client families. (See also Mittal & Wieling, 2006, for illustrations of the experiences of international CFT students.)

Postmodern understanding of how individuals are mindful of and make sense of things suggests that every interaction and discourse takes place between culturally diverse individuals. Indeed, every combination of people and setting is unique, and all participants need to be co-editors of the same story with mutually negotiated metaphors—which includes language. Both therapeutic and supervisory working alliances are enhanced when all participants accept multiple ways of understanding the phenomena with which they work (e.g., Inman, 2006), making feedback more understandable and useful.

Cultural Humility, Awareness, and Sensitivity

To be culturally competent is to expect and to understand complexities of culture—whether ethnicity, sexual orientation, or age, and so forth—and to keep them at the forefront of analysis around clinical work and supervision. To have cultural humility (Hook et al., 2013) is to attempt to see culture at the center of supervisory or clinical systems; to be curious about and respectful of clients' and trainees' situations and open to aspects of cultural identity that are important to clients and trainees. It also means we need to be self-reflective as supervisors about our own ideas and perceptions. This requires that trainees and supervisors be able to observe themselves and thereby to be aware of and examine their own experiences, limitations, perspectives, biases, and prejudices. It means that as relational supervisors, we are aware of our positions in these systems and seek to empower clients and trainees in terms of "power with" rather than "power over" (Hernández, 2008), and to utilize practices that honor context and selves of others. To do so requires us to concurrently consider the interplay of at least four features: selves, context, social location, and intersectionality of these factors. For example, imagine yourself as a Mexican-Latina supervisor of a Navajo male trainee, working on a Native American reservation. Cultural competence, from our view is that the supervisor does not need to "know" everything about the Navajo culture or what it is like to live on a reservation, but to be curious with the trainee about her own (as supervisor) experiences, the trainee's, and the clients' experiences as they impact therapy as resources or constraints. Mutual sharing at each level enhances safe relationships in all (Rigazio-DiGilio, 2016).

However, much work is needed in this area. Schomburg and Prieto (2011) reported that, in a study of trainees' multicultural case conceptualization, participants reported high levels of cultural competence on a widely used scale. However, in response to vignettes, these same participants did not recognize racial factors in their case conceptualizations. Christiansen and colleagues (2011) described struggles that participants in their study experienced as they attempted to learn cross-cultural therapy. Earlier, Marshall and Wieling (2003) reported that participants in their study found cross-cultural supervision beneficial and wanted more. Perhaps as we are able to heed these reports more, we will be able to do better at coaching trainees in cultural competence and humility (Hook et al., 2013).

Cross-cultural therapy or supervision suggests that we must be mindful that clients', trainees', and/or supervisors' identified cultures or social locations (see later in this chapter) are different one from another. However, it is important to remember that *culture* includes many aspects of experience, both internalized and external. Therefore, intra-cultural variances can be just as important as intercultural similarities and differences. One very important aspect of these differences has to do with power. Some cultures and some intra-cultural aspects have more power than others, and so it behooves supervisors to be as mindful and open as possible to power differentials in the supervisory and training systems.

Relational supervisors are aware of the differences between themselves and their trainees and, from our point of view, are not charged with inculcating their trainees with specific philosophies or approaches to therapy. Differing worldviews can enhance or impede therapist development, and supervisors are responsible for relational behaviors that are helpful rather than harmful to trainees and their client families. Of course, this suggests that supervisors ensure a strong working alliance. Inman (2006) reported that participants in a study of multicultural supervision reported a high correlation between the working alliance and satisfaction with supervision, which is likely still true. Although study results did not suggest higher multicultural awareness on the part of trainees, Inman suggested that becoming culturally competent is a developmental process and may need to begin with trainees' self-exploration before exploring clients' goals within a multicultural context. Inman also suggested that it is appropriate for trainees and supervisors to include enhanced cultural competence in the goals they establish for supervision.

Social Justice and Responsibility

We were revising this second edition of *The Contemporary Relational Supervisor* while isolating due to COVID-19 and also in the midst of economic, racial, and police protesting, and increasing awareness of systemic racism around the world, most especially in the United States. Omitting matters of social justice seemed to contribute further to the systemic racism and injustice that might be revealed in our text, and to our ideas about how to work within social discourse and actions that mightily and recursively affect our clients, trainees, selves, training systems, and larger contexts. How can this be pondered and discussed in supervisory relationships, when it involves so much that is both internal (family of origin, social location, other training) and external (professional standards and institutionalized racism)?

The Social Empathy Model (Segal, 2018), expanded and discussed by Domokos-Cheng Ham (2014), helps supervisors and trainees examine various parts of a situation, and builds on empathy, contextual understanding, and social responsibility, which together promote social justice. Segal's (2018) concept of Social Empathy conveys both understanding of personal positions and their location in at-times contradictory social systems. "Social empathy is … the ability to understand people and other social groups by perceiving and experiencing their life situations [through] learning about and understanding the historical context of group experiences, including the structural inequalities that have shaped communities" (Segal, 2018, p. 4).

> Domokos-Cheng Ham (2014) takes us through a decision-making process that leads to less-than-perfect, but thought-out resolutions to a dilemma a family faced: a Japanese mother's desire to control her own death from a terminal illness amid the other family members' strong objections. Domokos-Cheng Ham's trainee led the family through a process of listening to each other, working hard to empathically understand each other's views by considering responses in the context of each person's belief system (that is, both internal and external reasons, resources, and constraints for various decisions facing them). The trainee and Domokos-Cheng Ham had done the same thing in role play before the trainee approached the family. It was not easy, but the trainee viewed this process for both herself and the family *to be a socially responsible way of acting.* This action, as a whole, was considered in context of social justice and ethical behavior (considering autonomy, beneficence, nonmaleficence, fidelity, and justice). It was a growing process for everyone.

We believe that such processes can be difficult and time-consuming in supervision but are worthwhile. They "create spaces large enough to embrace the values, beliefs, and perspectives of each other" (Domokos-Cheng Ham, 2014, p. 20). They may not result in decisions that the trainee or supervisor would have made (or even thought of), but honor both the difficulty and the rights of members of the supervisory system—clients, trainee, and supervisor.

Social Location

The term *social location* refers to a person's place in society with respect to various categories of identity such as gender, race, social class, age, ability, religion, sexual orientation, and geographic locations (Watts Jones, 2016). (See wonderful illustrations in Brown et al., 2019. Moreover, Caldwell, 2011, may provoke useful debate.) As such, it is a complex presentation of one's identity, in a social system, that reflects a worldview. It is understood to be socially constructed as a perception of how things work, what is real, where things belong, and how they fit together. Thus, social location affects what is perceived as acceptable or unacceptable in various situations and often is stereotypical. This greatly affects identity, experience, and behavior. For example, a trainee who identifies as gay often lives at the margins of society and sometimes that part of the trainee's identity is invisible. However, from our perspective, this aspect of the trainee's identity is alive and influential in both clinical work and training, though perhaps invisible. This invisibility or marginalization not only gravely diminishes the individual, but may hinder training as an important aspect of self as a therapist, trainee, or supervisor unless openly addressed in some fashion.

Hays (1996) has developed a way of approaching different groupings that have been considered within the rubric of "diversity." The current authors expand the notion of diversity by using the term social location. It is more expansive in meaning and more clearly a social construction about who is at the center of society—and therefore has more influence, power, and privilege—and who is at the margins of society. Hays's approach, although limited to the areas she names, can help us examine and understand the uniqueness of all individuals, making visible the often assumed, stereotypical, or invisible. Hays uses the acronym ADDRESSING in her work: Age, Development, Disability, Religion, Ethnicity, Social Status, Sexual Orientation, Indigenous Heritage, National Origin, and Gender. Her position is that such factors or locations in society influence how we think about ourselves and others, and how others see and treat us. We would add that, although these aspects are social constructions (and there are others, such as Spirituality and Size), some have real effects in different places and in different ways. Stereotyping by skin, hair, facial features, dress, or other outward appearances or beliefs about someone leads to incorrect assumptions. We develop prejudices based on experiences with different people. For example, in some settings, "old" people are thought of as less intelligent, knowledgeable, or aware than those who are younger, and therefore unable to contribute to society. Indeed, even within a training system, people with accents, people of conservative or liberal political views, and people who are sexually attracted to members of their own sex or who enjoy sexual practices that are not in the mainstream, are often stereotypically mistreated or dismissed. Often, their ideas, opinions, needs, and potential contributions may tend to be disregarded or even pathologized. Zimmerman, Castronova, and ChenFeng (2016) suggested that one way to keep diversity in the supervisory relationship is to (a) make supervision a safe place for conversations and connection, (b) work toward expanding knowledge, awareness, and humility, and (c) recognize and manage power, privilege, and bias for all in the training system. One way to do this (Castronova, ChenFeng, & Zimmerman, 2020) is to use a "Social Location Map." This map accounts for social locations of clients, therapists, and supervisors (and perhaps others) and the privilege allotted (or not) to those locations. Using the ADDRESSING (Hays, 1996) or GRRAACCEESS (gender, race, religion, age, ability, class, culture, ethnicity, education, sexuality, spirituality) acronym, adding other social locations appropriate, listed vertically, as well as client, therapist, and supervisor, each party can be valanced according to more or less privilege in each area. Details can be added for each person in terms of intersectionality. For example, a client might be male, white, Christian, middle-aged, and so on, the trainee as female, Black, Muslim, and young, and the supervisor as female, Asian, Christian, and middle-aged. Patterns of privilege and oppression emerge as possibilities affecting the clinical work and supervision. In this example, the client has much privilege in all areas listed above, and the therapist and supervisor have privilege in some areas (e.g., female in a largely female context; supervisor's education) and less in others (trainee as minority religion in a largely Christian majority context; less education than supervisor but perhaps more than client). A discussion about similarities and differences may help the trainee understand nuances of therapy and relationships when viewed through these different lenses.

Through good CFT training, we know that we need to examine our attitudes about people who are different from ourselves so that we do not do harm to them as clients. The same is true for supervision. Trainees have described different experiences with male and female supervisors (see Nelson, 1991; Schiavone & Jessell, 1998) and, although these described differences may not apply to each of us, we should be sensitive to the felt experience of trainees as well as clients—as opposed to what we think we do as therapists or supervisors, or what we think may be their experiences. Persons of color often have experiences of mistreatment and it's important to be sensitive to and willing to discuss those experiences.

A number of resources have been cited throughout this text. Perhaps CFT's most contemporary view is provided by McGoldrick and Hardy (2019). This edited compendium is both comprehensive and sophisticated while providing solid general discussion informed by a systemic lens.

Intersectionality

Intersectionality refers to the presence of more than one area of diversity in a single person. None of us claims only one aspect of identity or background. We are men and women at the same time we are black, white, or brown; we are gay or straight, bisexual, transgender, or queer at the same time we are Latina or African American. Taylor, Hernández, Deri, Rankin, and Siegel (2006) interviewed ten ethnic minority CFT supervisors about how they address the intersections of diversity dimensions in their supervision of CFT trainees. In their literature review, Taylor, Hernández and colleagues noted that gender has received more attention in the literature than have other diversity dimensions such as ethnicity, social class, spirituality, and sexual orientation. Our own review suggests that the literature also focuses on sexual orientation and ethnicity/culture as well as other dimensions.

What about transgender participants in the training system? There are informed opinions by experienced clinicians but, overall, we could find nothing specifically about CFT supervisors who are transgender. However, transgender *therapists* are thought to be potential resources for training system growth because they may contribute unique and valuable perspectives into how gender organizes the therapeutic process (see Shipman & Martin, 2017). But at times they may "often need affirming, self-aware, competent, clinical supervisors, and peer support to ensure healthy development that safely guides them along" (p. 97), for example, when they are so far along in their transition process that clients perceive them as cisgender, or when roles are reversed and they are cast into the role of teacher for their supervisors and/or clients.

Cisgender supervisors of cisgender therapists who are working with transgender clients are cautioned to be alert for special challenges. Marjory Nichols (2019) cautions that working with this population forces both therapists and their supervisors to confront ingrained attitudes about gender binaries, roles, and expressions.

Robyak, Goodyear, and Prange (1987) focused on the supervisors' sex, focus of supervision, and experience as a supervisor. These factors combined to affect the kind of power they exhibited. For example, men and novice therapists in their sample preferred *referent* power (see Taylor, Peplau, & Sears, 2006), that which is earned as respect, to expert or legitimate power. These styles or preferences likely affect supervisory relationships in terms of fit between trainees and supervisors. Further, Hernández, Bunyi, and Townson (2007) discussed the interweaving of ethnicity and gender. Miller and Ivey (2006) and Miller, Korinek, and Ivey (2004) discussed the role of spirituality in training and even developed a scale (Miller et al., 2004). Their work encourages therapists and supervisors to be expansive in their thinking about diverse factors of our lives that impact our clients, therapy, and supervision. We would do well to avail ourselves of the existing literature and be alert for new articles, chapters, and books.

Hernández (2008) points us toward an understanding of how various contextual dimensions affect therapy and therefore should be considered vital for supervisors and supervision. Much of the literature focuses on one or two aspects of diversity, yet, at the same time, gives us ideas for thinking about other dimensions and how dimensions interact with each other (see, for example, Long and Bonomo's (2006) work on working with trainees and their biases toward and acceptance of LGBTQ clients. Their ideas can be applied to many areas of prejudice and bias). In supervision, this way of thinking helps us in several ways. It helps us become and remain aware of our own attitudes and behaviors about different diversity dimensions and the intersectionality of dimensions. It helps us attend to how we work with trainees around diversity dimensions as clinical factors and highlights how they affect our relationships and interpersonal dynamics with our trainees.

The Developing Selves of Trainees

Each of us as individuals can be placed along a variety of trajectories that include maturity level, family of origin position and role, training level, and clinical theory orientation. A relational supervisor works to help trainees identify among these factors and to determine goals that may help them move to more advanced stages of skill or competence and self-awareness. Relational supervisors also understand themselves in terms of their positions as supervisors and how their own positions interact with trainees' positions in both complementary and variant ways. To these ends, mutually determined goals for trainees, supervisors, supervisory systems, and training systems are important and helpful.

The developmental level of the trainee is also contextual and affects supervisory practice. Beginning therapists' programs often require focused and intense supervision that attends to aspects of cases or clinical skills (see Caldwell & Claxton, 2010; Stoltenberg & McNeill, 2010). There is much to be learned before one can be considered a skilled or competent therapist and it often is not clear where to begin. Graduate programs develop their own practices for introducing neophyte therapists to clinical work, some starting very slowly with observations and/or shadowing, and then one or two cases; others introduce students to clinical work with many cases very quickly. Some programs provide a lot of close, live supervision and others allow students to determine, on their own, how much case, live, or video supervision they want or need. Some of this may be personal preference and learning style as much as program requirements or supervisory preferences. Regardless, supervision for beginning therapists typically requires more close attention and oversight than for advanced trainees, something that some supervisors may not be equipped to do.

Intermediate trainees, those with perhaps 200–300 hours of completed clinical work, are often doing quite well with basic skills or competencies and are well on their way to proficiency as therapists. They may be working on clarifying their personal philosophies of therapy or change, exploring ideas beyond their early comfortable approaches, and stretching themselves clinically. This requires supervision that holds them to standards of basic care at the same time as providing a safe place to explore and develop their own styles. Supervision may take on more philosophical tones of theory and approach rather than specific models or practices. Discussions may include ethical practice in the abstract rather than related to specific situations and diversity as a fundamental construct that requires attention. This stage of training often is the longest and most intense, and is characterized by ups and downs of self-doubt and confidence. A very useful self-study by a group of CFT practicum students is described by Esmiol, Knudsen-Martin, and Delgado (2012).

Advanced trainees, those nearly ready for licensing or independent practice sometimes require a stance of watchful waiting on the part of supervisors. These trainees should be more capable of monitoring themselves, reflecting upon competencies and theory alike, and readying themselves for the next phases of their careers. Supervisors at this stage must be careful not to become complacent because there still are areas where trainees need assistance. However, supervision also may take on more of a mentoring tone. Here the mission is to assist trainees to be mature members of the mental health profession with all of the obligations and responsibilities of such positions. Supervisors must prepare trainees and themselves for change in the hierarchy from supervisor/trainee to colleagues, emphasizing that all therapists need consultation at times.

Selves of Supervisors

Clearly, supervisors' awareness of our own biases and prejudices greatly affects our ability to work with trainees around *their* biases, prejudices, and conscious and unconscious behaviors in therapy (Long & Bonomo, 2006). Awareness and sensitivity to our own biases and prejudices also affect our supervision interactions in both conscious and unconscious ways. Although there are no delineated competencies for supervision as there are for therapy (AAMFT, 2004; Nelson et al., 2007), wise and caring supervisors examine their own evolving attitudes and practices in the service of both good clinical work and good supervision.

Supervisors have much power over their trainees although some supervisors work from more flattened hierarchies than others. All supervisors, however, have the responsibility of gatekeeping for the profession and for clients and the ability to do it. Since we are likely to find ourselves supervising trainees who are impaired or not progressing in competence, we need to be able to work with them either to either change and improve or to find other careers. We must take this responsibility seriously as we work with trainees who are different from ourselves—and all are different in some manner or another—and strive to not use our power inappropriately. It is easy when we have personality conflicts with trainees, or when we do not like them for whatever reasons to treat them unfairly. We must guard against this lest we instigate power struggles and inappropriate triangles. Nelson and Friedlander (2001) cautioned that angry supervisors and power struggles lead to supervisory conflict, which is not conducive to a healthy working alliance and helping trainees in their professional growth, and which may isomorphically negatively impact the trainee's clinical work.

Supervisory Practices

One of the best ways we have found to work with trainees in different settings is to make ourselves conscious of the parameters of our involvement in each setting. We may be core faculty in a training program, and therefore have multiple roles with our trainees. So we need to be clear about the boundaries, requirements, and limits of each of those roles. We may supervise within agencies as employees of those agencies. In those cases, we may have financial stakes in the success and reputations of the agencies and need to be aware how that impacts our supervision with trainees, whether they be graduate practicum students or postgraduate trainees. We need to be aware of our levels of liability in each setting and help our trainees understand our practices and requirements within that context.

The best practice that we have found is direct dialogue with trainees about the setting, its policies and procedures, our various roles in it and with our trainees, and our intentions in each of our roles. Clear understanding and expectations go a long way toward avoiding confusion and problems. Tromski-Klingshirn (2006) provided some ideas about how to manage multiple roles, in this case, clinical and administrative supervising, that can present some challenges and opportunities for supervisors. Some supervisors manage multiple roles by conducting each in different places to help punctuate the differences in responsibilities and to help prevent boundary crossings or violations. Others find other ways to keep boundaries clear and avoid exploitation.

Similarly, best practices in therapy and in supervision call for clear and open dialogue with trainees about matters of sexuality, race, ethnicity, social class, and so forth. One exercise that we have found to be quite helpful is to ask trainees to describe a situation in which they felt oppressed, to deconstruct and understand that thoroughly, and then to do the same with a situation of privilege. This exercise helps trainees to understand themselves as both majority and minority in different situations and in complex ways. When done in a group, members learn new things about each other that are eye-opening and lead to better understandings and relationships. To the extent that a practice is congruent with a personal philosophy of supervision, supervisors can do the same for themselves, making these matters transparent and open for discussion, which can be very helpful during supervision of clinical cases. The Harvard Implicit Association Test (https://implicit.harvard.edu/implicit/takeatest.html) is a helpful personal tool that uses millisecond responses to privately discover our unconscious biases in several areas. We expect it to be helpful to all participants in a training system.

Another tool is Hardy and Laszloffy's (1995) cultural genogram. Trainees are invited to examine their intergenerational genograms, attending to many aspects of diversity and how those affect them personally as well as professionally. Just as this exercise is helpful in expanding sensitivity in clinical work, it also can be helpful when supervisors go over their own genograms with trainees and encourage dialogue about how supervision is impacted by the interaction among different factors.

The Cultural Context Model (see Almeida, Dolan-Del Vecchio, & Parker, 2007; Hernández & McDowell, 2010; Hernández, Siegel, & Almeida, 2009) delineates a practice of training and supervision wherein trainees learn about cultural sensitivity within cultural circles of clients and other trainees. The circles are designed to impact therapy and training with maximum accountability, "identifying and dismantling oppressive norms of family life across cultures" (Hernández, 2008, p. 12). This kind of immersion experience has a very different impact on training and trainees than does simply talking about diversity or reading about it in books or journal articles.

Trainees also may be asked to keep a daily journal of cultural critical events (see Lee & Vennum, 2010). These illuminating events occur "when individuals 'bump' into situations that do not fit their ways of thinking and behaving" (p. 239). Journaling can be an effective way to discover one's own culture. Trainees are asked to describe and then dissect each such situation. Trainees can discuss their entries as part of supervision. If there are many trainees, their total journal entries can be shuffled together and subjected to qualitative analyses.

Students have been positive about these experiences and supervisors of postgraduate trainees could use similar ones to assist their own trainees. I (Nelson) recall one role play with first semester graduate students. They thought they might please me and have fun by enacting a same-sex couple with communication difficulties. They surprised themselves by getting immersed in the role play and becoming emotional as one partner described his distress about how he was treated in his family and how he had to remain closeted at work. It was a valuable experience for all of us.

A number of exercises have been suggested for graduate programs that can be adapted for postgraduate training. For example, Laszloffy and Habekost (2010) devised exercises to meet five course objectives. Readers of this text may find these objectives useful and can consult the article for more ideas.

1 Examine the intersection among dimensions of diversity (e.g., class, race, gender, sexual orientation, religion, ability, and others) and the dynamics of oppression.
2 Understand the experiences of oppressed groups as well as how marginalization and oppression affect family and therapy processes.
3 Recognize how dimensions of diversity and dynamics of power and oppression shape students' identities and implications for their work as therapists.
4 Explore culturally competent practices.
5 Appreciate the importance of working on behalf of social justice in and outside of therapy.

Supervisors are encouraged to engage in practices that sensitize themselves and their trainees to multiple aspects of social location that affect clients, therapy, trainees, supervisors, supervision, and supervisory/training contexts. In addition, supervisors are encouraged to take initiative for engaging trainees in dialogue about matters of diversity (Taylor, Hernández et al., 2006), not waiting for clients or trainees to initiate these conversations or for trainees to see them as "issues." This requires making supervision a safe place to have differences and to explore the things we have written about in this chapter.

Exercises

1 Name three aspects of your own context that could easily impact your work negatively as a supervisor. How will you limit the potentially negative effects?
2 Name three aspects of your own context that could easily impact your work positively as a supervisor. How will you use these aspects to their best benefit?
3 Name an aspect of context with which you and your trainee might clash. How do/will you manage this so as to enhance rather than hinder the trainee's progress as a therapist?
4 Your trainee is having difficulty in a situation that you perceive is related to a clash of values between the trainee and his/her clients. How do/will you help the trainee with this situation?

11 Legal Aspects of Relational Supervision

As we get to the ethical (next chapter) and legal aspects of supervision, we are reminded of the depth of responsibility we carry as supervisors of therapists-in-training. Even as therapists, we often "forget" to pay attention to laws and ethics codes that govern our practice. I (Nelson) once taught an ethics workshop to more than 200 mental health practitioners. I asked how many had read the licensing laws in the past year; a few raised their hands. I then asked how many had read other laws that affect our profession (e.g., reporting suspected abuse, duty to warn, minors in therapy) and two people raised their hands. I asked how many had read their professional association's code of ethics in the last year; about 25 raised their hands. Finally, I asked how many knew that their professional association's ethics code was the law of the state in which we resided. Some raised their hands, but many looked at me rather wide-eyed. I told them that I thought I am fortunate because I am forced to read the laws, regulations, and ethics code several times a year because I teach supervision and ethics courses and workshops. It is very important for supervisors to know laws, rules, and codes regarding areas discussed in this chapter. As supervisors, we are responsible for our trainees' actions and for educating them about legal matters as they pertain to our work. Not knowing and keeping up on changes can be detrimental to all elements of the training system.

In this chapter, we go over some of the basic principles of law that supervisors need to know. The chapter might best be read in conjunction with a reading of your local laws, regulations, and the ethics codes under which you work. Typically, licensing laws and rules can be found on a state or provincial website, searching for [name of profession] licensing or doing a little digging using the keyword, *license.*

Organization of Laws and Regulations

Most people get confused and put off when reading laws and regulations related to laws. We both (Lee and Nelson) are fortunate that we have worked with licensure and regulation activities and learned how laws and rules are generally set up. What follows may seem dry and dull, but we believe it is important for supervisors to understand a bit about how regulatory laws are developed and what they entail.

Couple and family therapists are regulated in all 50 states and Washington, D. C., and two provinces in Canada (Sturkie & Paff Bergen, 2000). That was not

DOI: 10.4324/9781003099833-14

always so. Typically, a law-making body such as a legislature or congress was approached by a professional body concerned about citizens who believed they had been harmed but had no legal recourse. Occasionally, such laws began when a legislator was approached by a citizen. There were no laws governing the clinical services they had received. With regard to CFT, volunteers in our AAMFT professional divisions worked over many years to learn the political process of obtaining regulation of our profession in the various states and provinces. Legislators needed to pass laws that protected the public welfare, not the profession of CFT. These laws specified what were deemed to be the basic education and clinical experiences necessary to practice a profession. The details of these matters were left to regulatory or licensing boards to work out.

Clinical Practice: Licensure

In some states, professionals are licensed. Laws stipulate who can both use a title (e. g., CFT or MFT, psychologist) and provide certain services (e.g., CFT, psychotherapy), called *scope of practice*. In other states or provinces, certification is used. Anyone can perform services, but only those who meet specified criteria can identify themselves to the public by certain titles, for example, "Certified Public Accountant." Whether resulting in a license or other form of recognition and regulation, the underlying political and legislative processes are the same. Each of us has been involved in professional regulatory processes at one level or another. The process of getting licensure for a US state or Canadian province is quite interesting and almost antithetical for systemic therapists. As a systemic therapist, I (Nelson) was taught to attend to patterns and relational dynamics and less to content. Attending to content, we were taught, was a good way to get hooked into our own "stuff" or "hot topics" and to forget that systemic therapists attempt to help change processes. However, in the legislative process, it is all about content, even when we are politically required to bargain. For example, if CFT presses its case that the public is harmed when untrained individuals try to do therapy, we may be confronted with a counterclaim. Such a claim might be that couple and family therapists allegedly do not have sufficient training to diagnose physical problems that may be presenting as emotional or mental ones (e.g., depressive symptoms resulting from thyroid dysfunction). In such a case, we must be prepared to defend our position and our training.

The purpose of licensing laws is to protect the public from harm, and not to build CFT practices. However, at times there may be unnecessary conflict between these two goals. Therefore, it is important for CFTs as individual professionals and as professional organizations to participate in the development of licensing laws and regulations. In both positions we do this by staying alert to proposed legislation, commenting on it to our legislators, and sometimes serving as consultants.

At some point, a legislative body determines that a law is needed to certify or license individuals to engage in a specific scope of practice (e.g., the diagnosis and treatment of mental and emotional disorders, family therapy, etc.). The resultant law may discuss certain requirements, but does so in rather general terms. Specificity about the terms comes through rules or regulations set forth by appointed licensing or regulatory boards. For example, the law may specify that licensed marriage and family therapists must complete a course of educational training *to be determined by rule*. This means that the specifics of the training are left up to a licensing board or similar body. That body determines which courses, how many courses, and what kind of clinical experience is needed. Rules do not need legislative action to change them; licensing boards periodically announce proposed rule changes, such as requirements for continuing education or how therapy may be conducted (e.g., face to face or through phone or other technological means).

It is very important that supervisors understand the laws and rules of their areas quite well. I (Nelson) was brought up short when a supervisor candidate pointed out that the general licensing law for mental health in Utah requires that anyone contemplating an intimate (sexual) relationship with a former client must first undergo counseling themselves. I knew that sexual relations with clients is forbidden in Utah during therapy and for two years after terminating therapy, which is part of the *Marriage and Family Therapy* law, but had not read the overarching *Mental Health* law carefully. It is clear, then, that good supervisors and therapists pay attention to all of the laws, rules, and ethical codes that may apply to them.

Other Laws

In addition to licensing laws, therapists and supervisors need to be aware of other laws that affect the practice of CFT or mental health in general. Is client privilege or confidentiality protected? Under what circumstances may confidentiality be breached or broken? What happens if it is? Nearly all states require mental health professionals and other medical or school professionals to report suspected abuse of children or adults who cannot take care of themselves. How does a person go about making such a report? Does your area have laws regarding duties to warn or protect? If so, what is a professional supposed to do? Is it mandatory or optional? To whom should concerns be reported without breaching the laws around confidentiality?

How are client records to be treated? Do laws or regulations specify what should be in those records? How is that similar to or different from Health Insurance and Portability and Accountability Act (HIPAA, 1996) requirements? How long must you keep records? What arrangements must you make for your records in the event you are incapacitated, retire, or die? Under what conditions may you or must you release client records? What should you do if you don't want to release records or think that someone could be harmed if you did so? What should you do if a third party, an attorney, for example, sends you a subpoena for records?

May you treat minors without their parents present? Under what conditions should you or may you keep minors' conversations private? What if children's parents are divorced—to whom may you release records, report concerns, or report what happens in therapy? Below, we discuss a few of these questions.

Confidentiality

Confidentiality is the right of a client to determine for himself or herself what information is divulged in therapy to others. *Privilege* refers to the client's right to determine what confidential information is presented in court. You can see that they are similar but not the same thing. Regardless, as therapists and supervisors, we must protect our clients' confidentiality and their privilege except under certain circumstances, some of which are laid out below. In general, the safest way to be certain that divulging information is acceptable and that the client has full knowledge about the situation is to have the client sign a release of information and to discuss the situation with that person. This release should include the people to whom the information may go, details about what information may or may not be released, and a time frame or limit for releasing the information. As CFTs, we are obligated to obtain written consent to release any information about a case from every person who attended any sessions, even if they were considered consultants or visitors. It is very important that trainees' clients understand (in the client's Informed Consent to Treatment document) that an exception to this right to confidentiality is with the therapist's supervisor(s) or for mandatory reporting, but that supervisors are also held to the standard and may not divulge information without clients' permission or as allowed/required by law.

According to the AAMFT Code of Ethics (AAMFT, 2015a), trainees also have the right to have their conversations in supervision kept confidential and, perhaps, privileged. In some places, the AAMFT Code of Ethics has been included in licensing laws and therefore, breaking a trainee's confidence is also breaking the law.

Duty to Report

In most places, mental health and other licensed medical professionals are required or allowed to report suspected abuse or neglect of a child, vulnerable adult, or others who cannot take care of their own interests. Sometimes *all citizens are mandatory reporters* and are required to report suspicions of harm. In some locales there is a list of professionals who are mandated to report their suspicions. For these professionals, there are no options allowed by law. The named professionals must notify specified authorities in specified ways even if they know that they will be breaching confidentiality—which often is held to be the most sacrosanct of our duties. In most cases, this means that we can make these reports without fear that we will be breaking laws.

However, what many health professionals do not understand is that our duty or ability to talk about clients without breaching confidentiality is limited to the report only. Often, who in fact made the report may be kept private. Therefore, if a social worker, police officer, attorney, or other person wants more information, we cannot give that information without permission from our clients or a court order.

There may be many intricacies involved with abuse or neglect reports and it is important that supervisors make themselves aware of appropriate actions. Trainees need guidance because such situations usually provoke at least some anxiety and trainees need help navigating the procedures and dynamics of investigations and so forth. It is important to remember that such reports usually must be made on *reasonable suspicion* of abuse; therapists and supervisors are not investigators—child protective services or the police gather information that is needed.

As supervisors, we may find ourselves in delicate circumstances relative to duty to report. If we agree with our trainees and they have permission from their agencies to make such reports, it becomes a fairly straightforward process. If it is the first time a trainee has had to make such a report, it is important for us as supervisors to guide them through the process. It can be quite nerve wracking and upsetting, particularly when clients get upset and perhaps even threaten the therapist or ourselves. In those cases, supervisors often want trainees to talk with them before or during the process. After making a number of such reports, supervisors may be comfortable simply having the incidents reported to them and perhaps discussed a bit.

When trainees' agencies do not allow them to make reports of suspected abuse, it can be more complex for therapists-in-training and their supervisors. The AAMFT Code of Ethics (2015a; 6.1) says that when there is conflict, we should make our code known to the agency and attempt to resolve the conflict. However, the law is clear that it is *we*, those who are licensed, who must adhere to the laws and rules. Therefore, there may be times when therapists—even therapists-in-training—must act from their own professional beliefs and may, perhaps, need to make a report even when they disagree with their employers or us. On the other hand, if a trainee decides to *not* make such a report, we may need to do so ourselves and debrief the situation with the therapist afterward. In either case, it is important for supervisors to record notes of the situation, the process that was used to make a decision, the ultimate decision, and any further thoughts in supervision notes.

Duty to Warn or to Protect

A similar exception to the duty to maintain confidentiality is when we have good reason to believe that our clients are in danger of hurting themselves or someone else. The laws around duty to warn or protect someone often cite a case referred to as *Tarasoff*, in which a client told a university therapist in California that he was going to hurt his estranged girlfriend. The courts in California ruled that in such circumstances, when there is an identifiable victim, clear intent, statement, and means for imminent danger, therapists must not warn, but *protect* the intended victim or victims and the authorities. This California law has impacted laws in other jurisdictions although specifics may be different. This mandate may include notifying appropriate police departments, having clients taken into protective custody and held for observation, and notifying foreseeable victims. It is quite helpful for trainees and supervisors to know exact requirements and limits of laws *before* a situation arises.

States and provinces have different laws about breaking confidentiality in such dangerous situations. In some, the authorities may be informed (e.g., Texas), but not intended victims. In other states, therapists may report or must report such intent to authorities. It gets tricky, though, because we do not always know how serious our clients are when they make such statements. We must use our experience in general, our experience with a particular client, and a thorough understanding of the laws to help us make good decisions in such difficult circumstances. As supervisors, particularly new ones, it is easy for us to become anxious and not make wise decisions, whether acting too little or too much. Mentoring (supervision of supervision) is very helpful in such situations, just as supervision for new therapists is helpful. If you employ distance technology (e.g., supervision via the Internet or telephone), you will need to be conversant with the requirements of your trainees' and their clients' locales.

Minors in Therapy

Many or most couple and family therapists see children in their consultation or therapy practices. In those cases, it is important to know the limitations and requirements for seeing children. In some states and provinces, whoever brings the child to therapy, as long as they have legal authority to do so, now "owns" the case and can prohibit others, including other parents or guardians, from access to therapy or therapy records. In other places, they not only do not own such authority, they may *not* limit other legal guardians or representatives from access and therapists *must* cooperate with requests. It is very important that therapists and supervisors clearly understand jurisdiction limits and requirements for working with minors in therapy. In some places, therapists are allowed to see minors in therapy one time before securing parental consent. In all situations, the therapist must ensure that parents or guardians who provide consent are actually allowed or required by law to do so. This also applies to allowing information to be released to third parties.

The AAMFT (2015a) Code of Ethics (and many state laws) specifically forbids treating therapists from doing evaluations for custody or visitation in situations of divorce or separation. On occasion, treating therapists are subpoenaed or requested to testify in custody situations. It is vital that therapists and supervisors understand the limits of what can be reported in testimony, and exactly who must provide authorization. There are differences between therapist and expert witness testimony. The two roles must be kept separate. Similarly, therapists who conduct evaluations for purposes of custody or parenting time may not become treating therapists in the same cases (and a therapist in a case may not evaluate people in the same case).

Subpoenas

A subpoena is a legal request or demand for information or to appear at a certain place at a certain time with information. We cannot ignore subpoenas. We must either give what is requested or ask an attorney's help in *quashing* the order. However, we cannot give information without either the clients' permission or an order from a judge. It usually is best to seek the help of an attorney unless subpoenas are a routine part of one's job as a therapist or supervisor. A subpoena is typically a request by an attorney for case notes and, perhaps, the testimony of the therapist regarding the therapist's professional opinion about a client or what happened in therapy. Often, therapists can provide summaries of pertinent information rather than copying their notes. This is true for supervision notes as well as clinical notes. Therapists may release information if (a) all clients in the client system have signed authorization to release, or (b) ordered to release information by the court. A subpoena issued by an attorney does not allow or require us to release information—we must have court orders to do that. However, supervisors and their trainees may not simply ignore subpoenas and likely should consult an attorney for advice.

Therapists in training need to be guided through the distinctions between presenting facts (e.g., "the client reported improved parenting during the week") and interpretations or opinions (e.g., "the client's parenting improved" when this is known only through the client's report and not the therapist's observation). Supervisors, often removed from direct knowledge of what transpires in sessions, must help trainees with these distinctions. Careful reviews of oral reports and case notes alongside live or recorded sessions give supervisors information needed to help in such situations. This practice also helps the supervisor know how much confidence to place in oral reports and case notes, and provides data for coaching trainees in careful reporting.

Records and Other Documents

Another legal concern is supervision records as well as our counsel to trainees about their own case records. A few state or provincial regulations, as well as third party payers such as insurance companies, spell out what is required in client records and, as supervisors, we must know those requirements. We also need to know how to protect records and how they may be used in supervision. We are obliged to insist that all clinical records and recordings be available to us as supervisors. After all, civil lawsuits (e.g., concerning duty to protect the foreseeable victims of violence and suicidal behavior) have indicated that supervisors can be held liable for the actions of their trainees and their trainees' clients. Moreover, defensive trainees may cherry-pick records or recordings to show us, thus requiring that we have access to their records and recordings.

Both our trainees and we need to know laws and ethics rules around how to store records, how long to store them, and to make plans for the appropriate transfer or disposal of our records in case we are incapacitated or die.

Similarly, it is wise for supervisors to keep notes about what happens in supervision: which cases were discussed, what directives or suggestions were made and their rationale, how trainees responded, what general topics were discussed, follow up to previous consultations, and so forth. Just as therapists need records to remember what happened in therapy, supervisors need notes to help them remember what was discussed in supervision. Again, such notes also are helpful in situations where a therapist is investigated or involved in some sort of malpractice suit or licensing complaint. An important forensic dictum is "*if it isn't written down, it does not exist.*"

Documents and Billing Information in the Electronic Age

This discussion began in Chapter 5 with consideration of the unique practice complications of remote supervision and remote therapy. Aside from those unique issues, all supervisors need to be cognizant of the obligations across the entire training system created by the increased computerization of behavioral science practice. For example, the locations of their own and the therapists' client records and other identifying information probably have moved from locked file drawers to electronic storage and the security of these records has changed accordingly.

Client records typically include intake documents with extensive personal data, demographic and otherwise, as well as detailed authorizations to release some of that information to third parties. There also are diagnostic summaries, treatment plans, and formative and summative progress summaries and billing information. There also may be contingency forms with regard to emergencies, including lethality concerns, and legal issues. Typically, clients, their therapists, training supervisors, and administrative personnel and billing clerks have fluid access to some or all of these records. They also are requested by a variety of third parties.

Historically, these materials had been kept private and confidential by storing them in locked office furniture and by taboos—"files and/or their contents must not be removed from the premises"—enforced by draconian penalties. Many trainees remember sneaking a client file out of the building in order to work on it remotely, and then their panic when they forgot it in a restaurant, on a bus, and so on. This potential portability changed only a little when desktop computers replaced file cabinets and access to the computers as well as all the material stored on them was required to be protected by passcodes and/or encryption. Shortly thereafter, trainees and many of their supervisors discovered that thumb drives provided both an even better means of portability and another source of risk.

The Health Insurance Privacy and Accountability Act of 1996

Congress recognized that advances in electronic technology in the health care system could put at risk the privacy protections guaranteed to consumers that are stipulated in state health statutes, described in professional codes of ethics, and often simply assumed. It was clear that there needed to be a unifying federal law. Consequently, the US Congress passed the Health Insurance Portability and Accountability Act of 1996 (commonly referred to as HIPAA, not HIPPA). It mandated privacy protections for identifiable health information of individuals. Similar federal protections that had already been set in place for educational institutions—the Family Educational Rights and Privacy Act of 1974—were updated around the same time.

Federal law mandates, with the exception of session notes (see text box), that information in all records belong to the clients and they are allowed unencrypted access to them, and only they can allow the release of information contained in those records to be released to (revealed to) other parties. Federal law supersedes state law and therefore the rules of HIPAA are threshold obligations. There may be times when a local question arises that does not appear to be covered by the universal rules of HIPAA—for example, a question concerning the applicability of state regulations (e.g., duties to protect vulnerable citizens) as well as those of professional organizations. In such a case, the answer is determined by where the respective clients are physically located at the times at which those clients are receiving care. Clearly, supervisors therefore need to be aware of the privacy rules governing their supervises as well as the supervisees' individual clients (see Huggins, 2016a). Supervisors also need to ascertain privacy rules that apply to their training centers, whether they are supervising in an educational institution, agency, or privately. The authors recommend that readers consult legal resources of their respective professional organizations (for example, the Legal Counsel of the AAMFT), malpractice insurance, or local attorneys who are familiar with HIPAA and behavioral health laws.

HIPAA draws a distinction between formal formative and summative *progress* notes, and informal *session work* notes. The former often are required parts of a client file and belong to the clients. They have the right to inspect them and to obtain copies of them. In contrast, session or work notes are informal notes to themselves that therapists and supervisors use to jog their memories, gather their thoughts, and make note of their impressions. These notes are intended solely for the use of the person who has written them. The one requirement under HIPAA is that these notes be kept apart from official case files (US Department of Health and Human Services, 2017).

One solution, for Security's Sake: Business Associate Agreements

HIPAA rules, as well as state-specific regulations, apply not only to professional records, but also to institutional and private electronic messaging and billing processes. They also apply to emails and texting, and these will be covered in the next section. However, over the past decade, HIPAA-endorsed business associate agreements (BAA; HIPAA, 1996) use an optimal mechanism to "appropriately safeguard" protected health information. Health service providers—training centers, agencies, and group or private practice supervisors and therapists—enter into BAAs with a company or individual that guarantees it will safeguard the protected data exactly as required by HIPAA. This HIPAA-approved third party can handle not only required forms and records, but also billing mechanics and documentation (see below). If requested, a BAA can identify and track security breaches and documents. A well-conceived BAA also can specify and lock down what otherwise might be confusing arrangements, namely, rules, fees, security uncertainties, and expected responses.

We pointed out in Chapter 5 that we have observed that, while engaged in remote services (therapy, supervision, and supervision mentoring), CFTs have not universally obtained written informed consent on their various documents. In fact, HIPAA as well as state regulations and professional ethics codes require the privacy and security of signed consent forms, as well as the platforms used to provide the services. Several companies offer "HIPAA compliant, eSigning" at competitive prices, and this also may be a part of commercial practice management systems.

HIPAA-Compliant Billing

At the time of this text's publication, HIPAA-compliant billing mechanisms have been evolving, and some are more adequate than others. For example, a popular payment platform such as SQUARE could currently be used in a HIPAA-compliant way. However, PayPal could not. Again, almost all such platforms are in constant change and new ones are being created. Supervisors and therapists wanting to remain secure with regard to HIPAA will be interested in knowing that confidential billing can be made part of a BAA (see Huggins, 2016b). In addition, some online practice management systems are able to provide both confidential appointment-making, invoicing, and credit card payments (see Reinhardt, 2019).

Communication Pitfalls—Emails, Texting, and Telephone Voice Messages

Aspiring and current supervisors and their clientele should seriously think about the mechanisms and the processes involved when they use email and other forms of texting. Privacy may differ with the fastidiousness of the recipient. HIPAA does not require such messaging to be encrypted as long as the recipients have been warned of the risks involved. Such warnings should be in writing, discussed with and signed by trainees and clients, and made part of the supervisory and therapeutic records, respectively. It is important for supervisors also to consider the rules promulgated by their respective disciplines' ethical codes. A typical example is stated in AAMFT (2015a) Section 6.3, *Confidentiality and Professional Responsibilities*: "It is the therapist's or supervisor's responsibility to choose technological platforms that adhere to standards of best practices related to confidentiality and quality of services, and that meet applicable laws."

The authors understand that BAA protective mechanisms can include email providers. This may be worth investigating. Nevertheless, electronic transmission, be it voice mail, email, or text may be protected from outside hackers but, more important, once arrived, who hears or reads them cannot be guaranteed. They just are not secure. Consequently, one is advised to *never say or text anything that one could not say to one's mother*. And telephone messages should reveal as little as possible. ("This is Jane Doe. Please call me at xxx-xxx-xxxx.")

HIPAA has a special mandate for email. Whether therapists and their supervisors like them or not, they must attach email disclaimers—known as a "Confidential transmission notice"—to every professional email that they send. These warn the recipient that the message that they are receiving is not necessarily secure, the content is strictly confidential and, if they are not the correct contact, they are obligated to delete and forward the message. Five popular templates have been made available by Karen Green (2020).

Authorization for Release of Information

Related to HIPAA authorization to release therapy records to third parties is the issue of who is needed to give fully informed consent for any such release. The

Code of Ethics for couple and family therapists (AAMFT, 2015a) is quite specific about situations where we may divulge client information, often called Release of Information or Authorization to Release Information. One of these is with written client permission, which is logical. However, what is not always so apparent, is that CFTs must obtain written permission from *everyone* and *anyone* who attended *any* sessions of a case. This is because CFT considers the "case" or "client" to be a *system* and not just one individual. Simply creating separate folders for each member of a client system may be a logical, but not legal workaround. We strongly caution therapists and supervisors to check with knowledgeable legal counsel before releasing information, whether requested in a subpoena or otherwise. Clients, many attorneys, and even judges do not understand this difference between us and psychologists, social workers, counselors, or even physicians in terms of confidentiality. Supervisors must help trainees explain these rules to others when questioned about them. Once again, familiarity with the AAMFT Code of Ethics is important and helpful to the entire training system.

Summary

Practicing legally as a supervisory team or training system is important and it is interesting to us how many therapists and supervisors are not aware of the laws that govern their practices. We take the position that good supervisors help their trainees learn not only the details of laws that affect the practice of therapy, but also the importance of being aware of laws, knowing how to research them, and reviewing them periodically. Laws and rules change and licensing bodies are not required to tell us about those changes. Professional organizations tell only their members. Therefore, we believe that it is in our and our trainees' best interests to belong to such organizations and to check jurisdictional laws and rules regularly and with our trainees. In the case of AAMFT, members are eligible for free legal and ethics consultation, which can easily repay the cost of annual dues if used even once. Finally, supervisors and trainees should regularly attend legal and ethical practice workshops.

Exercises

1. What are the requirements in your area for practicing marriage and family therapy? What kind of graduate training, postgraduate training, and supervised experience is necessary?
2. What are the required qualifications and responsibilities of supervisors?
3. What are the qualifications for continuing education for both therapists and supervisors?
4. Under what circumstances might a license be limited, suspended, or revoked?
5. What recourse does the public have if it thinks it or someone may have been harmed in therapy? How does it access that process?
6. How often must a license be renewed? What are the current requirements for renewal of a license? Have any requirements changed since the last time a license was renewed?

7. Have there been any changes since the supervisor last checked that he or she must be aware of?
8. Research at least two areas of law that affect practice and thus supervision of CFT. How do/will you help your trainees learn these laws?
9. Suppose you are a supervisor "outside" an agency, that is, not a regular employee of that agency. Further suppose that the agency has different policies and procedures for keeping client notes than you prefer for yourself as a therapist. How will you work with the trainee and agency so that everyone is comfortable and not in a power struggle?

12 Ethical Considerations in Relational Supervision

Professional ethics often overlap with legal considerations. For one thing, state regulatory codes often overlap with ethical codes in the prescription (e.g., confidentiality, duty to protect) and prohibition (e.g., exploitation of clients, practice outside of one's area of expertise) of professional behaviors. Also, both state statutes and ethical codes have as their primary purpose the welfare of the public, not protection or promotion of a profession. Moreover, state regulations often may incorporate professional codes of ethics (see Sturkie & Paff Bergen, 2000). In that situation, violation of a professional code of ethics is the same thing as breaking the law. In this chapter, we discuss ethical considerations of the supervisory system and ways that supervisors instill ethical knowledge and behavior in trainees.

Overview

Ethics codes typically can be found on professional organizations' websites under *ethics* or *legal and ethics*. Be mindful of the date of the publication so that you are certain you have the latest draft. At this writing, the latest AAMFT Code of Ethics went into effect July 1, 2015 (see www.aamft.org). Ethics codes are based on five fundamental ethical principles (see Kitchener, 2000): autonomy (the right of clients to make decisions for themselves), beneficence (the obligation to be helpful), non-maleficence (the obligation to do no harm), fidelity (to keep promises), and justice (to act fairly). These principles are held within ethical theory and the interested reader is encouraged to read relevant books and articles. Further, there may be differences between personal (usually tied to personal values) and professional ethics (often tied to bad acts from the past) that would be good for supervisors and trainees to discuss. A debate exists about ethics as a set of professional behaviors (codified duties and proscriptions) versus aspirational endeavors. We touch on aspects of this debate in this chapter.

Our fundamental supervision and training goal is for trainees to be sufficiently skilled to practice therapy autonomously; to be competent in independent practice. We must accomplish this end with beneficence, that is, we must aim to treat our trainees well and help them grow in the profession in positive ways, just as we must treat our clients well. We must eschew maleficence—we strive to do no harm to our trainees and to allow no harm to come to their clients or the field. We keep our

DOI: 10.4324/9781003099833-15

promises to our trainees (fidelity) and treat them fairly and evenly (justice). Our trainees are expected to deal with their clientele in the same ways. Clearly these characteristics are central contributors to all working alliances.

However important it is for the above ethical principles to be expressed across behaviors in the training system, explicit knowledge of ethical practice also is a fundamental outcome goal for our trainees. Supervisors have the obligation to assure the community that trainees are operating in rational, learned, and ethical ways. For example, their communities give our new professionals the privilege of operating privately and behind closed doors. In so doing, the community trusts that our trainees will allow no harm to be done to its members.

Creating and Sustaining an Ethical Supervisory Climate

If we are to create and sustain a training system that is informed by professional and personal ethics, it may be useful to give ourselves a conceptual framework to organize our thinking. For example, Stoltenberg and McNeill (2010) suggested that educators and supervisors have three fundamental areas to influence: cognitive awareness of self and others; desire to change one's beliefs, feelings, and actions; and the ability to maintain the first two on one's own. Stoltenberg and McNeill observed that developmental factors should interact with these fundamental areas. For example, new trainees may be motivated to become therapists, but are focused on themselves while being dependent upon their supervisors and their clients. Because they want reassurance that they are doing no harm, they are quite focused on their own behavior (not to say that they don't care about their clients). More experienced trainees may be free of this fear and vacillate between wanting supervision and being on their own. They may have a tendency to focus on and identify with their clients. The most mature trainees have become able to accurately assess their own strengths and weaknesses as well as those of their clients. They have developed a "sense" for when things do not seem quite "right."

Supervisors wanting to cultivate training systems that facilitate productive moral and professional growth, do no harm, and are fair and just, need a posture that addresses this complexity (for example, again see Stoltenberg & McNeill, 2010). We would suggest that supervisors' first steps are to aspire genuinely to inculcate the five ethical principles of autonomy, beneficence, nonmaleficence, fidelity, and justice in relation to their trainees given in the overview to this chapter.

A Developmental Lens

All successful supervisors nurture, confront, interpret, direct, and otherwise promote change in their trainees and their trainees' clients (Stoltenberg & McNeill, 2010). However, as they do so, they recognize that trainees are diverse and they themselves are unique. Therefore, they not only address their trainees' developmental needs but also how these needs intersect with their own needs (see Falender & Shafranske, 2016). For example, beginning supervisors may experience confusion and frustration in reaction to their concerns about the immediate wellbeing of their trainees and trainees' clients. These supervisors might become anxious over relatively minor events and become irritable, avoidant, or overreactive. They might shift into an overly directive supervisory posture and thereby inhibit trainees' professional growth. What might beginning supervisors do instead? They could identify the contagious nature of trainee (and client) anxiety and its spread to themselves. Then, aware of their reactions, they could rationally assess them and, in so doing, strengthen the boundary between themselves and the others. From this more differentiated position, they also could plan interventions more useful to the entire system. For example, they could ask questions about trainees' expectations and presumptions. They also could practice self-help behaviors and suggest that their trainees do the same.

As trainees become increasingly mature, mature supervisors ideally join them in increasingly more collegial, consultative relationships. However, beginning supervisors may be uneasy when their trainees try to fly solo and ask sophisticated clinical questions. In defense, supervisors may reduce oversight and engage in more familiar kinds of relatedness (e.g., friendship, therapeutic, or micromanaging). We encourage supervisors to think not only about their trainees' developmental behaviors, but also their own and how the two interact. Thinking this way, similar to thinking about isomorphism as a metaskill, may generate ideas for resolving difficulties without blaming clients, trainees, supervisors, or others in the training system.

Contextual Lenses

Other aspects of therapy reflect the complexity of our observations when seen through systemic and contextual lenses wherein ethical and legal principles are part of the context and recursively interact with other parts. Previous versions of the AAMFT Code of Ethics, as well as the way graduate students often have been taught about ethics and ethical matters, have suggested that there are some clear and simple laws and rules that tell us what to do and not do that constitute "ethical behavior." However, as we have seen, this is a complex topic often calling for decisions, each of which may violate one or more of our ethical principles. For example, how do we manage a situation of potential harm to others that is not clear cut? To report the client to others means breaching confidentiality but to not report may put another person and the client in harm's way. The client systems' values and typical behaviors (e.g., related to child discipline) may conflict with state requirements, but are understandable when taking the total context into account? What do we do in those circumstances?

It is common for graduate instructors to require students to memorize an ethics code and expect that (a) it will be remembered and (b) it will be used. Our experience is that neither of these expectations is met after graduate school. Certainly, licensing boards and regulatory investigators know that many professionals neither learn nor heed basics of appropriate and inappropriate behavior, let alone the nuanced thinking that is required in many situations. This led the second author toward a requirement whereby students and postgraduate trainees must develop their own ethical decision-making approach for recognizing and resolving ethical dilemmas.

We believe that ethics should be a part of all graduate and postgraduate training, both in the abstract, and as it relates to cases. One of the best places to begin is through a thorough understanding of what constitutes one's own values and ethics and one's own perspective on what those concepts mean and how they apply in therapy and supervision beyond ethics codes. Bilot and Peluso (2009) describe the use of an ethics genogram in supervision based on Peluso's (2003, 2006) work. This genogram work, which we suggest for supervisors as well as therapists, helps therapists understand the origins of their ideas, morals, values, and behaviors in an intergenerational context that then can be used to examine stances relative to professional ethical behavior. This contextual lens both enhances and complicates more specific decisions because of factors other than laws and regulations.

Common Ethical Domains

Knowing one's own blind spots and being able to recognize or predict them is empowering. (Murray Bowen's 1978 explications about disparities in differentiation of self in clinical dyads are invaluable.) Blind spots exist with regard to family and personal defensive dynamics, microaggression, and various aspects of training systems. There are specific areas where supervisors', trainees', and clients' values and ethical sensitivities and blind spots may intersect, and about which training systems should consistently remain alert. Numerous useful vignettes illustrating these intersections are available at AAMFT (2015b).

Supervision and Power

Supervisory power is multifaceted. Power and differential possession of it pervades CFT training. It includes the power to reward, coerce, and positively direct and influence. It may be overt (didactic) or covert (modeling, manipulating). Some expressions of power are necessary or benign (see discussion by Castronova, Chen-Feng, & Zimmerman, 2020). A major ongoing task for ethical supervisors is to identify possible ethical blind spots in their trainees as well as themselves. The touchstone for what may be benign or trivial may be either party's perceived freedom to say "no."

Supervision and Multiple Relationships

Multiple relationships in supervision are typically ubiquitous. In graduate programs, supervisors who are faculty are also teachers, assistantship supervisors, and administrators, and have power over students' lives in terms of grades, time, their ability to stay in programs, and later, in the form of letters of reference. Supervisors of postgraduate trainees are often employers or administrative as well as clinical supervisors. Boundary crossings occur frequently and often are benign, such as an administrative supervisor reminding a trainee during clinical supervision that monthly reports are due. They can even be helpful, especially later in supervision when trainees and supervisors engage in collegial activities such as attending or presenting at conferences, or participating in local peer groups of mental health professionals. Nevertheless, boundary crossings can shift to boundary violations. Boundary violations parallel potential problems in therapy and include inappropriate self-disclosure, requesting or granting favors, business and financial interactions outside the supervision system, and outside social interactions. They usually involve power imbalances and exploitation of the more vulnerable party.

Several researchers (see a qualitative study by Aducci & Cole in 2011, and reviews in Zür, 2017) have discovered that in both psychotherapy and in supervision, multiple relationships may be complex, but they also can be beneficial because they potentially can increase the bonds between therapists and clients or trainees and supervisors, and that problems predicted by some theorists are not necessarily present. Therefore, blanket statements proscribing them are inappropriate. As the supervisees told Aducci and Cole (2011), three themes affect the valence and amount of influence that multiple relationships potentially have: the details of the situation, how much and in what way the relationship affects supervision and therapy, and how open all the parties can be with each other about their relationships.

Nevertheless, even though collegial multiple relationships may flatten the hierarchy, there is implicit hierarchy and power (e.g., Sude & Gambrel, 2017). For example, as supervisors, we have power to reward and coercive power over our trainees in part because of our evaluation and gatekeeping responsibilities. Other examples of relationships that could potentially muddy the supervisory relationship include *collegial* (current and former trainees; other business relationships), *friendships*, and those in *rural* and *small communities* where we may be neighbors, fellow members of religious or other organizations, have children who are friends with ours, trainees', or clients', and so forth. Further, potential power imbalances may linger with former trainees such as requests for letters of reference. We are certain you can think of other examples.

Therefore, we must be vigilant not to abuse our power. This caveat led to a reexamination of older AAMFT Codes of Ethics (2001, 2012) and resulted in a revised Code (2015a) that is more aspirational than proscriptive. In this latest Code, *the potential for exploitation* (i.e., exploiting our power position inappropriately) is raised as the major concern in multiple relationships rather than the relationship per se.

Exploitation

Even though collegial multiple relationships may flatten the hierarchy, we must remember implicit hierarchy and power. For example, we not only have positive power to reward our trainees but also, because of our evaluative and gatekeeping responsibilities, coercive power over them. Therefore, we must be vigilant not to abuse that power. Hence the latest AAMFT Code of Ethics (2015a) not only carries forward proscriptions about sexual harassment and intimacy with trainees, but also includes the potential for exploitation in other ways. An example might be using information from one setting (e.g., confidential content in supervision) to entertain or otherwise influence colleagues. The first author also remembers a senior supervisor who required her trainees to perform extensive housekeeping chores on "Clinic Clean-up Weekends" and who engaged in paperwork as they did so.

The key, as with clients, is to avoid exploiting trainees and, when multiple relationships cannot be avoided, to take steps to prevent exploitation. In nearly all cases, the CFT supervisor would do well to include plans for managing such situations in his or her personal supervision approach and to have relationships with other supervisory colleagues for consultation.

Shifts in Roles

Attempted shifts in preordained roles may be accompanied by intimidation, exploitation, and boundary violation. Common examples are when anxious supervisors look to their trainees for reassurance, supervisor–trainee roles morph into therapeutic ones, or supervisors and trainees become personal friends. Even where there is no coercion or obvious exploitation, the training system may suffer. For example, it may no longer be experienced as task-centered or a safe place for difficult training discussions—this is impaired judgment on the part of the supervisor. Further complicating matters, trainees who seek personal acceptance and comply with a supervisor's bids for or acceptance of shifts in role may choose to be less open and truthful about themselves or their cases, or their discomfort with such shifts.

As with therapy, the burden of managing relationships and boundaries falls on the higher person in the hierarchy, that is, the supervisor. Therefore, it is important for supervisors to keep themselves in good psychosocial repair lest they introduce or facilitate inappropriate agendas into their training systems. Continuing education and participation in organizational activities are major outside resources for supervisors aspiring to stay in touch with ethical thoughts, feelings, and action. Unhappily, the evidence indicates that few CFT supervisors and practicing CFTs take advantage of them (Lee, Nichols, Nichols, & Odom, 2004).

Effective teachers practice what they preach. They model attitudes and behaviors that they want trainees to emulate both inside and outside of training settings. It is equally important that training systems make ethical concerns and best professional practices explicit. Just as we must have explicit, clear, and defensible ethical decision-making approaches to support our work as supervisors and as therapists, we also must help our trainees develop them. If trainees have their own ethical decision-making mechanisms, they don't need to be reactive, "on the spot," or seek excessive supervisory direction. Instead, they will have a set of steps for working through the frequent and necessary decisions that supervisors and trainees must make. With such a mechanism, your trainees should find it easier to be thoughtful and thorough about decisions and less likely to make serious mistakes. Having such procedures in place also helps provide documentation for making such decisions should it be necessary or useful. Such experiences nurture a realistic sense of self-esteem in the service of professional autonomy.

Helping Trainees Develop Personal Ethical Decision-Making Models

As we have seen, legal statutes and ethical codes often overlap. Each tells professionals what they specifically must and must not do. Neither tells us how to make ethical decisions with regard to behaviors that are not specifically covered by these codes, fall into "gray areas," and, especially, occur under professional duress.

According to Mowery (2009a, 2009b), laws and regulations constitute the "floor" (minimum standard) and aspirational ethical codes constitute the "ceiling" (higher standard) of ethical behavior. She further suggested that looking only at the floor means we miss the ceiling and the middle of the room, where therapy and supervision typically take place. Therefore, if all we do is "train" trainees in the ethics code and relevant laws, we are focusing on compliance more than values. Consequently, it behooves educators and supervisors to focus on moral reasoning as well. That is, we can help aspiring therapists develop conceptual tools that go beyond specific legal and ethical mandates.

Zür (2007; Zürinstitute.com) observed that supervisors who focus only on legal and ethical standards are merely engaged in risk management for their respective institutions. However, if supervisors and trainees develop ethical aspirations, then their intention is to ensure supervisor, trainee, institution, and client wellbeing, and not simply to preserve their licenses. Supervisors and trainees might begin this developmental journey by taking a close look at themselves. One vehicle for this would be for them to look separately and together for answers to the following questions (Mowery, 2009b):

1 What do I presuppose about the nature and source of morals and ethics? What are my taken-for-granted ideas about good and bad, right and wrong, and how did I come to these ideas?
2 What kind of person do I want to be?
3 What duties or obligations push me in certain directions? To what extent do the five ethical principles (autonomy, beneficence, nonmaleficence, fidelity, justice) play a role? To whom am I obligated, personally and professionally?
4 What are the possible future consequences that might pull me in certain directions?
5 What are the contextual perspectives of all those who will be affected by my professional decisions? And who are they?
6 What are the qualities of the relationships in which I want to participate?
7 What does particular experience say about a specific situation?

From this perspective, our individual principles are about value-informed choices and, in particular, choices in therapy and supervision. Ethics codes reflect the values of the people who wrote and approved them and the people and other resources they consulted. Therefore, they may or may not be accurate reflections of the individuals for whom they are held. In those instances, individual values of desiring to remain members in good standing of a profession, keeping one's license to practice therapy, and trusting group process for a greater good (e.g., client wellbeing, reputation of a profession), may impel some supervisors to heed the code, even if they do not completely agree with all of its tenets. Conversely, personal ethics that go beyond a professional code of ethics will also influence one's behavior.

The next step after self-discovery is the development of explicit ethical decision-making models. A good illustration of how to proceed is Zygmond's and Borhem's (1989) still timely model of ethical decision making for therapists, including CFT practitioners. Practitioners begin with an intuitive level that includes the facts of a situation and ordinary moral sense. If an answer to a dilemma is not apparent, they then proceed to a critical-evaluative process that includes consulting professional ethical rules and laws, ethical principles, and ethical theory as they apply to clinical situations. Zygmond and Boorhem include a feminist perspective that equalizes power among the participants in the dilemma as appropriate. At the conclusion of this examination of the professional situation, a decision is made about what to do. At times, no action will be deemed necessary. At others, the action appears quite clear and thus there is no dilemma. When there *is* a dilemma, the model assists the therapist and supervisor in being thoughtful and thorough, and provides documentation of the decision-making process.

We have found that developing and using systematic processes for making decisions and documenting the process has helped us make decisions that avoid or reduce negative consequences. We have found additional ingredients that may be useful, particularly in the critical-evaluative phase of resolving an ethical dilemma, such as consulting with colleagues, and using attorneys and the AAMFT ethics and legal consultation services (www.aamft.org/Legal_Ethics/Consultations.aspx) whenever in doubt. Many licensing boards as well as some malpractice insurance companies have attorneys or others who can provide useful information. Supervisors should also find that guiding trainees through mock situations can substantially reduce their (and our) anxiety about predictable difficult situations.

Decision-making approaches need not be complicated and overly detailed. The second author has found that a few steps to keep in mind that can be modified or elaborated upon have been helpful in educating trainees about ethical decision making. She uses these in particular situations but also throughout supervision when discussing examples provided by others, allowing trainees to think about their own approaches outside emotionally charged, anxious situations. They are:

1 Pay attention to my own discomfort (intuition) regarding the facts of the situation. I call this my "itch" and I help trainees and ethics course participants identify where in their bodies they feel confusion or uncertainty or anger.
2 Ask myself what personal and professional values apply to my thinking. Is this my own issue? A clinical issue? A legal or ethical issue?
3 Review Informed Consents for Treatment or Supervisory Contracts to remind myself what I have promised or required (fidelity; critical evaluative level).
4 Review the AAMFT code of ethics and relevant jurisdictional laws and regulations.

5 Consult with clients or trainees when appropriate (autonomy).
6 Consult trusted colleagues and attorneys.
7 Analyze based on ethical principles of autonomy, beneficence, nonmaleficence, fidelity, and justice. Check in with my feelings about this analysis.
8 Determine course of action (if any).
9 Document my actions and decision-making process.
10 Evaluate the process and its consequences.
11 Amend Informed Consents for Treatment or Supervisory Contracts as necessary.
12 Did I mention documenting actions and process (each of the above steps)?

In addition to basic processes that can be used when faced with ethical dilemmas in therapy cases, it is wise for therapists and supervisors to have ideas about how they might recognize their own impairment (see Chapter 13) and a decision-making tree for addressing impairment issues. Remedies can range from enhancing self-care through stepping back from certain cases to suspending oneself for a time or permanently as a therapist. Greenwood (2010) is an attorney who has written an article for CFTs about planning ahead for impairment or even death. Although this is not a topic that supervisors typically broach with trainees, we believe it should be.

Topics for Educating CFT Trainees

Those reading this text will by now, we hope, have formulated many ideas about not only their ethical responsibilities as supervisors in relationships with their trainees, but also about educating their trainees about morals, values, ethics codes and laws, and processes for making decisions in ethical dilemmas. There are several areas that we would like to punctuate as important in this ethics education process in addition to helping your trainees develop their own ethical decision-making models.

Signs of Trouble

We believe that it is very important for therapists in training to learn the signs of trouble for themselves as well as for their clients. Supervisors must provide safe contexts for discussing mistakes and identifying signs of trouble. Careful reading of ethics codes as well as jurisdictional laws and rules and doing so regularly can help supervisors and trainees avoid trouble and provide clues to behavior that has the potential for resulting in difficulties or trouble. Two important signs include (a) ignoring a gut feeling that something is "off," and (b) reluctance to discuss something in supervision (for trainees) or with trusted colleagues (for supervisors).

Supervision Contracts

One of the best ways to avoid misunderstandings or ethical dilemmas in supervision is to anticipate situations and include them in supervisory contracts (see Chapters 3 and 14). Examples might include verbiage about not doing therapy with trainees and encouraging trainees to bring up discomforts as they arise in supervision and therapy. Both trainees and supervisors should have input to the contracts. Therapy trainees are adults being trained in professional behaviors related to therapy. They also are adults in supervision with advanced clinicians. Therefore, it is wise for trainees to carefully review their supervision contracts and work with supervisors to modify them appropriately for their specific situations.

Informed Consent for Treatment

Trainees may not fully appreciate the respect with which protective oversight and decision-making individuals regard therapy and therefore how crucial it is that their clients fully understand the implicit and explicit contracts—their own, their families', and their communities'—they are entering into with the trainee as a therapist. Therefore, supervisors should include the elements of appropriate informed consent in their education of therapy trainees:

> Marriage and family therapists obtain appropriate informed consent to therapy or related procedures and use language that is reasonably understandable to clients. When persons, due to age or mental status, are legally incapable of giving informed consent, marriage and family therapists obtain informed permission from a legally authorized person, if such substitute consent is legally permissible. The content of informed consent may vary depending upon the client and treatment plan; however, informed consent generally necessitates that the client: (a) has the capacity to consent; (b) has been adequately informed of significant information concerning treatment processes and procedures; (c) has been adequately informed of potential risks and benefits of treatments for which generally recognized standards do not yet exist; (d) has freely and without undue influence expressed consent; and (e) has provided consent that is appropriately documented.
>
> (AAMFT Code of Ethics, 2015a, Principle 1.2)

Boundaries

Just as CFT trainees learn about appropriate boundaries in therapy, they also must learn about appropriate boundaries in supervision. This element of trainees' education will help forestall many misunderstandings and help them speak up in supervision when they are confused or concerned about something. If they do not feel free to do this, the supervisor has not yet entered into an appropriate collegial relationship with the trainee and the situation must be repaired. It is appropriate to include language in contracts that hold trainees responsible for bringing up concerns.

Impairment

Many trainees are so concerned about interventions and avoiding harmful situations with their clients that they miss an important part of being a therapist: recognizing self-impairment and engaging in self-care. Indeed, many do not even know about the possibilities and, instead of confiding in their supervisors, pretend that they are not sick, distressed, made a mistake, burned out, or otherwise experiencing something that could impair their clinical judgment. Wood (2004), in a study of therapists who do not utilize therapy themselves, found that such therapists used religion/meditation, time with family, vacations, and exercise to help prevent burnout and increased those activities when they were feeling burned out. However, Wood's data also suggested that having networks of therapists to help manage the stress of difficult cases or caseloads may be helpful. Rosenberg and Pace (2010) also provided some ideas for early career therapists and supervisors on preventing and managing burnout, including consultation.

Situations for Discussion

It often is useful for supervisors to include sections in their supervisory contracts that make it clear that either the supervisor *or* the trainee may bring up topics for discussion, and to list a few appropriate topics. Otherwise trainees may not get help with clinical concerns that are important. Moreover, by collaborating with supervisors' diverse concerns, they will have the important cognitive and emotional experiences of having successfully asserted themselves in supervision and making known their professional needs. (Readers may appreciate reading Haug & Storm, 2014. They have useful suggestions for constructive processing of ethical challenges in the training system.)

Exercises

1 What are your state or provincial laws about ethical concerns?
2 Think of an example where you and your trainee are at similar developmental levels and the trainee calls you with concerns about a suicidal client. What do you think is the best way for you to proceed?
3 Think of a time when you either felt exploited as a trainee or could have. How would you have liked your supervisor to handle the situation instead?
4 Go through Mowery's questions for yourself—what did you discover about your most important personal values?
5 Write down the steps for your own ethical decision-making model.

Below are some situations you may want to use for practicing your decision-making model (suggested by J. T. Thomas, 2010; we suggest you consider this text, especially if you are supervising mandated therapists, perhaps those on probation from a licensing board or professional organization). You may think of others. Questions to ask yourself: Is this a situation with clinical, ethical, or legal implications or is there overlap? Which should take priority? Is there a boundary crossing or violation? If a boundary crossing, could it lead to a violation if care is not taken? What does an analysis using the five ethical principles (autonomy, beneficence, nonmaleficence, justice, fidelity) look like? Is this a situation where I should consult with the client or a colleague?

1 A trainee wants to provide hypnosis and has some training, but you have none.
2 You are contacted by a former trainee who has received her license and you would like to take her to dinner to celebrate.
3 Your trainee wants to develop and manage your website in exchange for supervision.
4 Your trainee has a serious mental health problem. What do you do?
5 Student trainees in group supervision complain because you require self-of-the-therapist exercises.
6 A colleague asks your opinion about a former trainee without the trainee's listing you as a reference.
7 A trainee tells you about a different supervisor's behavior that borders on boundary crossing or violation.

13 Self of the Therapist, Self of the Supervisor

A supervisor was facilitating a training group. At issue was the capacity of a chronically depressed woman from a marginalized urban family to mother several young children. "Is she Black?" asked the supervisor. A Black student spoke angrily and loudly: "Why would you assume that?" The faculty member replied that this was not an assumption, but a question. Urban Black, extended, multi-generational families have been described as unappreciated (by outsiders) as support systems for their members (Boyd-Franklin, 2003; McAdoo & Younge, 2009). "Perhaps one should not focus on this individual in isolation, but consider the entire custodial system which might be available to this family." The student glared back at the supervisor and then began to cry. The room otherwise was silent; a peer took the student in her arms. Everyone—including the supervisor—appeared uncomfortable. The supervisor then repeated the importance of assessing the total custodial system and moved the case discussion on from that point. The remainder of the session was awkward. Few students participated in the discussion and the African American student hurried away at the end. The supervisor emailed that student to schedule a private meeting at the supervisor's office.

Relational supervisors and their trainees will think about this event in the following ways: First, they will need to inhibit their natural tendency to react to what the trainee is exhibiting. They will need to expand their fields of view to the entire training system, that is, all of the individuals in the room in their institutional context, because the event involves the entire training system. This is a conceptual step above the common advice given to prospective supervisors: "Know your own stuff." "Know the trainees' stuff." To do this well requires that supervisors think about their own backgrounds, biases, and prejudices as well as helping their trainees examine theirs. And they need to understand systemic biases and prejudices.

The Russian philosopher Lev Vygotsky (1986) observed that individuals are not aware of their cultures until something "bumps" against them. For example, someone might not be aware that she thinks of men of a different race from herself as intimidating until she compares a chance meeting with such a person with a meeting of someone of her own race. These often-covert feelings must be made overt and examined in the tension of experiencing and revealing them to others or to oneself. Such momentary tensions provide opportunities for learning and growth. To increase sophisticated awareness of the selves of the therapists, supervisors and institutions rely on enlightened self-interest in these moments. Even though such

DOI: 10.4324/9781003099833-16

moments may feel unpleasant and one's tendency may be to escape tension, the opposite may be more productive: embrace the tension and inquire into it in a blameless, curious, and humane way. Thus, after attending to the clinical case and helping the therapist who was conducting the therapy, the supervisor could have led a general conversation about stereotypes, hypotheses, and cultural humility (Tervalon & Murray-Garcia, 1998) with the group. Then, the supervisor might have explored his or her concerns as well as the student's in individual supervision.

Training systems nevertheless need to be able to identify and remove barriers to effective interaction and growth. A number of factors on social and psychological continua contribute to lack of awareness of multiple realities, narrow perspectives, or over- or under-responsiveness to difficult situations. Relational supervisors are less concerned with the cause of such eccentricities as with their interpersonally dysfunctional effects. Interdependent supervisors wish to recognize barriers to effective interaction. We believe that effective relational supervisors and their training systems engage themselves in interpersonal consciousness raising. We believe that the ability to do this requires that supervisors be able to tolerate ideas and perspectives other than their own while, at the same time, critically analyzing their own and others' views.

Self of the therapist, self of the supervisor, and self-reflexivity within the entire training context come together at this point. It is vital to the training enterprise that they not be ignored. Some earlier writers (e.g., Lee & Everett, 2004) have addressed this educational goal under two separate headings: First, personal barriers to effective therapy and supervision, often called self-of-the-therapist (or -supervisor) issues or countertransference; and second, general social barriers often referred to as "cultural issues," and systemic racism as a way of dismissing prevalent and influential attitudes against oppressed people. The problem with separate approaches is that attention is diverted from the core, transcendental issue: addressing diversity as a means of increasing the effectiveness of diverse training systems composed of diverse individuals with diverse backgrounds in diverse contexts with diverse clients. This means both accepting and celebrating differences. In the opening vignette, there were two areas requiring attention: lack of application of valuable subcultural nuances, and the barriers to exploring this in the training group because of system dynamics. Barriers to constructive training system interactions carry over into clinical function. They must be addressed from the beginning and consistently throughout the training process as both self of therapist and supervisor and cultural competence/humility. Sahebi (2020) reminds us that the provision of remote supervision, as with remote therapy, can be influenced by and influence the unique subsystems of the entire training system.

Addressing the Self of the Professional as a Primary Goal of Supervision

Many experts have written about "working alliances" and have explored supervisors' parts in them (see reviews in Muran & Barber, 2010; Chapters 1, 2, 7, and 12 in this text). However, this collective wisdom can be reduced to the following maxim: Central to any potential collaboration are shared goals and enough of a relationship to support work on them. Call it "establishing rapport," "joining," or acquiring a "working relationship," the bottom line is that, without these two factors—shared goals and a supportive relationship—significant constructive work is not likely.

Establishing a working alliance should be considered a social law in therapy and certainly constitutes a huge part of the effective outcome of therapy (e.g., Safran et al., 2014). It also influences the course of any consultation including supervision. In the course of therapy and in the course of supervision, questions often arise of "what to do first" and "where to go now." There is only one response: "Always attend to your working relationship." *The state of this relationship takes precedence over any other matter.* This dictum, of course, should not block steps required for client, other, and community safety. Such legal and ethical requirements always take precedence.

Supervisors can be expected to take the lead: "I perceive some discomfort, confusion, bias, etc., here. That's a good sign that this might be a good learning opportunity. Let's hold up, have a quiet moment, and then see if we can process it." If they are in a group setting, supervisors have two goals: (a) to grow the group process in an experience of safe participation—an application of the "working alliance" rule—while (b) helping the group recognize whether a sensitivity or insensitivity has occurred. If there has been an insensitivity, how that might be a barrier both to effective supervision (including the group process) and therapy must be discussed as well as how to address it.

In the opening vignette, there clearly were group-in-context processes to be addressed. Not only the complainant but also the other trainees may have felt uneasy at challenging their supervisor. After all, they were in an institutional setting where they were students "under" a faculty member, in the supervisor's institutional seminar room. One wonders how this matter would have been dealt with more openly in another setting (e.g., off-campus) or if the supervisor were not present, had not been the one who triggered the sensitivity, or had addressed the group and asked for feedback. Beyond these contextual matters, positive learning might have occurred if the group setting had provided a forum for discovery instead of being accepting, consoling, and/or avoidant. The group goal would be to nurture a calm exploration by everyone, informed by curiosity without the hint of blame. Doing so would no doubt have increased the probability of two desirable things: The group might have had a corrective emotional experience of dealing constructively with potentially prickly matters while acquiring cognitive subcultural awareness of the client's (and trainee's) context. Again, note that this would require the supervisor to be aware of and sensitive to his- or herself. Most important, such learning is systemic. Members of the training system learn not only about experienced insensitivity and microaggression, but also the protections afforded the ostensible victims when interacting with their peers in their training contexts. The credibility, richness, and here-and-now learning through experience attendant upon such opportunities should not be minimized. In contrast, surveys of "worst supervisory" experiences (Anderson, Schlossberg, & Rigazio-DiGilio, 2000; Piercy et al., 2016) indicate that where such educational processes do not occur, beliefs and feelings are learned that pose barriers to effective training and therapy. Years after their negative experiences, respondents in the Anderson and colleagues' study described experiences in individual and group supervision of having not been heard, feeling put down, and otherwise inhibited in supervision. This may be so general an experience by trainees that these barriers to constructive interaction should be addressed up-front in new supervisory relationships.

It is important to recognize that some trainees are so sensitive and even reactive to perceived supervisors' or others' slights that they present ongoing barriers to good training. In such situations, it is helpful for supervisors to be willing to examine their own attitudes, words, and actions and, if necessary, consult with trusted colleagues for help in managing themselves and the supervisory situation.

Activities to Raise Self-Awareness within the Immediate Training System

There are some commonly cited experiential approaches to self-awareness in clinical situations. One of these is to have trainees immediately review videotapes of their therapy sessions and to describe what they were thinking and feeling at specific points (e.g., Cook, Welfare, & Sharma, 2019; Routon, 2018), and debriefing of clients about their therapeutic experiences (e.g., Dwyer, 1999). Supervisors and their trainees also can discuss responses to therapeutic or working alliance scales (see compilation in meta-analysis by Martin, Garske, & Davis, 2000). There also are self-discovery operations specific to individual CFT models, for example, Emotionally Focused Therapy (Soloski & Deitz, 2016), Person of the Therapist (Aponte & Kissil, 2016; Rober, 2017), and Functional Analytic Psychotherapy (Tsai et al., 2009). Also noteworthy are the diverse articles on person of the therapist in training and supervision compiled in the October 2009 issue of the *Journal of Marital and Family Therapy*.

Appreciation of Personal Barriers—Live or in Debriefing

To the extent that one person is not sensitive to another person's nonverbal and verbal communications or cues, or, having been sensitive to them, does not respond in a timely and appropriate manner (in size or kind), it is assumed that the person is experiencing the other through a distorting filter. In other cases, there may be a palpable lack of enthusiasm, initiative, or discomfort. For example, someone (supervisor or therapist) might become anxious or irritated with self, the client, or the supervisor in ways that are not customary for that individual or situation.

For example, in response, the training system nonjudgmentally explores what its participants might be thinking and feeling and the extent to which it is congruent with what might be experienced in a different situation. If it is appropriate to the training setting, the participants might explore where the meaning came from (e.g., family of origin or other experiences).

Activities to Raise Self-Awareness Outside of the Training System

The previous section highlights interactions within the immediate training system. However, the training system is just one of many systems in which the members exist. They also are living parts of friendship systems, families, communities, and so on. Attitudes and biases, sensitivities and insensitivities exist and are facilitated by the entire ecosystem in which these other systems are involved. Trainees have designated (personal communications) some educational activities as having been helpful in discovering their own cultures as well as those of others. Many have spoken of how the specific pieces of cognitive learning were interesting, but what was most valuable was the appreciation that prejudicial filters limited and determined their experiences of self and others across their social contexts.

A few directed approaches to overall cultural self-awareness employ the cultural genogram (Hardy & Laszloffy, 1995; Keiley et al., 2002), self-exploration questions processed in a group (compiled by Lee & Everett, 2004; Totsuka, 2014), and daily journaling of so-called "critical incidents" (Lee & Vennum, 2010). This last approach does not ask the participants to be deficit detectives. Instead, it invites them to be cultural anthropologists. As the participants go about their daily lives in school, on the streets, and in their abodes, they are to make brief entries into journals when they experience the tension of Vygotsky's "cultural bumps." In their journals, trainees describe the critical incident or "bump," their reaction, and then reflect upon it. At the end of the term, they review their journals and write what they may have learned about themselves and others. They may or may not be asked to share their personal insights in the larger group. Participants have described the credibility and excitement of this enterprise. In time, they said, they came to look forward to discoveries and intentionally placed themselves in what they thought might be provocative settings. (See Chapter 10 for more ideas on exploring cultural contexts.)

Supervisors' and Trainees' Self-Care

An important aspect of being a professional and understanding one's self as a therapist or supervisor is knowing one's limits, both professionally and personally. This includes knowing what to do (or not do) and when to do it to take care of oneself. Not doing so leads to burnout and impairment, two unhappy consequences that affect not only therapists and supervisors, but also clients, family and friends, and colleagues, and can affect the reputation of our field.

One approach to training may ideally be suited to a sense of wellbeing as part of the self of the professional. Solution-focused training (e.g., Nelson, 2014) can be used as an exclusive training model or its ideology and techniques can be used in appropriate circumstances with other supervision or therapy approaches. Although purists might decry its use as such, solution-focused conceptualizations and techniques are wondrous tools to carry in your kit and unpack as needed. When supervisors or trainees are confused, frustrated, bogged down, despondent, bored, or pessimistic, they can obtain great emotional relief and direction by asking themselves or having other members of the training system ask them, "When supervision/therapy is going a little better, what are you doing? What are the others doing?" More specifically, "In the past few sessions, when things were going a little better with these clients, that is, you were feeling good in the session and after it, what was different? How do you think you accomplished that?" The training system might also explore what "a little better" would look like for each of its members.

Solution-focused training systems also concern themselves with goal setting: realistic, clearly observed, positive action behaviors in the here-and-now, and ostensibly under the participants' control, mirroring well-formed goals in therapy (e.g., De Jong & Berg, 2013). Trainees can be asked not what they think is wrong or bad, but what they have done well, or what they might be doing instead or more of, and what they have done in the past in similar situations. The training system might explore how they would know that progress was being made: what participants would see, hear, and/or experience. They could construct scales that would measure progress toward their goals. They also could ask themselves a variation of the "miracle question" (de Shazer et al., 2007): "Suppose a miracle happened and your dreams of being the best therapist possible came true. What would be the first thing you would notice that would tell you this miracle happened? What would others notice?"

Resiliency

"Resiliency" has been defined as a "synergistic collection of attributes of individuals and their groups that allows them to (a) stand up to stress and (b) grow from it (see Walsh, 2016). Resiliency is a process that mediates the interaction of individual and contextual attributes. As others have uncovered, individuals are resilient to the extent to which they perceive themselves as active agents in what happens to them, have optimistic outlooks toward life, and can find and recruit the help of external resources when necessary. Their social contexts, in turn, share these adaptive beliefs, and also contain resources that are both easily apparent to and capable of being used by its members under duress. Individuals in interdependent relationships might wish to do a self-inventory (e.g., a brief 5-factor assessment scale by Lee, 2013). No matter how a training system assesses its resiliency, its members will benefit from appreciating what they as a group already do well and exploring what "growing edges" might benefit from more cultivation.

Some time ago Lee and his students (Lee, Eppler, Kendal, & Latta, 2001) carefully explored what a cohort of family therapy trainees found stressful. What turned out to be both the source of their greatest stress as well as their greatest resource for dealing with overall stress was their myriad social memberships: supervisor training group, peers in training, relationships with significant others, and family, church, and social groups. When a professor or supervisor, parent or child, mate or friend ignored demands being made of their lives because of multiple commitments, they were distressed. However, these same relationships were important sources of renewable energy. A training group or the entire training system might benefit from drawing personal ecomaps (Hartman, 1995) and considering the implications of these in their professional lives.

Assessing Impairment

As a practical matter, uncovering dysfunctional processes of the self is a universal life-long enterprise. For training system purposes, the touchstone is the extent to which a personal or group process interferes with effective therapy or membership in a training system. If the barrier to effective functioning is of sufficient impact toward training goals or security obligations, and simpler solutions do not work (e.g., notes to the self; limitation to live supervision), external aid must be identified and used (see Russell, DuPree, Beggs, Peterson, & Anderson, 2007 for suggestions for remediation actions and consequences used in COAMFTE graduate programs. Many of these apply to postgraduate training as well). In this regard, formal documentation of concerns should be in supervision or training files. This documentation should include concerns with explicit examples of observed behaviors and their consequences. The documentation then provides the rationale and evidence for Performance Improvement Plans. Performance Improvement Plans are based on clearly observable, auditable behaviors, a statement of what would indicate the course of necessary progress and perhaps how this will be accomplished, a timeline, and specification of clearly stated consequences should the behavior not change. These formal Performance Improvement Plans must be signed and dated by the supervisor, trainee, and any others involved in the development of the plan.

Cultural Lenses: Biased Expectations Based on Group Membership

Participants in a training system uniquely view their respective worlds through lenses created by their cultures and subcultures. The naive think about culture as "something the other person has" (see Lee & Nelson, 2014, page 157). They are unaware of the dominating influence of their own. This is unfortunate because "unconscious biases in emotions, motivations, fund of knowledge, and information processing may prejudice the expert, as can ethnic, racial, and cultural biases against the evaluee, which an internal dialogue may limit" (Aggarwal, 2012, p. 116). Consequently, for several decades, both master's and doctoral accredited CFT therapy programs have sought to infuse gender and cultural sensitivity by interspersing specific courses throughout their curricula and with experiential programming (Winston & Piercy, 2010; Kumar, Karabenick, Warnke, Hany, & Seay, 2019). Guidebooks (e.g., Purtilo, Doherty, & Haddad, 2019) are available to help supervisors and aspiring supervisors as they attempt to identify cultural biases in their training systems and to manage them in order to create a safe and buoyant climate for learning. Qualitative studies have revealed that an important variable associated with the success of these efforts has been (Laszloffy & Habekost, 2010) and continues to be (Campbell, 2018) the participants' perceived level of commitment and transparency regardless of context.

Microaggressions

Some cultural biases may be blind spots that seem benign. However, all of them have the potential to obstruct the authenticity necessary to professional growth. Others are toxic. Microaggressions, first identified in the literature 40 years ago (Pierce, Carew, Pierce-Gonzales, & Wills, 1977), typically are brief and commonplace verbal, behavioral, and/or environmental narratives that—although defended by many people as harmless—are experienced as insulting, degrading, and otherwise demoralizing by their recipients. In a classic compendium, Sue (2010/2020) has discussed how this model has fruitfully been extended from racism to a wide range of target individuals in diverse subcultures—gender, age, social class, regional and national identity, religion, and perceived mental or physical challenges, to name a few.

Evolution of Supervisors Requires Tolerance of Ambiguity

Contemporary supervisors recognize that social constructivism is an epistemology meeting the requirements of a new age in therapy. They recognize that multiple ways of knowing and meaning inform diverse belief systems with attendant values, emotions, and action tendencies. They have long become used to looking into and thinking about things to the point where they become confusing, and they have developed a tolerance for this ambiguity (see Knight, Kenny, & Endacot, 2016; McLain, Kefallonitis, & Armani, 2015; Sung, Antefelt, Choi, & Jin, 2017). Although entertaining dynamic complexity can be anxiety-producing and tempt one to over-simplification through reductionistic models, these new-age supervisors and therapists appreciate that openness to multiple possibilities is an opportunity for learning. Such professionals are not technicians whose perceptions, thoughts, and consequent interventions are determined by therapeutic models. In contrast, they are client-focused, integrative, and evolving. They see assessment and interventions as applied family science.

Concurrently, research (see review in Kattari, 2019) has demonstrated that these experiences of identity-related microaggressions negatively influence emotional and physical well-being, and contribute to work fatigue, decline in productivity, and difficulty in learning.

Another Valuable and Straightforward Research Opportunity

Supervisors have a duty to take steps to prevent activities that adversely intrude into their educational and training processes and make the training system feel unsafe to any or all of its members: "Effective supervision is based on shared goals and a relationship (good enough) to sustain those goals" (Chapter 1, p. 13). Albeit scientific support for the psychotherapeutic common factors model is lacking (Cuijpers, Reijnders, & Huibers, 2019), it seems reasonable to hypothesize that, in relational therapy and in its supervision, positive processes and outcomes will be found to involve common facilitative factors such as a positive working alliance and corrective supervisory experiences (see Watkins, 2018).

And Yet Another Research Opportunity

Microaggressive beliefs, with their attendant emotions and action tendencies, that have been documented by researchers to exist between therapists and their clients could reasonably be expected to exist *throughout the training system* and to influence outcomes for the respective participants. Race- and gender-based prejudicial assumptions have been investigated extensively. Other negative biases, not so much.

Similar inquiries about the association of meta-aggressions or systemic biases—if any, in what way, and how much—within *training system* processes and outcomes strike us as invaluable choices for dissertation topics and, later, integrated programs of scholarly research. A good example has been a scholarly program investigating the association of affirming CFT faculty beliefs about LBGTQ with their pedagogy (McGeorge, Carlson, & Toomey, 2015). Specifically, those faculty members who reported more positive beliefs about LGB clients were more likely to include LGBTQ affirmative therapy content in classroom and practicum syllabi, and their trainees demonstrated that positive influence in their clinical work.

Inquiry about the probable influences of affirming and nonaffirming biases throughout the training system could consider, to name a few, entities such as weight bias (see Pratt et al., 2016), overt religiosity (Maxwell, Davis, Miller, & Woolley, 2018), heterocentrism (Hartwell, Serovich, Reed, Boisvert, & Falbo, 2017), and negative expectations related to manifest transgender identification (e.g., Shipman & Martin, 2017).

Supervisors want to cultivate and nurture a safe workplace. Therefore, they manage toxic influences by first operating in ways that these will be identified and then, as with other apparent glitches, regard them with respect. They are welcome learning opportunities. Recognizing and managing them will promote the effectiveness of everyone engaged in their corporate mission. To ignore or regard microaggressions in a hostile or defensive manner probably results in a familiar downward spiral: Anxiety leads to fight or flight; "walking on eggshells" leads to resentment. In contrast, benign, so-called "empathic" confrontation is concerned with nurturing sensitivity and safety for the wellbeing of all. It is part of a narrative that begins with a sincere, "I care about myself and I care about you, and I care about us." Supervisors can uncover plentiful pragmatic guidance in human relations and self-help literature, in print and online (e.g., St. Louis County, 2014; Sue, 2010/2020).

Exercises

1. We assume that you at least contemplated one or more of the exercises suggested in this chapter. What did you learn about yourself? About how you interact with others?
2. Imagine you are watching a video recording with a trainee in which a client may have experienced some microaggression (seemingly small but important hurt) and the trainee does not see it. Write at least three ways you could open a discussion with the trainee about this.
3. Imagine that a trainee has just confronted you about your own behavior toward another member of the training group regarding a perceived inappropriate religious comment. How would you like to think you would handle the situation? What factors about the reporting trainee, the apparently harmed trainee, yourself, and the training context inform your actions/words?
4. Addressing experienced microaggression communicated by supervisors. What might facilitate this and what might create barriers? How to manage cases where one party doesn't see the big deal.

Part 4

Troubleshooting and Writing a Personal Philosophy of Supervision Paper

An Overview

DOI: 10.4324/9781003099833-17

14 Troubleshooting and Pragmatics in the Relational Training System

Readers will expect this chapter to immediately address problematic circumstances between supervisors and trainees. It will do that—eventually. However, it usually is helpful to have a big conceptual map that offers training glitches as understandable and predictable predecessors to the clinical growth of all parties to the training. Such a map also facilitates the creation—on the spot or otherwise—of acceptable interventions. Therefore, the materials in this chapter begin with conceptual overviews followed by situation-specific pragmatics.

Appreciating the Interpersonal Context of Training

Supervisory Environment

When trainees reflect upon what has characterized their "best" supervisory experiences they unanimously cite exciting-but-safe environments conducive to taking risk while facilitating multifaceted discovery (see Anderson, Schlossberg, & Rigazio-DiGilio., 2000; Drake Wallace, Wilcoxin, & Satcher, 2010; Piercy et al., 2016). Supervisors recognize that most individuals have had an uneven relationship with authority figures over their life spans, and now are concerned with their professional adequacy. The stage is set for the emergence of toxic emotions associated with power, evaluation, and advice giving (see discussions in Chapter 12; Sude & Gambrel, 2017).

The first supervisory goal must be to *develop an environment characterized by safety conducive to constructive openness*, that is, one that fosters a trusting relationship between supervisors, trainees, trainees' clients, and the training system in which all are embedded. As in therapy, the absence of this characteristic diminishes the probability of desirable processes and events.

The second fundamental goal of supervision is the *maintenance* of this atmosphere in ways compatible with the needs of the entire training system. This includes the three units above as well as the contexts in which all of them (and the interventions) are situated. For example, trainees' trust and security should not be achieved in an unholy alliance against other stakeholders. Such a stance requires that supervisors have minimal, and keep alert to, overlapping baggage with both trainees and outside authorities, and recognize and question things that are being assumed, both in the

DOI: 10.4324/9781003099833-18

supervisory relationship and between trainees and their clients. For example, supervisors must maintain confidentiality and its limitations as described and agreed to in the supervisory contract. Remember our mantra: When supervisors consider their priorities at any time—except for significant dangers posed to readily foreseeable others—they should first look to the establishment and maintenance of a good-enough supervisor–trainee relationship within the parameters of the overall training context. For example, breaching confidentiality except as described and limited in the contract will surely disrupt or break the relationship.

From that viewpoint supervisors might be wise to resist the temptation to reduce uncertainty and "set things clear." It might prove better to appreciate *everyone's* uncertainty and their reactions to it. Paradoxically, the solution to setting things clear is asking good questions and actively listening, and thereby taking charge in a positive way that will model a constructive and safe, accepting atmosphere. Many difficulties arise when trainees do not disclose concerns or mistakes because they feel unsafe. Therefore, establishing a safe context for discussing *anything* can pre-empt many troubles and difficulties. Nelson vividly remembers a situation where a trainee confronted her privately about something Nelson had said in group supervision that the trainee found offensive and hurtful. Nelson was appalled at what she had said and the hurt it caused, apologized, and asked what she could do to right the wrong. After apologizing to the whole group, Nelson participated in a discussion about both what she had said, what it might indicate about herself, what she had learned from it, and general talk about how to admit mistakes, make up for them, and recover from them. We all learned that it is easy to become defensive, but then to do what we can to make up for our transgressions.

Supervisors need to appreciate multiple realities in their workplaces. If resistance is a sign of folks feeling threatened, its presence means that they must be seeing things differently than their supervisors because most supervisors do not want their trainees to feel threatened. This is a time when supervisors should remind themselves to remain calm, non-defensive, and to promote exploration of thoughts and feelings in an atmosphere of safety and openness.

Such discussions are both difficult and desirable. They are opportunities to model openness to the diversity of experience. Modeling good interviewing technique logically follows. "Your body language and your voice suggest that you are uneasy. What is it I am not seeing/hearing/understanding?" Such questions are asked benignly and the exploration is comprised of active listening. One is not dismissive or defensive no matter what the resulting information might be. Whatever it is, it is the other's view, they believe it, and they will not calm down or feel that they are in a safe relationship unless they appreciate your genuine interest. In fact, it may be that their very capacity to share this information is a clue to the level of trust possible within the training system. Therefore, instead of responding with one's own view, give a simple, "Ok. Thank you. You've given me a lot to think about." If the awkwardness of the moment hinders processing the situation, it might be wise to table the matter and let some time go by. Things should become discussable after that. "Remember last session? What you said was … I could see that you were upset. … and I'd like to talk about this." And then *listen* non-defensively

Multiple Roles

Supervisors simultaneously hold multiple roles in which they have multiple and even competing responsibilities to both their trainees and training settings (see Chapters 2, 10, and 11). With respect to trainees, supervisors concurrently are teachers, mentors, and evaluative administrators (Sude & Gambrel, 2017; Whitman & Jacobs, 1998). Difficulties can arise when these roles conflict or when boundaries are ambiguous. The latter—blurred boundaries—facilitate boundary crossings and even boundary violations. Supervisors also need to recognize that these multiple, overlapping roles as well as the training system are embedded in larger environments: education, training, and service environments; neighborhoods; and state and national regions. Navigating roles through these systems is not always easy. All environments are informed by diverse needs for safety and wellbeing. Some supervisory roles are defined in policies and best practices regulated by legislatures, professional organizations, federal agencies, special interest groups, training programs, universities, agencies, and supervision contracts. Moreover, supervision of clinical practice may be voluntary or mandated, further complicating the mix of roles between clinical supervision and gatekeeping. In each role, stakeholders expect supervisors to pay attention to and contribute to the safety and wellbeing of not only their trainees but also various institutions and the public. Supervisory candidates often hear this news with trepidation, fearing that it will be difficult to keep roles separate. It is an awesome and sometimes seemingly impossible obligation. Yet, it is an obligation well met when supervisors understand their various roles and ways to manage the mix so that trainees and others are not harmed. This is not a time for "ignorance is bliss."

The path of responsibility for the welfare of various stakeholders leads back to the supervisors involved. This fact has been consistently affirmed by clients, institutions, personal injury attorneys, judges, and juries. These precedents lead to pragmatics outlined in the following sections.

"The Best Defense is a Good Offense"

Fortunately, the touchstone is "prudence": When presented with facts, a jury of a supervisor's peers should be able to agree with the supervisor with regard to obligations and that the best tools available were used to arrive at reasonable judgments and actions regarding them. Consequently, it is fundamentally important for trainees and supervisors to understand the ethics and laws related to supervision (see Chapters 11 and 12 in this text; AAMFT, 2015a) and to be open to available resources. Books and help lines for legal and ethical advice (e.g., AAMFT Legal Counsel) underscore this opinion.

From the very beginning of each supervisory relationship, prudent supervisors let their understanding of their multiple obligations help determine essential supervisory structures:

- Comprehensive introductory interviews, preliminary systemic assessment of trainees' skills and understanding of therapy and supervision, and introduction to the supervisor's philosophy and administrative tools;
- Discussion with trainees about potential and actual multiple roles, with plans for how each can recognize them and call out the supervisor when necessary;
- Essential tools used consistently: written supervision contracts, adequate observation supported by documentation packages, explicit evaluative processes and their consequences, and detailed policies and procedures of the training system.

Systemic Assessment: The Training System in Its Largest Environment

Supervisors should be conversant with Imber-Black's (1988) classic text *Families and Larger Systems: A Family Therapist's Guide Through the Labyrinth*. She advises supervisors and therapists to consider the larger systems in which all parties are living units. Members should explore:

- Each person's areas of responsibility. *Where do these areas overlap?*
- The beliefs and expectations of each about roles for themselves as well as others in the system. This includes beliefs about each other. *Where do these conflict?*
- The goals of each, that is, that which each stakeholder considers to constitute "success."
- *Are these compatible with one another?*

How do the supervisor and trainee fit in terms of the larger context? Are their beliefs, understandings, and expectations about supervision sufficiently congruent that reasonably smooth supervision of clinical work can take place? Do they understand each other's backgrounds well enough to determine whether or not there is a good fit in the relationship? Does each have the capacity to discuss differences and arrive at acceptable solutions?

Initial Interview

The initial interview is not an event, but a process. It should thoroughly explore the needs, expectations, and concerns of all parties in or out of the consultation room (that is, not just the supervisors and trainees, but also administrative hierarchies, regulatory boards, and the like). Trainees should be introduced to ethical codes (e.g., AAMFT, 2015a) as well as applicable statutes regarding scope of practice, confidentiality, privilege of confidential material, child and elder protection, duty to protect or warn, and so forth. Later, they should be held accountable for the information in those documents in an ongoing manner.

Legal advisors to the helping professions also advise that fewer inflammatory complications arise when there is an open, amiable, and compassionate relationship among the stakeholders. Therefore, the initial interview is the best place to start to establish a trusting relationship between the supervisor and trainee to test whether this will be sufficiently strong to have the kinds of discussions that will be needed to forestall mistakes and their consequences, and to manage when either the trainee or supervisor does make mistakes.

Supervisors and supervisor candidates can explore the following three questions in an introductory session and document their mutual understanding of the answers as part of the written supervision contract:

1 What are the obligations that must be met by each person?

   a Provision of specified content
   b Fulfillment of specific requirements
   c Protection of reasonably identifiable victims

2 To whom are the obligations owed?

   a Clients and their significant others
   b The supervisor and trainee
   c The training system
   d Relevant social communities
   e Training institutions
   f Educational institutions
   g Service-providing institutions
   h Governmental regulatory bodies
   i Professional organizations

3 How will these obligations be audited and what reports will be made and to whom?

Comprehensive Written Supervision Contract

Supervision is an undertaking with a high degree of uncertainty. Individuals differ in their tolerance of uncertainty and, when that threshold is exceeded, react strongly to reduce it. The best preventative may be structure. This includes explicit statements describing how your mutual business will be done, supported by a reasonable rationale that is easily defended, and expectations for each person regarding ways to address potential difficulties or problems.

Legal advisors observe that if something "isn't written, it doesn't really exist." A written contract, reviewed and signed by all parties subsequently can be used to structure, review, and defend supervision processes. When spelled out, expectations and consequences make it much easier to deal with difficulties later on. Supervisors need to understand that, from a legal viewpoint, it is very difficult to apply consequences if a rule has not been stated in advance and documented by a signature and date. However, many contracts typically address the concerns of supervisors and not necessarily those of trainees. Supervision contracts that are arrived at collaboratively between supervisors and trainees presumably are understood and followed better than those that are dictated by supervisors. Moreover, supervisors must live up to the terms of these contracts if the contracts are to be taken seriously. For example, if a contract specifies punctuality and preparedness, supervisors themselves should arrive on time, not leave early, or be prepared. Similarly, if trainees are expected to be prepared for supervision, supervisors are not helpful if they ignore the breaches or are not themselves prepared. See Chapters 3 and 14 for more discussion of supervisory contracts.

Documentation Packages

Documentation packages, at their minimum, include supervision process notes and periodic evaluative and planning summaries. The latter include review and modification of supervision goals. There also needs to be a final evaluative summary that indicates capacities and recommendations for further work. The mechanisms and criteria of evaluation should be agreed upon at the beginning of supervision by both supervisors and trainees, as well as "non-negotiable" items such as sobriety, notifications, and confidentiality in both supervision and trainee client consultations.

Evaluative Processes and Their Consequences

The range of consequences for negative evaluations should be addressed. These may range from "Performance Improvement Plans" to "immediate termination" (see Russell, DuPree, Beggs, Peterson, & Anderson, 2007 for ideas from a sample of COAMFTE-accredited potential actions) with notification of appropriate authorities. Supervision contracts may include clauses that specify that supervisors may notify further supervisors and/or others such as educational faculty or licensing boards if the supervision is terminated prematurely. Trainees who sign contracts with this clause are thereby giving consent to such notifications.

Addressing Difficulties

Although serious, immediate concerns must be quickly and clearly addressed, wise supervisors also think in terms of the context in which these issues exist as well as broader supervisory structures that may prevent such issues in the future. They recognize that (a) barriers to supervisory efficacy require a maintenance structure. That is, reciprocal behaviors lead to and maintain the status quo including "crises of the week." Thus, wise supervisors think about their own parts in the difficulties that are happening. They also recognize that (b) barriers can begin at any level of the training system and flow up and down. For example, if clients experience what they perceive to be wonderful results from an intervention, their empowerment, optimism, and pleasure are transmitted to their therapists, and thence to the supervisors.

Positive supervisors (see Chapter 9 with regard to metaskills) no doubt empower trainees and, through them, clients. Conversely, if things go sour, negative reactions spread throughout systems, resulting in disappointment in self and others and perhaps oppositional behavior or indifference. Sensitive supervisors respond to both positive and negative ripples in the pond that is the training system by exploring the thoughts, emotions, and actions of everyone, including the messages trainees and supervisors give to themselves and others. For example, any one situation may lead to the excitement of discovery or the reinforcement of difficulties. Notice that central to establishing positive or negative consequences is the capacity of at least one member of the training system to head off automatic negative reactions by self and/ or others. One of the authors remembers a masterful preschool teacher's response to a dropped ice cream cone and tears: "Oh, look! See how happy those ants are! You've given them a treat! Good for you!" (Yes, other globs of ice cream then began hitting the ground.)

Troubleshooting the Nuclear Subsystem: Supervisor↔Trainees↔Clients

Unholy alliances within the system, impasses, bogging down, avoidance of issues, negative affect, even boredom are all training barriers. One historically fundamental assumption has undergirded all approaches to trouble shooting: *The training system must have the capacity to observe itself.* This is an extension of the original psychoanalytic concept of the "observing ego," which has been considered a prerequisite for psychodynamic interventions (Ormont, 2001). Notice that we emphasize "training system" here. Relational supervisors do not believe that a narrow focus on a singular part of a system will lead to an adequate response and is not a good learning experience for relational trainees. Moreover, once one member of the training system ascertains that there is a potential barrier to training or intervention efficacy, other parties must be able to see it. In a classic case example (Lee, 1999) there is a description of a long impasse wherein all parties to the case—client, therapist, supervisor, and supervisory mentor—viewed circumstances in the same way. When the supervisory mentor was finally able to question common assumptions, broad and deep progress ensued.

This assumption—that the training system must be able to observe itself—is the *sine qua non* of efficacious, relationship-aware supervision. It embodies the insights of Bowen (1978), postmodern epistemology, and solution-focused approaches. It is intuitively reasonable and has been passed on formally and informally by family therapy trainers for decades. However, it is important to appreciate that, although this assumption "makes sense" and is defended by substantial anecdotal evidence, it is not empirically validated. Some supervisors would even disagree with it. Empirical validation will be of great value.

Now, once both supervisors and trainees agree that something is a potential barrier to effective supervision, they must also agree that it is important enough that change is desirable (from Pinsof, 1983). If so, then extending solution-focused approaches to the training system may be useful:

1 This barrier must be made observable and therefore auditable by both parties. Ideally, if a behavior is to be diminished, the goals should consist of a positive presentation, that is, what the trainee, supervisor, or interaction should be "doing instead."
2 Both parties must agree on methods of auditing and change that are realistic, situated in the here and now, and under their control.

3 The parties should agree to evidence indicating that they are on the right track, document necessary data, and explore all the reciprocities that have been involved in barrier maintenance.
4 All parties should agree on a deadline for meeting the performance goal or revisiting the plan.

Regardless of good intentions, we nearly all perceive some situations as conflictual, and this applies to the supervisory relationship as well as in other parts of our lives. Korinek and Kimball (2003) suggested that conflict in the supervisory system, the same as in other systems, often is a result of perceptions of incompatible goals, scarce resources, and/or interference in reaching certain goals. They listed a number of other areas that can lead to conflict. These include perceived incompetence, differences in learning style, theory of therapy, and personality. They also include role ambiguity and role conflict (e.g., stemming from multiple relationships), unconscious attempts to replicate other relationships (transference, countertransference, unfinished business), and plain, old "differences." Disagreements can develop over case conceptualization, areas of influence, case management, reporting issues, and the supervisory process itself. The latter can include dissonance in developmental expectations and perceived performance by either the supervisor or the trainee.

Qualitative studies by supervision researchers (e.g., Drake Wallace, Wilcoxin, & Satcher, 2010; Nelson & Friedlander, 2001; Piercy et al., 2016) have revealed that trainees are likely to perceive a number of situations that lead to or contextualize conflict in the supervisory system. These include supervisors who are not invested in the supervisory process or the trainee, supervisors who are unwilling to own their own responsibility in communication or dynamics difficulties, perceptions of too much work with too little supervision, power struggles, and angry supervisors. The message to us is that, to the extent participants can co-construct supervisory settings that avoid such difficulties, they are likely to avoid dysfunctional conflict.

Korinek and Kimball (2003) also provided some remedies to minimize conflict, including factors we have discussed previously and repeatedly: healthy supervisory relationships or working alliances, clear contracts that include expectations for both supervisors and trainees as well as consequences for not meeting those expectations, and positive and supportive supervision. They noted that "deficit detectives" (see Liddle, 1988) typically do not do well. They suggested that supervisors provide balance in hierarchy and power, attend to diversity, and constructively manage their anxiety. They also suggested that we "pick our battles," which historically has been wise advice for both supervisors and parents!

Examples of Common Barriers to Effective Supervision

Some barriers pose serious threats to the wellbeing of others and may or may not be intractable. These grave situations are discussed later in this chapter. In this section, we present examples of common blockages to constructive growth in the supervision and therapy that can be addressed reasonably easily.

Vignette 1

In an initial session of group supervision, the supervisor noticed that one trainee appeared uneasy in his posture, refrained from eye contact, and did not join the group discussion. When the supervisor attempted to engage him, the trainee responded tersely. The supervisor then said, "I observe from your body language and participation that you are uneasy right now." The trainee replied, "Yes. I do not want to be here." "Why not?" asked the supervisor. The trainee replied, "Because I have been told that you are a very critical and arrogant person." The supervisor responded, "What evidence do *you* have for that?" The trainee exclaimed, "I don't need this!" and left the room, went to an administrator, and asked to be assigned to another supervisor. That wish was immediately granted.

This example illustrates systemic dysfunction in all of its transacting units. The supervisor had a need to be liked and a low tolerance for insecurity. In the service of that, he intervened immediately and in a confrontational manner. Instead, the supervisor could have allowed the trainee time and space to come to a different opinion about the assigned supervisor and group. The supervisor could have said something like, "I'm sorry you have that impression of me; it is not my intention. Can we agree that you will observe me for yourself and let me know what behaviors may feel critical or arrogant? Then, perhaps I can change them or we can at least discuss them."

The trainee's expectations were influenced by recent hostile interactions with an important senior family member. The trainee had been harshly criticized by a parent and not supported by other family members. Consequently, the trainee distrusted the supervisor and did not expect other group members to be helpful. The group members were taken by surprise by the trainee's outburst and had mixed feelings about what they were experiencing.

The administrator liked to help students in apparent need. The end result was that this system was deprived of an excellent opportunity for positive growth. One wonders what would have happened if the supervisor had been patient and his subsequent interactions in the group provided a corrective emotional experience, the group had asked for and been given time to collect itself, and the administrator encouraged all parties to process their experiences in a common setting rather than acting unilaterally.

Vignette 2

A trainee consistently did not ask clients about substance use or relationship violence. After reviewing several recent cases with the trainee, the supervisor took an opportunity to bring these lapses to the trainee's attention. However, several weeks later, the lapse occurred during several intake sessions. The trainee, looking at this evidence, agreed that this oversight was a problem that needed to be corrected. The trainee placed an index card ("Ask client about ...") in each case file as a reminder. The lapses no longer occurred. However, the trainee experienced considerable discomfort in raising these questions with clients. Those moments and discussion about them led the trainee to pursue personal therapy.

Vignette 3

A trainee came late to individual supervision. The supervisor thought that the two of them had been at an impasse for several sessions and observed, "You are late. You must not have wanted to come." "No," said the trainee, "the traffic was terrible." One wonders whether it would have been more productive had the supervisor waited for more evidence to accrue, such as a pattern of tardiness or inattentiveness, and then addressed concerns through discussion of these patterns.

Vignette 4

A supervisor explored the exhausted tone he thought a trainee had when talking about a particular client. The trainee affirmed this; the client wasn't making progress. The trainee subsequently expressed both anger at the client and at herself: "I ought to be able" to do something to move matters along. She wondered if she were talented enough to be a therapist. The supervisor noted aloud that she perhaps was a harsh judge of herself (affirmed), invited her to consider the realism of her expectations (not very), and observed that a therapist was only as useful as clients let them be. This became a recurrent theme throughout the course of supervision.

Pragmatics: Facilitating Effective Supervision

Unhappily, there is no empirically based literature on the efficacy or effectiveness of supervision. There also are no reviews of extant supervisory theoretical approaches. Therefore, the authors are compelled to provide what they believe to be a good-enough synthesis of effective practices.

Dealing with Impasses

Overall, we suggest that we all begin with the presumption that every course of supervision will bog down for a brief or a prolonged time at some point. When this occurs, any number of dynamics may be in operation (e.g., Todd, 1997). Historically, relational supervision experts have reminded both supervisors and trainees to think systemically and thereby to recognize that dynamics in one level of the system may be mirrored in other relationships (see Lee & Everett, 2004; Liddle, 1988). This has been called "isomorphism," a concept that has been nicely elucidated by Mark White and Candyce Russell (1997). A hypothesis of isomorphism may not only facilitate discovery of barriers to efficacy but also system-wide resolution. For example, the blindness of a trainee and her client to their interpersonal dynamics can be maintained if it is mirrored in the relationships of the trainee and the supervisor, and the supervisory candidate and the supervisory mentor (see case illustration by Lee, 1999).

Whether or not the hypothesis of isomorphism informs one's supervisory outlook, contemporary supervision experts can use a developmental model of training. They believe that identification of barriers to efficacy and their resolution are positive opportunities for professional and personal growth for all stakeholders—at a minimum, supervisors, therapists, and clients (see Chapter 1 and articulation in Chapters 3, 6, 9, and 11.) Although purists decry moving from the interventions of one model to another, most training teams like the flexibility afforded by models that fit the way they and their clients make sense of things. These diverse models (e.g., modernist or postmodern; Bowen Family Systems, Emotionally Focused, Structural, Solution-Focused, and so on) come with respective interventions that can be extended to supervisory impasses. At risk of over-simplification, two somewhat generic interventions come to mind. The first intends to promote clinical insight to unaddressed issues. The second may seem to sacrifice insight in favor of behavior change, but cognitive and emotional progress also may come from processing the interventions in terms of what generally works for the therapist. The reader will think of other ways to approach impasses.

Because impasses are ubiquitous, we believe it is useful to discuss this with trainees in the first interview. One supervisor candidate said that in such interviews, he always mentions that there will be times when he and the trainee don't agree or that there is an impasse that needs to be discussed: It's not personal, it happens to everyone. Then, when something comes up, the supervisor is able to say, "Remember when I told you ...? Well, this is one of those times." This allows the trainee to take a breath, move into discussion mode, and each hold the other accountable for a discussion rather than either ignoring the difficulty or having an unproductive argument about it.

Unaddressed Issues

Many barriers to growth take this form, something like "ignoring the elephant" in the supervisory room. In this case, trainees and/or their supervisors are not aware of or are ignoring systemic dynamics. They view but don't *see*, listen but don't *hear*. They make assumptions, value judgments, and avoidance maneuvers. The prudent training team will remain alert for indications of these situations. Some situations may be driven by trainees' (or supervisors') anxiety (Hill, 2009), which can come from many areas and need limited exploration in supervision or suggestions for outside consultation or therapy if supervision or trainees' therapy work is negatively impacted.

Otherwise, systemic reciprocity may maintain the barriers. The first step at resolution is for someone to bring the issue to light, which requires a safe environment for doing so. Various major family therapy models suggest remedies such as careful process questions, reflecting teams, and even therapeutic approaches to supervision. At the minimum, there must be a system-wide alertness for unaddressed issues, resulting in insight-provoking questions in a safe-enough environment: "*I wonder what we are not talking about?*" "*What are we assuming?*" "*What do we imagine happening if we were to 'go there'?*" One of us (Nelson) had a small stuffed animal in her conference room. The rule was that whenever someone had something to bring up but felt a bit unsafe in doing so, that person invoked the toy. This meant that everyone had to listen nonjudgmentally and work toward common, accepted solutions to the difficulty. Simply having the toy available often made it easier for people to bring up issues before they became intractable.

We have avoided writing about specific situations lest readers of this text look for answers. We have preferred encouraging overall philosophical and relational processes that, when managed well, handle most situations. There is one situation, however, that is often an elephant in the room and neglected in supervision that we want to mention: sexual attraction. This includes attraction toward or from clients and therapist, and between therapist and supervisor. Harris (2001) wrote that this topic is not handled well in graduate programs although it is ubiquitous and trainees suffer when this is not included in topics of professional development. Harris encourages us to be proactive in our discussion with trainees about sexual attraction in therapy and in supervision. Note that there is a sparsity of literature on this topic, which means that we, as supervisors, must be proactive and alert to concerns that affect our trainees, their clients, or ourselves.

Solution-Focused Approaches

The tools of this model are very valuable for any supervisor. They immediately instill hope and a sense of wellbeing, empowerment, and direction. They can be used when supervisors or trainees feel bogged down and even when either of them is tired, confused, or otherwise not feeling up to hard conceptual work. For example, supervisors can ask themselves to "think of a time in the past few weeks when things were going better" or "What did we do during a recent time like this that was helpful? What was I doing and what was the trainee doing?" Supervisors can make the same inquiry of trainees with regard to their clients. An entire strengths-oriented, as-needed supervisory dialogue can be scripted by extending solution-focused goal setting and approaches to supervision. (For concise compilations of solution-focused tools, see Nelson, 2010).

Emergencies

The best time to consider what should be done in an emergency is before such an unhappy event occurs. During emergencies, emotions may run high and interfere with constructive thought and memory. However, a checklist and assessment plan can be drawn up in quiet times for use should an emergency actually occur. Such action tools can even be included in policies and procedures manuals. Then trainees and supervisors need only retrieve the appropriate document from close at hand, follow its instructions, and put the time-dated and signed document in clients' treatment files. Trainees and supervisors are thus reminded of their obligations, what to assess, how to make judgments, and actions to take. All the while, trainees and supervisors are indicating to all involved in these cases, including outside parties, that they were prudent and, where required, followed the dictates of the law. For example, consider the following happenstance: A 23-year-old male client, a US Marine, had returned from active duty in Afghanistan. He was under medication for post-traumatic stress, a condition exacerbated by his discovery that his girlfriend had given birth to a son. The client was out of the country when the baby was conceived. He kept visualizing his girlfriend having sex with the other man and he could not shut these images out despite the pain they caused. He could not sleep and did not eat. He was showing high tension and alternated between tears and rage. He expressed murderous impulses toward the man who "invaded his life" and "stole his woman." In this case, the trainee and the supervisor found that the checklist given in Table 14.1 was extremely valuable.

Readers may wish to modify the tool to fit their own circumstances and settings, including adding resiliency or signs of safety. Our point is that wise forethought will help trainees know what to do in a variety of situations and what to do if they don't know what to do (e.g., consult with the supervisor or other clinician). Role-play during supervision can be very helpful. Decision-making models for emergencies and ethical dilemmas, much like articulated approaches to therapy, provide wonderful guides, prevent anxiety, and reduce mistakes. Also, such documentation on the part of both the therapist and supervisor may come in handy should there be legal consequences. Knowledgeable attorneys have told us

Table 14.1 A Violence Assessment Tool

Probability increases with the following:	*Motive (loss of love and/or self-esteem)*
	Capacity/opportunity (stated inclination, owns weapons, has access to potential victims)
	Gender (male)
	Age (under 25 years old)
	Substance use (e.g., pathological intoxication or frequent abuse)
	Mental health diagnosis (post-traumatic stress disorder; explosive and/or paranoid personality disorder; psychosis)
	Past history of violence (The best indicator of what a person will do in the future is what s/he has done in the past)
Action required by law: (Document Who, What, and When)	
	Reasonably foreseeable victims (names)
	Notified police in area(s) where reasonably foreseeable victims reside and work
	Notified the above foreseeable victims
	Notified supervisor
	Taken steps to hospitalize the predicted perpetrator. If not, why not?
Reason for ceasing action, namely, prudent indications that no further action need be taken; the potential victims are secure. For example, you have been notified by the police that the potential perpetrator has been taken into protective custody and will be held by the regional assessment center.	

Note: This table both applies contemporary actuarial statistics and reflects the statutes of the state in which the professional-client relationship existed.

that even when there have been mistakes in judgment or decision, following a predetermined and defensible decision-making plan that is documented reduces risk of legal consequences for the therapist.

Decisions about Handling Dysfunction or Deficiencies

Sometimes, preventative plans, training interventions, and notes to oneself do not work: Individuals prove unable to function constructively in therapy or within supervision. They may appear to be intractably incapacitated in supervision, their therapy, or both, or unable to maintain functional relationships with peers, supervisors, or others in the training system. The first step is for supervisors and trainees to agree that a problem exists, that it limits professional efficacy to a specified extent, and it has resisted typical attempts to fix it. The individuals are invited to co-create performance improvement plans. In any case, the explicit goal is the removal of the barrier to effective therapy. The supervisor and trainee must agree to and document visible evidence of change and a time frame for reaching certain goals. Contracts should include language about due process should the trainee disagree with or refuse to collaborate on a plan or feels mistreated. Russell and colleagues (2007) outline a number of reasonable consequences for inadequate or problematic behavior, including increased supervision, decreased client load, decrease in certain kinds of clients, coursework, therapy, and other potentially helpful measures. We strongly recommend this article.

It is important for supervisors to recognize that they can be concerned only with barriers that are behaviorally evident in actual clinical work. They have authority and responsibility over nothing that allegedly occurs outside of the training system. For example, a program administrator was told that a trainee often got drunk and was promiscuous. The informant had to be told that this alleged behavior occurred outside of the training setting and, while worrisome, could not be addressed by the training institution because no illegal activity had taken place (as prohibited by the training contract or policies and procedures manual) and there was no apparent negative impact on the trainee's therapy or clients. The institution could legally concern itself only with documented dysfunction in the classroom, supervision sessions, and therapy unless other behaviors were specified in training contracts. However, contracts can include that trainees must be professional as identified within the training system, and to maintain themselves as positive members of the system. Examples of the latter might include appropriate clothing, grooming, verbal expressions, and acting in public in ways that damage the reputation of the setting.

Early Termination of Training Relationships

The training process should be prudently structured so that risks to the community, client, therapist, and supervisor are appropriately addressed. For example, these may include limitations in what cases the trainee is to be involved with and the conditions under which the clinical interventions are to take place. For example, a trainee proved to be both alcoholic and unable to establish appropriate boundaries with a client. Until the latter condition was remedied, the trainee was allowed to see clients only in mornings because that was a time period in which there was a higher probability of appropriate behavior, and under live supervision.

The readers will notice that this training consequence recognized the contemporary legal climate in which training and supervision existed. Supervisors were empowered only with regard to events that took place within the training and supervision, and that could reasonably be expected to have foreseeable serious negative consequences for readily identifiable people.

Training relationships must be terminated when supervisors and their administrators recognize that trainees are so limited in cognitive, affective, and/or behavioral flexibility that documented performance-improvement plans are or have been substantially ineffectual. As a result, clients, supervisors, institutions, and communities may be at risk of harm. In such circumstances this decision is best informed by a remediation plan, consultation with an appropriate neutral authority, and documentation specifying the observable behaviors, probable consequences, remedial interventions, rationale for termination from the training or supervision, and notice that the supervisor may determine that the situation needs to be discussed with other supervisors, agency administrators, or even the licensing board.

Prudent training systems often specify non-negotiable prohibitions in their training contracts. For example, training contracts may state outright, "Sexual exploitation of clients, violations of privileged communications, or intoxication in sessions will result in termination." Policies can also define other expectations and deficiencies that may merit remediation plans or termination of the supervisory relationship. Training institutions have discovered to their chagrin that such terms must be written, introduced, and their acceptance documented before the training relationship begins. Otherwise, they legally cannot be used as grounds for dismissal.

As a general rule, termination from supervision should occur when

- Individuals refuse to participate in developing or executing performance improvement plans;
- The performance improvement plans are not successful at removing what prudent professionals would consider to be significant barriers to training and/or clinical ability;
  OR
- Individuals do not respect practice limitations, thereby putting some segment of the clinical population or training setting at reasonable risk of maltreatment.

If training takes place in an educational institution, these criteria should be part of the training syllabus or program policies and procedures manual. In other settings, they should be in written, signed, and dated supervisory contracts. Due process should be described and available. Clinical work may be suspended during a process of determining steps to be taken. Should trainees quit supervision or be terminated without amelioration, a signed document can be helpful should the supervisor decide it is necessary to discuss the situation with other supervisors, agency administrators, or even the licensing board. Without such a signature, doing so would be a breach of confidentiality.

At the same time, relational supervisors may agree to supervise therapists or other supervisors who have been sanctioned by licensing boards or professional organizations. These therapists may be allowed to continue to practice therapy and/or supervision and, as a condition of this, be supervised by a person approved by the board or organization. J. T. Thomas (2010) includes a chapter about the ethical challenges of supervising mandated therapists and some wise advice for supervisors. It is not something we advise for novice supervisors.

Concluding Remarks

Ideally, supervision is smooth: Trainees do well, supervision is enjoyable, and clients are well served. Unfortunately, it is not uncommon for there to be bumps in the road in relationships that may span two or more years, where individuals change, and where relationships also change. We hope that our ideas of being prepared and thinking systemically when there are problems are helpful.

Exercises

1. Name a situation in which you were a trainee or supervisor and there was some sort of impasse. Think through at least three different ways the situation could have been handled, both well and badly, in addition to what actually happened.
2. You have flexed on a boundary about supervision times during a period when your trainee was grieving the loss of a close relative, and you expressed sympathy appropriately. However, now your trainee seems to think that this temporary flex can be more permanent and frequently comes in late to supervision or comes unprepared. How might you address this with your trainee? How might you do this and avoid a confrontation or unhelpful conflict?
3. Revisit the supervisory contract you developed for Chapter 4. What might you change about it now that you have read other chapters, including this one?
4. Choose one of the vignettes from this chapter and describe at least two ways you might handle the situation.
5. Under what conditions do you think you would terminate a supervisory relationship? How would you do that? What documentation would you keep? What might you share with others and who might those others be?

15 Developing Your Personal Philosophy of Supervision Paper

This chapter is more personal than the others. We intend to provide you with the opportunity to actually reflect on and integrate your ideas for your personal Philosophy of Supervision paper. This paper is one of the requirements for gaining the AAMFT designation as an Approved Supervisor. It also is a major requirement in AAMFT-approved courses on the fundamentals of CFT supervision. Even if you are not planning on securing the AAMFT designation, we have found it useful in the same way that it is useful to think about and articulate a theory of therapy as a clinician. If you have kept notes throughout this text about your own ideas, it may be rather easy to pull them together into an articulated integrative philosophy.

As consumers of supervision, you have had varying experiences that were likely both good and bad. For those of you who have been supervising, you also can think of situations that worked well and some that did not, as well as how systemic your supervision was. We hope that you are prepared to bring those experiences to the fore as you think about your own approach to relational supervision. Figley (2000) noted that for many, the philosophy of supervision paper can be a major barrier to completing the requirements for the approved supervisor designation. Many who review this text have not written academic papers in a long time, and may feel intimidated by the process. We hope to provide you with outlines and tools to help you focus on your ideas rather than on the writing process. The paper does not need to be publishable. Instead it should be an accurate reflection of your ideas about relational supervision.

For each area of the requirements, we suggest that you develop a section that corresponds to your chosen format for the paper (see ideas below). Your task then is to reflect on, consolidate, and substantiate your ideas as much as you can to demonstrate familiarity with literature. Your document is meant to be highly personal about what you believe with regard to supervision (Storm, 2000b). Personal pronouns (e.g., "I" and "my") are acceptable and usually preferred. The paper will cover broad, philosophical ideas such as your general approach and goals of supervision. It also will cover specific ideas such as your preferences for individual and group supervision, or live, recorded, or case consultation formats, and how you might or might not use technology.

The AAMFT (2014) guidelines call for four single-spaced pages or approximately 1,500 to 2000 words, exclusive of references or appendices. Some instructors and

DOI: 10.4324/9781003099833-19

supervisor mentors might ask for appendices of glossaries or more detailed descriptions of approaches to therapy to help keep the main body of the paper focused on your supervision ideas and limited in length. The paper may be written early in the supervision mentoring process as part of a course, which we recommend. We would expect that a supervisor candidate's ideas would change over time and that reviewing and revising the paper near the end of the supervision mentoring period is wise. We also think that it is useful for supervisors to review their approaches on occasion, just as we believe that it is useful for therapists to periodically review their approaches to therapy.

Content Requirements

Just as evaluating trainees best begins with clarity of the goals to be accomplished, the same can be said of your philosophy of supervision paper. That is, it may be helpful to understand expectations for the paper and the rubrics used for grading. Below, we list the AAMFT Approved Supervisor educational guidelines for the philosophy of supervision paper.

1 Evidence of systemic thinking.
2 Clarity of purpose and goals for supervision.
3 Clarity of supervisory roles and relationships.
4 Evidence of supervisory contracts, and of evaluation of trainees and self.
5 Evidence of awareness of personal and professional experiences that impact supervision (e.g., person of the supervisor).
6 Preferred supervision model or practices and their connection with the candidate's own therapy model.
7 Evidence of sensitivity and attention to contextual factors such as developmental phase of the trainee, training setting, culture, ethnicity, race, sexual orientation, age, sex, gender, economics, and so forth.
8 Familiarity with modes of supervision (individual/group, case consultation/live/audio-video, and technology-assisted).
9 Evidence of sensitivity to and competency in ethics and legal factors of supervision.
10 Awareness of requirements for AAMFT membership, regulatory agencies, and the standards for the Approved Supervisor designation.
11 Integrated MFT supervision literature. (AAMFT, 2014)

The last area—integrated MFT literature—does not need to be a separate section. It indicates that supervisors should be familiar with literature that pertains to the Approved Supervisor designation or activities. In this sense, each other area of the paper should include appropriate citations with references, thereby demonstrating substantiation for your ideas. Alternatively, some references may suggest areas where you have different ideas, but the general topic is contained in some literature. Your course instructor and/or mentor will guide you about what this means for a course or for finishing the supervisor candidate training period.

Criteria for evaluating each area are outlined in the AAMFT *Approved Supervisor Designation: Standards Handbook.* They include a 5-point Likert-type evaluation scale that goes from insufficient (0) to exceptional response (4). For their final evaluation before submitting their materials for the designation, supervisor candidates must score at least "2" in each area (that is, they name and provide basic definitions, but do not illustrate them) and an overall average of "3" (they name, define, and illustrate concepts). Course instructors may have their own requirements for passing a paper, but supervisor mentors, who evaluate the paper at the time the candidate is ready to submit material for the designation, must use the AAMFT evaluation criteria.

Process

You may prefer to use your own writing style. However, it may be easier for course instructors and mentors to read your paper when you carefully follow outlines. Moreover, you may find it easier to write your paper this way.

There are a number of formats that you can use for your paper (see below). Some course instructors or supervision mentors may require specific formats. Be sure to check with them about this. Others allow whatever format you choose as long as you cover all required areas. Make certain you are clear about your instructor's or supervisor mentor's preferences.

The first task is to choose a format and formulate ideas within each section, whether you start writing with the first section or move around. We have found it beneficial to keep lists of ideas and notes that you might use in other sections of the paper as you work on each one. Regardless, you will want to be certain that each section is concise yet complete—this may help you be concise yet complete, staying on topic for each area. Evaluating the papers usually entails looking for whether or not certain ideas are named, described, and, perhaps, illustrated, and the extent to which every area is included and complete. Keep case material to a minimum, using it to briefly illustrate your ideas.

We also find it useful to go back and forth from the big picture to details. Think about detailed processes such as developing contracts, setting goals, and determining evaluation devices and procedures as well as your overall thoughts about the purpose and goals of supervision. Think about the process of supervision, picturing it in your head, and telling your reader about how you use certain interventions and rationale for preferences.

It is vital that you keep a systemic perspective as you write the paper. One of the requirements is evidence of systemic thinking, but many supervisor candidates and course participants have attempted to satisfy this requirement by simply naming a few system concepts. Evaluators will be looking for how well you demonstrate your understanding of system ideas (defining and illustrating, preferably in supervision) and integrate them throughout the various sections of the paper. This is a big picture idea.

The paper is required for the Fundamentals of Supervision Course that AAMFT oversees, and the course instructor will evaluate that paper. It may or may not fit requirements that your AS Supervisor mentor requests, but must fit the course requirement. It is not required that your mentor oversee, read, or approve this paper—it's purpose is for the course. When you have nearly completed your training requirements, you will need to revise your paper to fit your mentor's desires and because you have had more experience since the course and have a better idea about your philosophy. Your last mentor will evaluate and approve the paper before you apply for your Approved Supervisor designation, but you will not submit your paper with your application. Consult the latest version of the Handbook for details.

Formats

One format that is obvious uses the areas cited earlier. Use each point as a heading so that your instructor or supervision mentor can easily follow your thinking, and add details about each area.

Other foci can be added to the above. Lee and Everett (2004) suggest the following format:

- Supervisory roles and goals for both you and your trainees, and therefore your ground rules for supervision.
- Major CFT models that inform your model.
- Integration of models and approaches.
- Developmental concerns—yours and your trainees'.
- Attention to contextual factors, personal and environmental (larger system influences).
- Ethical and legal concerns.
- Contractual and administrative concerns.

Note that although the paper can be written in sections that correspond to the above formats, much of a person's philosophy is integrated into many areas. Therefore, "sensitivity … to contextual factors such as …" should not be an "issue" or singular section. Instead, there should be some evidence for such factors as they are important in many areas. For example, explain your ideas about how supervisory roles and relationships intersect with context such as a white male supervisor needing to develop a different relationship with Latina females than he has with white males.

You also may find that some formats reflect your thinking better than others. This may be acceptable to your course instructor or supervision mentor. However, be certain that whatever format you use incorporates all areas of the requirements.

Filling in the Details

As much as you can, visualize the supervisory process step by step. Where do you start? How do you prepare to do that? What are you interested in during an initial interview that helps you decide whether there is a good fit between you and the trainee? If trainees are assigned to you, how do you decide what you will do in areas where there may not be a good fit?

Think about your goals for supervision for both trainees, for the process, as well as any goals you identify for yourself that you might discuss with your supervisor mentor. For example, most supervisors agree that one long-term goal for trainees is the development of a competent therapist. Beyond that, the goals may get more specific to your personal philosophy. If part of your philosophy includes self-of-the-therapist growth based on examining background and/or family of origin experiences (e.g., Aponte, 1994), how will you do that with the trainee and how will you define boundaries so that you do not stray into doing therapy with the trainee? How will you evaluate progress toward or completion of goals? How will you involve trainees (or not) in this process?

For supervisors, short-term goals often include such things as establishing a safe environment so that trainees will feel comfortable bringing up mistakes and difficult issues. Goals also may include increasing trainees' professional maturity, mentoring them into the CFT profession, and preparing them for the next phases of their careers (Lee & Nichols, 2010). One of Nelson's personal goals in supervision is to learn something from trainees and the supervision process.

What are the roles that you will take on for each goal? What other roles will you find important, and how much will they relate to other roles? How will you help trainees learn systemic thinking or contextual sensitivity (see Chapter 8)? How much will you focus on different developmental phases of training? How much will you want to know about what is going on in the trainee's life outside of therapy? How much of yourself will you share with your trainees?

What experiences in your life, both personal and professional, guide your philosophy and your ideas about the process of supervision? Are you a beginning supervisor and therefore perhaps focusing more on helping the trainee work with particular clients? Or are you more experienced as a supervisor and focused on the trainee's progress in general? What do you think your role is in helping trainees learn about specific client populations?

If you already have been supervising, as many who read this text will have done, what ideas have this text and other material, perhaps from a supervision course, informed your philosophy, reinforced your ideas, and perhaps changed them? What have you learned about your idealized preferences versus realities of specific settings, trainees, and yourself? What have you learned about yourself?

For each of the areas of the paper, think about questions you might be asked in an oral conversation and how you would answer them, looking back at different chapters of this text. As much as possible without compromising length, be concrete. For example, instead of saying simply that you prefer video review, explain your rationale and what you do: "I prefer video review because live observation is not available and it is a good way to see what is happening in therapy." "I like to ask the therapist to come prepared with five minutes of review of something they think they did well and five minutes of something they would like to have done better or a place where they were feeling stuck. We then discuss the case and what they think would be good to do next." Be sure to use citations and references.

Connecting Your Therapy and Supervision Approaches

Although most supervisors no longer use single models of therapy as their supervision approach, we do tend to use aspects of certain models integrated into our approaches. Ratliff (2000) wrote an interesting article about this integration. It is worth your time to read it if you can find it (it is now out of print and not available through university electronic libraries; see References). We have found his metaphor to be so useful that we will attempt to reconstruct his ideas for you.

Ratliff uses "cut flowers" to capture the essence of eclectic therapy and supervision—using a bit of this and a bit of that with little connecting them. "Potted plants" use a single model, often in incomplete and inflexible ways without taking into consideration factors that might suggest being more in tune with specific contexts. Ratliff used an example of structural therapy with a stepfamily during which their 13-year-old girl ran away. The supervisor candidate had discouraged the therapist from using literature on stepfamilies, saying the information was inconsistent with a structural approach and that the running away was a change in the system. The system would have to change in response, and therefore the case was a success. Ratliff further pointed out that this perspective did not acknowledge structural family therapy tenets of maintaining structural stability while promoting change (see Thomas, 1994) and thus was incomplete.

"Transplants" are what Ratliff considered to be competent uses of single theories. He compared this kind of integration to a well-rooted plant that has been transplanted to a new context. This approach is more flexible than a potted approach in that it has flexibility to account for differences in situations. To further the analogy, Ratliff wrote about "grafted" plants—those that connect two approaches well. There is a synergy between the approaches such that the assumptions are similar enough that the plants "take" to each other because there is a strong foundation with connected techniques from each initial approach.

Finally, in a "grown from seed" integration, Ratliff considered a seasoned clinician to be one who has internalized the approaches to an extent that it is difficult to articulate them. Theory has less influence than experience. Nevertheless, supervisors are never free of their obligation to explain their rationale for their procedures to their trainees.

Common Mistakes to Avoid

The biggest mistake that supervisor candidates make is omitting an area completely. Another mistake is mentioning something, but not defining or explaining it. This leaves instructors or supervision mentors to infer meaning, which can be confusing or incorrect. Sometimes, candidates do not integrate systemic or contextual factors into other areas. Our field has come a long way in terms of cultural sensitivity, but it is important to think about how trainees consider culture in their clinical work and how we think about it in supervision. Therefore, it is important to articulate this sensitivity so that it isomorphically transfers from supervision to the entire training system. Instead, some candidates have thought it adequate to simply state that they pay attention to context without defining it or explaining what they mean or do.

If using the sections that Lee and Everett (2004) delineated, be sure to include ideas about trainee development and the isomorphism between your approach to therapy and to supervision and, ideally, among all the different levels of the system. Many write about their models of therapy but not how those ideas translate into supervision. Yingling (2000) has some good ideas for how to remedy this. Integrate current literature throughout the paper as appropriate, but be sure to use citations accurately. Astute instructors will know when you are plagiarizing or have not actually read something you cite.

Final Words

Think about your target audience as you write the paper. You are not writing for academic journal publication. Instead, you are writing for your course instructor, your supervisor mentor, and, most of all, for yourself and perhaps your trainees. Think about what you would tell them about your supervisory approach.

Take pity on your instructor and supervisor mentor and group your materials within a clear outline of headings and subheadings. This allows you to keep your readers within your flow of thought. Do your best to use proper grammar and punctuation, and cite references for your thinking throughout. Follow your instructor's guidelines about such things as formatting style, such as the American Psychological Association's (APA) current version (American Psychological Association, 2020). Be sure that your citations and references correspond to each other and that your reference list is complete.

Use your supervisor mentor as a sounding board for different sections of the paper. Although the Philosophy of Supervision paper may seem a daunting task, it will help if you approach it in small chunks as you go through this text or a course. By the time you finish the course or text, you may be able to simply polish the paper, ensure appropriate knowledge of extant literature, and update ideas in places where you have gained experience.

Exercises

1. Compare two or more formats for your personal philosophy of supervision paper to determine which might be best for you. Compare that to the requirements of AAMFT.
2. What is it that makes this your *personal* philosophy of supervision?
3. After writing a draft of your paper, compare it to the AAMFT requirements.

Appendix A: Major Marriage and Family Therapy Models

Developed by Thorana S. Nelson, PhD and Students

STRUCTURAL FAMILY THERAPY

LEADERS

- Salvador Minuchin
- Charles Fishman

ASSUMPTIONS:

- Problems reside within a family structure (although not necessarily caused by the structure)
- Changing the structure changes the experience the client has
- Don't go from problem to solution, we just move gradually
- Children's problems are often related to the boundary between the parents (marital vs. parental subsystem) and the boundary between parents and children

CONCEPTS:

Family structure

- Boundaries
  - Rigid
  - Clear
  - Diffuse
  - Disengaged
  - Normal Range
  - Enmeshment
  - Roles
  - Rules of who interacts with whom, how, when, etc.
- Hierarchy
- Subsystems
- Cross-Generational Coalitions
- Parentified Child

GOALS OF THERAPY:

- Structural Change
  - Clarify, realign, mark boundaries
- Individuation of family members
- Infer the boundaries from the patterns of interaction among family members
- Change the patterns to realign the boundaries to make them more closed or open

STRUCTURAL FAMILY THERAPY

ROLE OF THE THERAPIST:

- Perturb the system because the structure is too rigid (chaotic or closed) or too diffuse (enmeshed)
- Facilitate the restructuring of the system
- Directive, expert—the therapist is the choreographer
- See change in therapy session; homework solidifies change
- Directive

ASSESSMENT:

- Assess the nature of the boundaries, roles of family members
- Enactment to watch family interaction/ patterns

INTERVENTIONS:

- Join and accommodate
    - mimesis
- Structural mapping
- Highlight and modify interactions
- Unbalance
- Challenge unproductive assumptions
- Raise intensity so that system must change

Interventions

- disorganize and reorganize
- Shape competence through Enactment (therapist acts as coach)

CHANGE:

- Raise intensity to upset the system, then help reorganize the system
- Change occurs within session and is behavioral; insight is not necessary
- Emotions change as individuals' experience of their context changes

TERMINATION:

- Problem is gone and the structure has changed (2nd order change)
- Problem is gone and the structure has NOT changed (1st order change)

SELF OF THE THERAPIST:

- The therapist joins with the system to facilitate the unbalancing of the system
- Caution with induction—don't get sucked in to the content areas, usually related to personal hot spots

EVALUATION:

- Strong support for working with psychosomatic children, adult drug addicts, and anorexia nervosa.

STRUCTURAL FAMILY THERAPY

RESOURCES:

Minuchin, S. (1974). *Families and family therapy*. Cambridge, MA: Harvard University Press.

Minuchin, S., & Fishman, H. C. (1981). *Family therapy techniques*. Cambridge, MA: Harvard University Press.

Minuchin, S., Rosman, B. L., & Baker, L. (1978). *Psychosomatic families*. Cambridge, MA: Harvard University Press.

Fishman, H. C. (1988). *Treating troubled adolescents: A family therapy approach*. New York: Basic Books.

Fishman, H. C. (1993). *Intensive structural therapy: Treating families in their social context*. New York: Basic Books.

NOTES:

STRATEGIC THERAPY (MRI)

LEADERS:

- John Weakland
- Don Jackson
- Paul Watzlawick
- Richard Fisch

ASSUMPTIONS:

- Family members often perpetuate problems by their own actions (attempted solutions) –the problem is the problem maintenance (positive feedback escalations)
- Directives tailored to the specific needs of a particular family can sometimes bring about sudden and decisive change
- People resist change
- You cannot not communicate–people are ALWAYS communicating
- All messages have report and command functions– working with content is not helpful, look at the process
- Symptoms are messages – symptoms help the system survive (some would say they have a function)
- It is only a problem if the family describes it as such
- Based on work of Gregory Bateson and Milton Erickson
- Need to perturb system – difference that makes a difference (similar enough to be accepted by system but different enough to make a difference)
- Don't need to examine psychodynamics to work on the problem

STRATEGIC THERAPY (MRI)

CONCEPTS:

- Symptoms are messages
- Family homeostasis
- Family rules – unspoken
- Cybernetics
  - Feedback Loops
  - Positive Feedback
  - Negative Feedback
- First order change
- Second order change
- Reframing
- Content & Process
- Report & Command
- Paradox
- Paradoxical Injunction
- "Go Slow" Messages
- Positive Feedback Escalations
- Double Binds
- "One down" position
- Patient position
- Attempted solutions maintain problems and become problems themselves

GOALS OF THERAPY:

- Help the family define clear, reachable goals
- Break the pattern; perturb the system
- First and second order change- ideally second order change (we cannot make this happen– it is spontaneous)

ROLE OF THE THERAPIST:

- Expert position
- Responsible for creating conditions for change
- Work with resistance of clients to change
- Work with the process, not the content
- Directive

ASSESSMENT:

- Define the problem clearly and find out what people have done to try to resolve it
- Elicit goals from each family member and then reframe into one, agreed-upon goal
- Assess sequence patterns

STRATEGIC THERAPY (MRI)

INTERVENTIONS:

- Paradox
- Directives
  - Assignments ("homework") that interrupt sequences
- Interrupt unhelpful sequences of interaction
- "Go slow" messages
- Prescribe the symptoms

CHANGE:

- Interrupting the pattern in any way
- Difference that makes a difference
- Change occurs outside of session; insession change is in viewing; homework changes doing
- Change in viewing (reframe) and/or doing (directives)
- Emotions change and are important, but are inferred and not directly available to the therapist

TERMINATION:

- Client decides when to terminate with the help of the therapist
- When pattern is broken and the client reports that the problem no longer exists
- Therapist decides

SELF OF THE THERAPIST:

- Therapist needs to be VERY careful with ethics in this model; it can be very manipulative (paradox) and a lot of responsibility is on the therapist as an expert

EVALUATION:

- Very little research done
- Do clients report change? If so, then it is effective

RESOURCES:

Watzlawick, P., Weakland, J., &, Fisch, R. (1974). *Change: Principles of problem formation and problem resolution.* New York: Norton.

Fisch, Richard, John H. Weakland, and Lynn Segal (1982). *The tactics of change: Doing therapy briefly.* San Francisco: Jossey-Bass.

Watzlawick, P., J. B. Bavelas, and D. J. Jackson. (1967). *Pragmatics of human communication.* New York: W. W. Norton.

Lederer, W. J., and Don Jackson. (1968). *The mirages of marriage.* New York: W. W. Norton.

NOTES:

STRATEGIC THERAPY (Haley & Madanes)

LEADERS:

- Jay Haley
- Cloe Madanes
- Influenced by Minuchin

ASSUMPTIONS:

- Family members often perpetuate problems by their own actions (attempted solutions) –the problem is the problem maintenance (positive feedback escalations)
- Directives tailored to the specific needs of a particular family can sometimes bring about sudden and decisive change
- People resist change
- You cannot not communicate–people are ALWAYS communicating
- All messages have report and command functions– working with content is not helpful, look at the process
- Communication and messages are metaphorical for family functioning
- Symptoms are messages – symptoms help the system survive
- It is only a problem if the family describes it as such
- Based on work of Gregory Bateson, Milton Erickson, MRI, and Minuchin
- Need to perturb system – difference that makes a difference (similar enough to be accepted by system but different enough to make a difference)
- Problems develop in skewed hierarchies
- Motivation is power (Haley) or love (Madanes)

CONCEPTS:

- Symptoms are messages
- Family homeostasis
- Family rules – unspoken
- Intergenerational collusions
- First and second order change
- Metaphors
- Reframing
- Symptoms serve functions
- Content & Process
- Report & Command
- Incongruous Hierarchies
- Ordeals (prescribing ordeals)
- Paradox
- Paradoxical Injunction
- Pretend Techniques (Madanes)
- "Go Slow" Messages

GOALS OF THERAPY:

- Help the family define clear, reachable goals
- Break the pattern; perturb the system
- First and second order change- ideally second order change (we cannot make this happen– it is spontaneous)
- Realign hierarchy (Madanes)

STRATEGIC THERAPY (Haley & Madanes)

ROLE OF THE THERAPIST:

- Expert position
- Responsible for creating conditions for change
- Work with resistance of clients to change
- Work with the process, not the content
- Directive
- Skeptical of change
- Take a lot of credit and responsibility for change; however, therapist tells clients that they are responsible for change
- Active

ASSESSMENT:

- Define the problem clearly and find out what people have done to try to resolve it
- Hypothesize metaphorical nature of the problem
- Elicit goals from each family member and then reframe into one, agreed-upon goal
- Assess sequence patterns

INTERVENTIONS:

- Paradox
- Directives
    - Assignments ("homework") that interrupt sequences
- Interrupt unhelpful sequences of interaction
- Metaphors, stories
- Ordeals (Haley)
- "Go slow" messages
- Prescribe the symptoms (Haley)
- "Pretend" techniques (Madanes)

CHANGE:

- Breaking the pattern in any way
- Difference that makes a difference
- Change occurs outside of session; insession change is in viewing; homework changes doing
- Change in viewing (reframe) and/or doing (directives)

TERMINATION:

- Client decides when to terminate with the help of the therapist
- When pattern is broken and the client reports that the problem no longer exists
- Therapist decides

SELF OF THE THERAPIST:

- Therapist needs to be VERY careful with ethics in this model; it can be very manipulative (paradox) and a lot of responsibility is on the therapist as an expert

EVALUATION:

- Very little research done
- Do clients report change? If so, then it is effective

STRATEGIC THERAPY (Haley & Madanes)

RESOURCES:

Madanes, Cloe. (1981). *Strategic family therapy*. San Francisco, CA: Jossey-Bass.
Madanes, Cloe. (1984). *Behind the one-way mirror: Advances in the practice of strategic therapy*. San Francisco, CA: Jossey-Bass.
Madanes, Cloe. (1990). *Sex, love, and violence: Strategies for transformation.* New York: W. W. Norton.
Madanes, Cloe. (1995). *The violence of men: New techniques for working with abusive families*. San Francisco: Jossey-Bass.
Haley, Jay. (1980). *Leaving home*. New York: McGraw-Hill.
Haley, Jay. (1984). *Ordeal therapy: Unusual ways to change behavior*. San Francisco, CA: Jossey Bass.
Haley, Jay. (1987). *Problem-solving therapy* (2nd Ed.). San Francisco: Jossey-Bass.

NOTES:

MILAN FAMILY THERAPY

LEADERS:

- Boscolo
- Palazzoli
- Prata
- Cecchin

ASSUMPTIONS:

- problem is maintained by family's attempts to fix it
- therapy can be brief over a long period of time
- clients resist change

CONCEPTS:

- family games (family's patterns that maintain the problem)
  - dirty games
  - psychotic games
- there is a nodal point of pathology
- invariant prescriptions
- rituals
- positive connotation
- difference that makes a difference
- neutrality
- hypothesizing
- therapy team
- circularity, neutrality
- incubation period for change; requires long periods of time between sessions

GOALS OF THERAPY:

- disrupt family games

MILAN FAMILY THERAPY

ROLE OF THERAPIST:

- therapist as expert
- neutral to each family member – don't get sucked into the family game
- curious

ASSESSMENT:

- Family game
- Dysfunctional patterns (patterns that maintain the problem)

INTERVENTIONS:

- Ritualized prescriptions
- Rituals
- Circular questions
- Counter paradox
- Odd/even day
- Positive connotation
- "Date"
- Reflecting team
- Letters
- Prescribe the system

CHANGE:

- Family develops a different game that does not include the symptom (system change)
- Requires incubation period

TERMINATION:

- Therapist decides, fewer than 10–12 sessions

EVALUATION:

- Not practiced much, therefore not researched
- Follow up contraindicated

RESOURCES:

Campbell, D., Draper, R., & Huffington, C. (1989). *Second thoughts on the theory and practice of the Milan approach to family therapy.* New York: Karnac.

Campbell, D., Draper, R., & Crutchley, E. (1991). The Milan systemic approach to family therapy. In A. S. Gurman & D. P. Kniskern (Eds.), *Handbook of Family Therapy (Vol. II)* (pp. 325–362). New York: Brunner/Mazel.

Cecchin, G. (1987). Hypothesizing, circularity, and neutrality revisited: An invitation to curiosity. *Family Process, 26*(4), 405–413.

Cecchin, G. (1992). Constructing therapeutic possibilities. In S. McNamee & K. J. Gergen (Eds.), *Therapy as social construction* (pp. 86–95). Newbury Park, CA: Sage.

Palazzoli, M. S., Boscolo, L., Cecchin, G., & Prata, G. (1978). *Paradox and counterparadox: A new model in the therapy of the family in schizophrenic transaction.* New York: Jason Aaronson.

Palazzoli, M. S., Boscolo, L., Cecchin, G., & Prata, G. (1978). A ritualized prescription in family therapy: Odd days and even days. *Journal of Marriage and Family Counseling, 48,* 3–9.

Palazzoli, M., & Palazzoli, C. (1989). *Family games: General models of psychotic processes in the family.* New York: W. W. Norton & Company.

NOTES:

SOLUTION-FOCUSED BRIEF THERAPY

LEADERS:

- Steve de Shazer
- Insoo Kim Berg
- Yvonne Dolan
- Eve Lipchik

ASSUMPTIONS:

- Clients want to change
- There's no such thing as resistance (clients are telling us how they cooperate)
- Focus on present and future except for the past in terms of exceptions; not focused on the past in terms of cause of changing the past
- Change the way people talk about their problems from problem talk to solution talk
- Language creates reality
- Therapist and client relationship is key
- A philosophy, not a set of techniques or theory
- Sense of hope, "cheerleader effect"
- Nonpathologizing, not interested in pathology or "dysfunction"
- Don't focus on the etiology of the problem: Solutions are not necessarily related to problems
- Assume the client has strengths, resources
- Only need a small change, which can snowball into a bigger change
- The problem is not occurring all the time

CONCEPTS:

- Problem talk/ Solution talk
- Exceptions
- Smallest difference that makes a difference
- Well-formed goals (small, concrete, measurable, important to client, doable, beginning of something, not end, presence not absence, hard work)
- Solution not necessarily related to the problem
- Clients are experts on their lives and their experiences
- Therapeutic relationships: customer/ therapist, complainant/sympathizer, visitor/host

GOALS OF THERAPY:

- Help clients to think or do things differently in order to increase their satisfaction with their lives
- Reach clients' goals; "good enough"
- Shift the client's language from problem talk to solution talk
- Modest goals (clear and specific)
- Help translate the goal into something more specific (clarify)
- Change language from problem to solution talk

SOLUTION-FOCUSED BRIEF THERAPY

ROLE OF THERAPIST:

- Cheerleader/Coach
- Offer hope
- Nondirective, client-centered

ASSESSMENT:

- Assess exceptions—times when problem isn't there
- Assess what has worked in the past, not necessarily related to the problem; client strengths
- Assess what will be different when the problems is gone (becomes goal that might not be clearly related to the stated problem)

INTERVENTIONS:

- Help set clear and achievable goals (clarify)
- Help client think about the future and what they want to be different
- Exceptions: Amplify the times they did things that "worked" when they didn't have the problem or it was less severe
- Compliments:
  - "How did you do that?"
  - "Wow! That must have been difficult!"
  - "That sounds like it was helpful; how did you do that?"
  - " I'm impressed with .... "
  - "You sound like a good .... "

INTERVENTIONS:

- Formula first session task: Observe what happens in their life/relationship that they want to continue
- Miracle question:
  - Used when clients are vague about complaints
  - Helps client do things the problem has been obstructing
  - Focus on how having problems gone will make a difference
  - Relational questions
  - follow up with miracle day questions and scaling questions
  - pretend to have a miracle day
- Scaling questions
- Midsession break (with or without team) to summarize session, formulate compliments and bridge, and suggest a task (tasks used less in recent years; clients develop own tasks; therapist may make suggestions or suggest "experiments"), sometimes called "feedback" (feeding information back into the therapy with a difference)
- Predict the next day, then see what happens

TERMINATION:

- Client decides

SELF OF THE THERAPIST:

- Accept responsibility for client/therapist relationship
- Expert on therapy conversation, not on client's life or experience of the difficulty

SOLUTION-FOCUSED BRIEF THERAPY

EVALUATION:

Therapy/Research:

- Simple (not necessarily easy)
- Can be perceived that therapist as insensitive- "Solution Forced Therapy"
- Crucial that clients are allowed to fully express struggles and have their own experiences validated, BEFORE shifting the conversation to strengths
- Techniques can obscure therapist's intuitive humanity
- Many outcome studies show effectiveness, but no controlled studies

Progress of therapy:

- Can clients see exceptions?
- Are they using solution talk?

RESOURCES:

de Shazer, S. (1982). *Patterns of brief family therapy: An ecosystemic approach.* New York: Guilford.

de Shazer, S., Dolan, Y., Korman, H., Trepper, T., McCollum, E., & Berg, I. K. (2007). *More than miracles: The state of the art of solution-focused brief therapy.* New York: Haworth.

Berg, I. K., & Miller, S. (1992). *Working with the problem drinker.* New York: Norton.

Berg, I. K. (1994). *Family-based services: A solution-focused approach.* New York: Norton.

De Jong, P., & Berg, I. K. (2007). *Interviewing for solutions* (3rd ed.). Pacific Grove, CA: Brooks/Cole.

Dolan, Y. (1992). *Resolving sexual abuse.* NY: W.W. Norton.

Lipchik, E. (2002). *Beyond technique in solution focused therapy.* New York: Guilford.

Miller, S. D., Hubble, M. A., & Duncan Barry L. (Eds.). (1996). *Handbook of solution-focused brief therapy.* San Francisco: Jossey-Bass.

Nelson, T. S., & Thomas, F. N. (Eds.). (2007). *Handbook of solution-focused brief therapy: Clinical applications.* New York: Haworth.

Nelson, T. S. (2019). *Solution-focused brief therapy with families.* New York, NY: Routledge

---

NOTES:

NARRATIVE THERAPY

LEADERS:

- Michael White
- David Epston
- Jill Freedman
- Gene Combs

ASSUMPTIONS:

- Personal experience is ambiguous
- Reality is shaped by the language used to describe it – language and experience (meaning) are recursive
- Reality is socially constructed
- Truth may not match historic or another person's truth, but it is true to the client
- Focus on effects of the problem, not the cause (how problem impacts family; how family affects problem)
- Stories organize our experience & shape our behavior
- The problem is the problem; the person is not the problem
- People "are" the stories they tell
- The stories we tell ourselves are often based on messages received from society or our families (social construction)
    - People have their own unique filters by which they process messages from society

CONCEPTS:

- Dominant Narrative – Beliefs, values, and practices based on dominant social culture
- Subjugated Narrative – a person's own story that is suppressed by dominant story
- Alternative Story: the story that's there but not noticed
- Deconstruction: Take apart problem saturated story in order to externalize & re-author it (Find missing pieces; "unpacking")
- Problem-saturated Stories – Bogs client down, allowing problem to persist. (Closed, rigid)
- Landscape of action: How people do things
- Landscape of consciousness: What meaning the problem has (landscape of meaning)
- Unique outcomes – pieces of deconstructed story that would not have been predicted by dominant story or problem-saturated story; exceptions; sparkling moments

GOALS OF THERAPY:

- Change the way the clients view themselves and assist them in re-authoring their story in a positive light; find the alternative but preferred story that is not problem-saturated
- Give options to more/different stories that don't include problems

ROLE OF THERAPIST:

- Genuine curious listener
- Question their assumptions
- Open space to make room for possibilities

ASSESSMENT:

- Getting the family's story, their experiences with their problems, and presumptions about those problems.
- Assess alternative stories and unique outcomes during deconstruction

NARRATIVE THERAPY

INTERVENTIONS:

- Ask questions
  - Landscape of action & landscape of meaning
  - Meaning questions
  - Opening space

CHANGE:

- Occurs by opening space; cognitive
- Client can see that there are numerous possibilities
- Expanded sense of self

Interventions

- Preference
- Story development
- Deconstruction
- To extend the story into the future
- Externalize problems
- Effects of problem on family; effects of family on problem
- Restorying or reauthoring
  - Self stories
- Letters from the therapist
- Certificates of award

TERMINATION:

- Client determines

SELF OF THE THERAPIST:

- Therapist's ideas, values, prejudices, etc. need to be open to client, "transparent"
- Expert on conversation

EVALUATION:

- No formal studies

RESOURCES:

Freeman, Jennifer, David Epston, and Dean Lobovits. (1997). *Playful approaches to serious problems: Narrative therapy with children and their families*. New York: W.W. Norton.

Freedman, Jill, and Gene Combs. (1996). *Narrative therapy: The social construction of preferred realities*. New York: W. W. Norton.

White, Michael, and David Epston (Eds.). (1990). *Narrative means to therapeutic ends*. New York: W.W. Norton.

White, Michael. (2007). *Maps of narrative practice*. New York: W.W. Norton.

NOTES:

COGNITIVE-BEHAVIORAL THERAPY

LEADERS:

- Ivan Pavlov
- Watson
- Thorndike
- B. F. Skinner
- Bandura
- Dattilio

ASSUMPTIONS:

- Family relationships, cognitions, emotions, and behavior mutually influence one another
- Cognitive inferences evoke emotion and behavior
- Emotion and behavior influence cognition

CONCEPTS:

- Schemas- core beliefs about the world, the acquisition and organization of knowledge
- Cognitions- selective attention, perception, memories, self-talk, beliefs, and expectations
- Reinforcement – an event that increases the future probability of a specific response
- Attribution- explaining the motivation or cause of behavior
- Distorted thoughts, generalizations get in way of clear thinking and thus action

GOALS OF THERAPY:

- To modify specific patterns of thinking and/or behavior to alleviate the presenting symptom

ROLE OF THERAPIST:

- Ask a series of question about assumptions, rather than challenge them directly
- Teach the family that emotional problems are caused by unrealistic beliefs

ASSESSMENT:

- Cognitive: distorted thoughts, thought processes
- Behavioral: antecedents, consequences, etc.

INTERVENTIONS:

- Questions aimed at distorted assumptions (family members interpret and evaluate one another unrealistically)
- Behavioral assignments
- Parent training
- Communication skill building
- Training in the model

CHANGE:

- Behavior will change when the contingencies of reinforcement are altered
- Changed cognitions lead to changed affect and behaviors

TERMINATION:

- When therapist and client determine

SELF OF THE THERAPIST:

- Not discussed

EVALUATION:

- Many studies, particularly in terms of marital therapy and parenting

COGNITIVE-BEHAVIORAL THERAPY

RESOURCES:

Jacobson, N. S., & Margolin, G. (1979). *Marital therapy: Strategies based on social learning and behavior exchange principles.* New York: Brunner/Mazel.

Jacobson, N. S., & Christensen, A. (1998). *Acceptance and Change in Couple Therapy: A Therapist's Guide to Transforming Relationships.* New York: Norton.

Epstein, N. B., & Baucom, D. H. (2002). *Enhanced cognitive-behavioral therapy for couples.* Washington, DC: APA Books.

Resources

Dattilio, F. M. (1998). *Case studies in couple and family therapy: Systemic and cognitive perspectives.* New York: Guilford.

Dattilio, F. M., & Padesky, C. (1990). *Cognitive therapy with couples.* Sarasota, FL: Professional Resource Press.

Beck, A. T., Reinecke, M. A., & Clark, D. A. (2003). *Cognitive therapy across the lifespan: Evidence and practice.* Cambridge, UK: Cambridge University Press.

NOTES:

CONTEXTUAL FAMILY THERAPY

LEADERS:

- Ivan Boszormenyi-Nagy

ASSUMPTIONS:

- Values and ethics are transmitted across generations
- Dimensions: (All are intertwined and drive people's behaviors and relationships)
  - Facts
  - Psychological
  - Relational
  - Ethical
- Trustworthiness of a relationship (relational ethics): when relationships are not trustworthy, debts and entitlements that must be paid back pile up; unbalanced ledger gets balanced in ways that are destructive to individuals and relationships and posterity (e.g., revolving slate, destructive entitlement)

CONTEXTUAL FAMILY THERAPY

CONCEPTS:

- Loyalty: split, invisible
- Entitlement (amount of merit a person has based on trustworthiness)
- Ledger (accounting)
- Legacy (we behave in ways that we have been programmed to behave)
- Relational ethics
- Destructive entitlement (you were given a bad ledger and it wasn't fair so it's ok to hand it on to the next person—acting out, neglecting important others)
- Revolving slate
- Posterity (thinking of future generations when working with people) this is the only model that does
- Rejunctive and disjunctive efforts

GOALS OF THERAPY:

- Balanced ledger

ROLE OF THE THERAPIST:

- Directive
- Expert in terms of assessment

ASSESSMENT:

- Debts
- Entitlements
- Invisible loyalties

INTERVENTIONS:

- Process and relational questions
- Multi-directional impartiality: Everybody and nobody feel special—all are attended to but none are more special
- Exoneration: Help people understand how they have been living out legacies and debts-ledgers—exonerate others
- Coach toward rejunctive efforts

CHANGE:

- Cognitive: Awareness of legacies, debts and entitlements
- Behavioral: Very action oriented—actions must change

TERMINATION:

- Never- totally up to the client

SELF OF THE THERAPIST:

- Must understand own legacies, entitlements, process of balancing ledgers, exoneration

EVALUATION:

- No empirical evaluation

CONTEXTUAL FAMILY THERAPY

RESOURCES:

Boszormenyi-Nagy, I. (1987). *Foundations of contextual therapy: Collected papers of Ivan Boszormenyi-Nagy*. New York: Brunner/Mazel.

Boszormenyi-Nagy, I., & Krasner, B. (1986). *Between give and take: A clinical guide to contextual therapy*. New York: Brunner/Mazel.

Hargrave, T. D., & Pfitzer, F. (2003). *The new contextual therapy: Guiding the power of give and take*. New York: Brunner-Routledge.

van Heusden, A., & van den Eerenbeemt, E. (1987). *Balance in motion: Ivan Boszormenyi-Nagy and his vision of individual and family*. New York: Brunner/Mazel.

NOTES:

BOWEN FAMILY THERAPY

LEADERS:

- Murray Bowen
- Michael Kerr (works with natural systems)
- Edwin Friedman

ASSUMPTIONS:

- The past is currently influencing the present
- Change can happen—individuals can move along in the process of differentiation
- Differentiation: ability to maintain self in the face of high anxiety (remain autonomous in a highly emotional situation)
  - Change in experience of self in the family system
  - Change in relationship between thinking and emotional systems
- Differentiation is internal and relational—they are isomorphic and recursive
- Anxiety inhibits change and needs to be reduced to facilitate change
- High intimacy and high autonomy are ideal
- Emotions are a physiological process—feelings are the thoughts that name and mediate emotions, that give them meaning
- Symptoms are indicators of stress, anxiety, lower differentiation
- Anyone can become symptomatic with enough stress; more differentiated people will be able to withstand more stress and, when they do become symptomatic, recover more quickly

BOWEN FAMILY THERAPY

CONCEPTS:

- Intimacy
- Autonomy
- Differentiation of Self
- Cutoff
- Triangulation
- Sibling position
- Fusion (within individual and within relationships)
- Family projection process
- Multigenerational transmission process
- Nuclear family
- Emotional process
- 4 sub-concepts (ways people manage anxiety; none of these is bad by itself – it's when one is used to exclusion of others or excessively that it can become problematic for a system):
  - Conflict
  - Dysfunction in person
  - Triangulation
  - Distance
- Societal emotional process
- Undifferentiated family ego mass

GOALS OF THERAPY:

- Ultimate—increase differentiation of self (thoughts/ emotions; self/ others)
- Intermediate—detriangulation, lowering anxiety to respond instead of react
- Decrease emotional reactivity—increase thoughtful responses
- Increased intimacy one-on-one with important others

ROLE OF THERAPIST:

- Coach (objective)
- Educator
- Therapist is part of the system (non-anxious and differentiated)
- Expert—not a collaborator

ASSESSMENT:

- Emotional reactivity
- Degree of differentiation of self
- Ways that people manage anxiety/ family themes
- Triangles
- Repeating intergenerational patterns
- Genogram (assessment tool)

BOWEN FAMILY THERAPY

INTERVENTIONS:

- Genogram (both assessment and change tool)
- Plan for intense situations (when things get hot, what are we going to do – thinking; process questions)
- Process questions– thinking questions: "What do you think about this?" "How does that work?"
- Detriangulating one-on-one relationships, one person with the other two in the triangle
- Educating clients about the concepts of the model
- Decrease emotional reactivity— increase thoughtful responses
- Therapist as a calm self and calm part of a triangle with the clients
- Coaching for changing own patterns in family of origin

CHANGE:

- Reduced anxiety through separation of thoughts and emotions – cognitive
- Reduced anxiety leads to responsive thoughts and actions, changed affect, changed relationships
- When we think (respond), change occurs (planning thinking) – when you know how you would like to behave in a certain emotional situation, you plan it, it makes it easier to carry through with different consequences

TERMINATION:

- Ongoing—we are never fully differentiated

SELF OF THE THERAPIST:

- Important with this model; differentiated, calm therapist is main tool
- We don't need to join the system
- We must be highly differentiated so we can recognize and reduce reactivity
- Our clients can only become as differentiated as we are; we need coaching to increase our own differentiation of self

EVALUATION:

- Research suggesting validity: not much, not a lot of outcome
- Did not specify symptom reduction
- Client report of different thoughts, actions, responses from others, affect is evidence of change

RESOURCES:

Bowen, M. (1978). *Family therapy in clinical practice.* New York: Jason Aaronson.

Friedman, E. (1987). *Generation to generation: Family process in church and synagogue.* New York: Guilford.

Kerr, M. E., & Bowen, M. (1988). *Family evaluation: An approach based on Bowen theory.* New York: W. W. Norton and Company.

NOTES:

PSYCHODYNAMIC FAMILY THERAPY (OBJECT RELATIONS)

LEADERS:

- Freud
- Erik Erikson
- Nathan Ackerman
- Several others who were trained, but their models were not primarily psychodynamic: Bowen, Whitaker, etc.
- Object relations: Scharff & Scharff
- Attachment theory: Bowlby

ASSUMPTIONS:

- Sexual and aggressive drives are at the heart of human nature
- Every human being wants to be appreciated
- Symptoms are attempts to cope with unconscious conflicts over sex and aggression
- Internalized objects become projected onto important others; we then evoke responses from them that fit that object, they comply, and we react to the projection rather than the real person
- Early experiences affect later relationships
- Internalized objects affect inner experience and outer relationships

CONCEPTS:

- Internal objects- mental images of self and others built from experience and expectation
- Attachment- connection with important others
- Separation-individuation- the gradual process of a child separating from the mother
- Mirroring- When parents show understanding and acceptance
- Transference-Attributing qualities of someone else to another person
- Countertransference – Therapist's attributing qualities of self onto others
- Family Myths- unspoken rules and beliefs that drive behavior, based on beliefs, not full images of others
- Fixation and regression-When families become stuck they revert back to lower levels of functioning
- Invisible loyalties- unconscious commitments to the family that are detrimental to the individual

GOALS OF THERAPY:

- To free family members of unconscious constraints so that they can interact as healthy individuals
- Separation-Individuation
- Differentiation

ROLE OF THERAPIST:

- Listener
- Expert position
- Interpret

ASSESSMENT:

- Attachment bonds
- Projections (unrealistic attributions)

PSYCHODYNAMIC FAMILY THERAPY (OBJECT RELATIONS)

INTERVENTIONS:

- Listening
- Showing empathy
- Interpretations (especially projections) Family of origin sessions (Framo)
- Make a safe holding environment

CHANGE:

- Change occurs when family members expand their insight to realize that psychological lives are larger than conscious experience and coming to accept repressed parts of their personalities
- Change also occurs when more, full, real aspects of others are revealed in therapy so that projections fade

TERMINATION:
Not sure how therapy is terminated

EVALUATION:

RESOURCES:

Sander, F. (2004) Psychoanalytic Couples Therapy: Classical Style in Psychoanalytic Inquiry Issue on Psychoanalytic Treatment of Couples ed. By Feld, B and Livingston, M. Vol 24:373–386.

Scharff, J. (ed.) (1989) Foundations of Object Relations Family Therapy . Jason Aronson, Northvale N.J.

Slipp, S. (1984). *Object relations: A dynamic bridge between individual and family treatment.* Northvale, NJ: Jason Aronson.

NOTES:

EXPERIENTIAL FAMILY THERAPY

LEADERS:

- Carl Whitaker
- Virginia Satir

ASSUMPTIONS:

- Family problems are rooted in suppression of feelings, rigidity, denial of impulses, lack of awareness, emotional deadness, and overuse of defense mechanisms
- Families must get in touch with their REAL feelings
- Therapy works from the Inside (emotion) Out (behavior)
- Expanding the individual's experience opens them up to their experiences and helps to improve the functioning of the family group
- Commitment to emotional well being

EXPERIENTIAL FAMILY THERAPY

CONCEPTS:

- Honest emotion
- Suppress repression
- Family myths
- Mystification
- Blaming
- Placating
- Being irrelevant/irreverent
- Being super reasonable
- Battle for structure
- Battle for initiative

GOALS OF THERAPY:

- Promote growth, change, creativity, flexibility, spontaneity, and playfulness
- Make the covert overt
- Increase the emotional closeness of spouses and disrupt rigidity
- Unlock defenses, enhance self-esteem, and recover potential for experiencing
- Enhance individuation

ROLE OF THE THERAPIST:

- Uses their own personality
- Must be open and spontaneous, empathic, sensitive, and demonstrate caring and acceptance
- Be willing to share and risk, be genuine, and increase stress within the family
- Teach family effective communication skills in order to convey their feelings
- Active and directive

ASSESSMENT:

- Assess individual self-expression and levels of defensiveness
- Assess family interactions that promote or stifle individuation and healthy interaction

INTERVENTIONS:

- Sculpting
- Choreography
- Conjoint family drawing
- Role playing
- Use of humor
- Puppet interviews
- Reconstruction
- Sharing feelings and creating an emotionally intense atmosphere
- Modeling and teaching clear communication skills (Use of "I" messages)
- Challenge "stances" (Satir)
- Use of self

CHANGE:

- Increasing stress among the family members leads to increased emotional expression and honest, open communication
- Changing experience changes affect; need to get out of head into emotions; active interventions change experience, emotions

EXPERIENTIAL FAMILY THERAPY

TERMINATION:

- Defenses of family members are broken down
- Family communicating openly
- Family members more in touch with their feelings
- Members relate to each other in a more honest way
- Openness for individuation of family members

SELF OF THE THERAPIST:

- Through the use of humor, spontaneity, and personality, the therapist is able to unbalance the family and bring about change
- The personality of the therapist is key to bringing about change

EVALUATION:

- This model fell out of favor in the 80s and 90s due to its focus on the emotional experience of the individual while ignoring the role of family structure and communication in the regulation of emotion
- Emotionally Focused Couples Therapy (Sue Johnson) and Internal Family Systems Therapy (Richard Schwartz) are the current trend
- Need to assess in-therapy outcomes as a measure of success due the fact that they often result in deeper emotional experiences (and successful sessions) that have the potential to generalize outside of therapy

RESOURCES:

Satir, V. (1967). *Conjoint family therapy*. Palo Alto, CA: Science and Behavior Books.
Satir, V. (1972). *Peoplemaking*. Palo Alto, CA: Science and Behavior Books.
Napier, A. Y., & Whitaker, C. A. (1978). *The family crucible*. New York: Harper & Row.

NOTES:

EMOTIONALLY FOCUSED THERAPY

LEADERS:

- Susan Johnson
- Les Greenburg

ASSUMPTIONS:

- "The inner construction of experience evokes interactional responses that organize the world in a particular way. These patterns of interaction then reflect, and in turn, shape inner experience" (Johnson, 2008, p. 109)
- Individual identity can be formed and transformed by relationships and interactions with others
- New experiences in therapy can help clients expand their view and make sense of the world in a new way
- Nonpathologizing, not interested in pathology or "dysfunction"
- Past is relevant only in how it affects the present.
- Emotion is a target and agent of change.
- Primary emotions generally draw partners closer. Secondary emotions push partners away.
- Distressed couples get caught in negative repetitive sequences of interaction where partners express secondary emotions rather than primary emotions.

CONCEPTS:

- Attachment needs exist throughout the life span.
- Negative interactional patterns
- Primary and secondary emotions
- Empathic attunement
- Cycle de-escalation
- Blamer softening
- Withdrawer re-engagement

GOALS OF THERAPY:

- Identify and break negative interactional patterns
- Increase emotional engagement between couple
- Identify primary and secondary emotions in the context of negative interactional pattern
- Access, expand, and reorganize key emotional responses
- Create a shift in partners' interactional positions.
- Foster the creation of a secure bond between partners through the creation of new interactional events that redefine the relationship

EMOTIONALLY FOCUSED THERAPY

ROLE OF THERAPIST:

- Client-centered, collaborative
- Process consultant
- Choreographer of relationship dance

ASSESSMENT:

- Assess relationship factors such as:
    - Their cycle
    - Action tendencies (behaviors)
    - Perceptions
    - Secondary emotions
    - Primary emotions
    - Attachment needs
- Relationship history, key events
- Brief personal attachment history
- Interaction style
- Violence/abuse/drug usage
- Sexual relationship
- Prognostic indicators:
    - Degree of reactivity and escalation- intensity of negative cycle
    - Strength of attachment/commitment
    - Openness – response to therapist – engagement
    - Trust/faith of the female partner (does she believe he cares about her).

INTERVENTIONS

- Reflection
- Validation
- Evocative questions and empathic conjecture
    - Self-disclosure
- Tracking, reflecting, and replaying interactions
- Reframe in an attachment frame
- Enactments
- Softening
- Heightening and expanding emotional experiences

EMOTIONALLY FOCUSED THERAPY

TERMINATION:

Therapy ends when the therapist and clients collaboratively decide that the following changes have occurred:

- Negative affect has lessened and is regulated differently
- Partners are more accessible and responsive to each other
- Partners perceive each other as people who want to be close, not as enemies
- Negative cycles are contained and positive cycles are enacted

SELF OF THE THERAPIST:

- Accept responsibility for client/therapist relationship
- Expert on process of therapy, not on client's life or experience of the difficulty
- Collaborator who must sometimes lead and sometimes follow

EVALUATION:

Therapy/Research:

- Difficult model to learn
- When using the EFT model, it is important to move slowly down the process of therapy. This can be difficult to do.
- Learning to stay with deepened emotions can sometimes be overwhelming, but the therapist must continue to reflect and validate.
- Empirically validated, 20 years of research to back up.

CHANGE:

- Change happens as couples have a new corrective emotional experience with one another.
- When couples are able to experience their own emotions, needs, and fears and express them to one another and experience the other partner responding to those emotions, needs, and fears in an accessible, responsive way.

RESOURCES:

Johnson, S. M. (2004). *The practice of emotionally focused couple therapy* (2nd ed.). New York: Brunner-Routledge.

Johnson, S. M., Bradely, B., Furrow, J., Lee, A., Palmer, G., Tilley, D., & Wolley, S. (2005). *Becoming an emotionally focused couple therapist: The workbook.* New York: Routledge.

Johnson, S. M. (2008). Emotionally focused couple therapy. In A. S. Gurman (Ed.), *Clinical handbook of couple therapy* (4th ed., pp. 107–137). New York: Guilford.

Johnson, S. M., & Greenburg, L. S. (1994). *The heart of the matter: Perspectives on emotion in marital therapy*. New York: Brunner/Mazel.

NOTES:

Gottman Method Couple Therapy

LEADERS:

- John Gottman
- Julie Gottman

ASSUMPTIONS:

- Therapy is primarily dyadic
- Couples need to be in emotional states to learn how to cope with and change them
- Therapy should be primarily a positive affective experience
- Positive sentiment override and friendship base are needed for communication and affect change

CONCEPTS:

- Negative interactions (four horsemen) decrease acceptance of repair attempts
- Most couples present in therapy with low positive affect
- Sound marital house
- Softened startup
- Love maps

GOALS OF THERAPY:

- Empower the couple
- Problem solving skills
- Positive affect
- Creating shared meaning

ROLE OF THE THERAPIST:

- Coach
- Provide the tools that the couple can use with one another and make their own

ASSESSMENT:

- Four horsemen are present and repair is ineffective
- Absence of positive affect
- Sound marital house

INTERVENTIONS:

- Sound Marital House
- Dreams-within-conflict
- Label destructive patterns
- Enhancing the Marital friendship
- Sentiment override

CHANGE:

- Accepting influence
- Decrease negative interactions
- Increase positive affect

TERMINATION:

- When couples can consistently develop their own interventions that work reasonably well

SELF OF THE THERAPIST:

- Not discussed

EVALUATION:

- Theory is based on Gottman's research

RESOURCES:

The Marriage Clinic

NOTES:

Appendix B: AAMFT Core Competencies

Number	Subdomain	Competence
Domain 1: Admission to Treatment		
1.1.1	Conceptual	Understand systems concepts, theories, and techniques that are foundational to the practice of marriage and family therapy
1.1.2	Conceptual	Understand theories and techniques of individual, marital, couple, family, and group psychotherapy
1. 1. 3	Conceptual	Understand the behavioral healthcare delivery system, its impact on the services provided, and the barriers and disparities in the system
1. 1. 4	Conceptual	Understand the risks and benefits of individual, marital, couple, family, and group psychotherapy
1. 2. 1	Perceptual	Recognize contextual and systemic dynamics (e.g., gender, age, socioeconomic status, culture/race/ethnicity, sexual orientation, spirituality, religion, larger systems, social context)
1. 2. 2	Perceptual	Consider health status, mental status, other therapy, and other systems involved in the clients' lives (e.g., courts, social services)
1. 2. 3	Perceptual	Recognize issues that might suggest referral for specialized evaluation, assessment, or care
1. 3. 1	Executive	Gather and review intake information, giving balanced attention to individual, family, community, cultural, and contextual factors
1. 3. 2	Executive	Determine who should attend therapy and in what configuration (e.g., individual, couple, family, extrafamilial resources)
1. 3. 3	Executive	Facilitate therapeutic involvement of all necessary participants in treatment
1. 3. 4	Executive	Explain practice setting rules, fees, rights, and responsibilities of each party, including privacy, confidentiality policies, and duty to care to client or legal guardian
1. 3. 5	Executive	Obtain consent to treatment from all responsible persons

(Continued)

Number	Subdomain	Competence
1. 3. 6	Executive	Establish and maintain appropriate and productive therapeutic alliances with the clients
1. 3. 7	Executive	Solicit and use client feedback throughout the therapeutic process
1. 3. 8	Executive	Develop and maintain collaborative working relationships with referral resources, other practitioners involved in the clients' care, and payers
1. 3. 9	Executive	Manage session interactions with individuals, couples, families, and groups
1. 4. 1	Evaluative	Evaluate case for appropriateness for treatment within professional scope of practice and competence
1. 5. 1	Professional	Understand the legal requirements and limitations for working with vulnerable populations (e.g., minors)
1. 5. 2	Professional	Complete case documentation in a timely manner and in accordance with relevant laws and policies
1. 5. 3	Professional	Develop, establish, and maintain policies for fees, payment, record keeping, and confidentiality
Domain 2: Clinical Assessment and Diagnosis		
2. 1. 1	Conceptual	Understand principles of human development; human sexuality; gender development; psychopathology; psychopharmacology; couple processes; and family development and processes (e.g., family, relational, and system dynamics)
2. 1. 2	Conceptual	Understand the major behavioral health disorders, including the epidemiology, etiology, phenomenology, effective treatments, course, and prognosis
2. 1. 3	Conceptual	Understand the clinical needs and implications of persons with comorbid disorders (e.g., substance abuse and mental health; heart disease and depression)
2. 1. 4	Conceptual	Comprehend individual, marital, couple, and family assessment instruments appropriate to presenting problem, practice setting, and cultural context
2. 1. 5	Conceptual	Understand the current models for assessment and diagnosis of mental health disorders, substance use disorders, and relational functioning
2. 1. 6	Conceptual	Understand the strengths and limitations of the models of assessment and diagnosis, especially as they relate to different cultural, economic, and ethnic groups
2. 1. 7	Conceptual	Understand the concepts of reliability and validity, their relationship to assessment instruments, and how they influence therapeutic decision making

(Continued)

Number	*Subdomain*	*Competence*
2. 2. 1	Perceptual	Assess each client's engagement in the change process
2. 2. 2	Perceptual	Systematically integrate client reports, observations of client behaviors, client relationship patterns, reports from other professionals, results from testing procedures, and interactions with client to guide the assessment process
2. 2. 3	Perceptual	Develop hypotheses regarding relationship patterns, their bearing on the presenting problem, and the influence of extra therapeutic factors on client systems
2. 2. 4	Perceptual	Consider the influence of treatment on extra-therapeutic relationships
2. 2. 5	Perceptual	Consider physical/organic problems that can cause or exacerbate emotional/interpersonal symptoms
2. 3. 1	Executive	Diagnose and assess client behavioral and relational health problems systemically and contextually
2. 3. 2	Executive	Provide assessments and deliver developmentally appropriate services to clients, such as children, adolescents, elders, and persons with special needs
2. 3. 3	Executive	Apply effective and systemic interviewing techniques and strategies
2. 3. 4	Executive	Administer and interpret results of assessment instruments
2. 3. 5	Executive	Screen and develop adequate safety plans for substance abuse, child and elder maltreatment, domestic violence, physical violence, suicide potential, and dangerousness to self and others
2. 3. 6	Executive	Assess family history and dynamics using a genogram or other assessment instruments
2. 3. 7	Executive	Elicit a relevant and accurate biopsychosocial history to understand the context of the clients' problems
2. 3. 8	Executive	Identify clients' strengths, resilience, and resources
2. 3. 9	Executive	Elucidate presenting problem from the perspective of each member of the therapeutic system
2. 4. 1	Evaluative	Evaluate assessment methods for relevance to clients' needs
2. 4. 2	Evaluative	Assess ability to view issues and therapeutic processes systemically
2. 4. 3	Evaluative	Evaluate the accuracy and cultural relevance of behavioral health and relational diagnoses
2. 4. 4	Evaluative	Assess the therapist client agreement of therapeutic goals and diagnosis
2. 5. 1	Professional	Utilize consultation and supervision effectively

(Continued)

Number	*Subdomain*	*Competence*
Domain 3: Treatment Planning and Case Management		
3. 1. 1	Conceptual	Know which models, modalities, and/or techniques are most effective for presenting problems
3. 1. 2	Conceptual	Understand the liabilities incurred when billing third parties, the codes necessary for reimbursement, and how to use them correctly
3. 1. 3	Conceptual	Understand the effects that psychotropic and other medications have on clients and the treatment process
3. 1. 4	Conceptual	Understand recovery-oriented behavioral health services (e.g., self-help groups, 12-step programs, peer-to-peer services, supported employment)
3. 2. 1	Perceptual	Integrate client feedback, assessment, contextual information, and diagnosis with treatment goals and plan
3. 3. 1	Executive	Develop, with client input, measurable outcomes, treatment goals, treatment plans, and aftercare plans for clients utilizing a systemic perspective
3. 3. 2	Executive	Prioritize treatment goals
3. 3. 3	Executive	Develop a clear plan of how sessions will be conducted
3. 3. 4	Executive	Structure treatment to meet clients' needs and to facilitate systemic change
3. 3. 5	Executive	Manage progression of therapy toward treatment goals
3. 3. 6	Executive	Manage risks, crises, and emergencies
3. 3. 7	Executive	Work collaboratively with other stakeholders, including family members, other significant persons, and professionals not present
3. 3. 8	Executive	Assist clients in obtaining needed care while navigating complex systems of care
3. 3. 9	Executive	Develop termination and aftercare plans
3. 4. 1	Evaluative	Evaluate progress of sessions toward treatment goals
3. 4. 2	Evaluative	Recognize when treatment goals and plan require modification
3. 4. 3	Evaluative	Evaluate level of risks, management of risks, crises, and emergencies
3. 4. 4	Evaluative	Assess session process for compliance with policies and procedures of practice setting
3. 4. 5	Evaluative	Monitor personal reactions to clients and treatment process, especially in terms of therapeutic behavior, relationship with clients, process for explaining procedures, and outcomes
3. 5. 1	Professional	Advocate with clients in obtaining quality care, appropriate resources, and services in their community

(Continued)

Number	*Subdomain*	*Competence*
3. 5. 2	Professional	Participate in case-related forensic and legal processes
3. 5. 3	Professional	Write plans and complete other case documentation in accordance with practice-setting policies, professional standards, and state/provincial laws
3. 5. 4	Professional	Utilize time management skills in therapy sessions and other professional meetings
Domain 4: Therapeutic Interventions		
4. 1. 1	Conceptual	Comprehend a variety of individual and systemic therapeutic models and their application, including evidence-based therapies and culturally sensitive approaches
4. 1. 2	Conceptual	Recognize strengths, limitations, and contraindications of specific therapy models, including the risk of harm associated with models that incorporate assumptions of family dysfunction, pathogenesis, or cultural deficit
4. 2. 1	Perceptual	Recognize how different techniques may impact the treatment process
4. 2. 2	Perceptual	Distinguish differences between content and process issues, their role in therapy, and their potential impact on therapeutic outcomes
4. 3. 1	Executive	Match treatment modalities and techniques to clients' needs, goals, and values
4. 3. 2	Executive	Deliver interventions in a way that is sensitive to special needs of clients (e.g., gender, age, socioeconomic status, culture/race/ethnicity, sexual orientation, disability, personal history, larger systems' issues of the client)
4. 3. 3	Executive	Reframe problems and recursive interaction patterns
4. 3. 4	Executive	Generate relational questions and reflexive comments in the therapy room
4. 3. 5	Executive	Engage each family member in the treatment process as appropriate
4. 3. 6	Executive	Facilitate clients' developing and integrating solutions to problems
4. 3. 7	Executive	Defuse intense and chaotic situations to enhance the safety of all participants
4. 3. 8	Executive	Empower clients and their relational systems to establish effective relationships with each other and larger systems
4. 3. 9	Executive	Provide psychoeducation to families whose members have serious mental illness or other disorders
4. 3. 10	Executive	Modify interventions that are not working to better fit treatment goals

(Continued)

Number	*Subdomain*	*Competence*
4. 3. 11	Executive	Move to constructive termination when treatment goals have been accomplished
4. 3. 12	Executive	Integrate supervisor/team communications into treatment
4. 4. 1	Evaluative	Evaluate interventions for consistency, congruency with model of therapy and theory of change, cultural and contextual relevance, and goals of the treatment plan
4. 4. 2	Evaluative	Evaluate ability to deliver interventions effectively
4. 4. 3	Evaluative	Evaluate treatment outcomes as treatment progresses
4. 4. 4	Evaluative	Evaluate clients' reactions or responses to interventions
4. 4. 5	Evaluative	Evaluate clients' outcomes for the need to continue, refer, or terminate therapy
4. 4. 6	Evaluative	Evaluate reactions to the treatment process (e.g., transference, family of origin, current stress level, current life situation, cultural context) and their impact on effective intervention and clinical outcomes
4. 5. 1	Professional	Respect multiple perspectives (e.g., clients, team, supervisor, practitioners from other disciplines who are involved in the case)
4. 5. 2	Professional	Set appropriate boundaries, manage issues of triangulation, and develop collaborative working relationships
4. 5. 3	Professional	Articulate rationales for interventions related to treatment goals and plan, assessment information, and systemic understanding of clients' context and dynamics
Domain 5: Legal Issues, Ethics, and Standards		
5. 1. 1	Conceptual	Know state, federal, and provincial laws and regulations that apply to the practice of marriage and family therapy
5. 1. 2	Conceptual	Know professional ethics and standards of practice that apply to the practice of marriage and family therapy
5. 1. 3	Conceptual	Know policies and procedures of the practice setting
5. 1. 4	Conceptual	Understand the process of making an ethical decision
5. 2. 1	Perceptual	Recognize situations in which ethics, laws, professional liability, and standards of practice apply
5. 2. 2	Perceptual	Recognize ethical dilemmas in practice setting
5. 2. 3	Perceptual	Recognize when a legal consultation is necessary

Number	*Subdomain*	*Competence*
5. 2. 4	Perceptual	Recognize when clinical supervision or consultation is necessary
5. 3. 1	Executive	Monitor issues related to ethics, laws, regulations, and professional standards
5. 3. 2	Executive	Develop and assess policies, procedures, and forms for consistency with standards of practice to protect client confidentiality and to comply with relevant laws and regulations
5. 3. 3	Executive	Inform clients and legal guardian of limitations to confidentiality and parameters of mandatory reporting
5. 3. 4	Executive	Develop safety plans for clients who present with potential self-harm, suicide, abuse, or violence
5. 3. 5	Executive	Take appropriate action when ethical and legal dilemmas emerge
5. 3. 6	Executive	Report information to appropriate authorities as required by law
5. 3. 7	Executive	Practice within defined scope of practice and competence
5. 3. 8	Executive	Obtain knowledge of advances and theory regarding effective clinical practice
5. 3. 9	Executive	Obtain license(s) and specialty credentials
5. 3. 10	Executive	Implement a personal program to maintain professional competence
5. 4. 1	Evaluative	Evaluate activities related to ethics, legal issues, and practice standards
5. 4. 2	Evaluative	Monitor attitudes, personal wellbeing, personal issues, and personal problems to ensure they do not impact the therapy process adversely or create vulnerability for misconduct
5. 5. 1	Professional	Maintain client records with timely and accurate notes
5. 5. 2	Professional	Consult with peers and/or supervisors if personal issues, attitudes, or beliefs threaten to adversely impact clinical work
5. 5. 3	Professional	Pursue professional development through self supervision, collegial consultation, professional reading, and continuing educational activities
5. 5. 4	Professional	Bill clients and third-party payers in accordance with professional ethics and relevant laws and policies, and seek reimbursement only for covered services
Domain 6: Research and Program Evaluation		
6. 1. 1	Conceptual	Know the extant MFT literature, research, and evidence-based practice

(Continued)

Number	*Subdomain*	*Competence*
6. 1. 2	Conceptual	Understand research and program evaluation methodologies, quantitative and qualitative, relevant to MFT and mental health services
6. 1. 3	Conceptual	Understand the legal, ethical, and contextual issues involved in the conduct of clinical research and program evaluation
6. 2. 1	Perceptual	Recognize opportunities for therapists and clients to participate in clinical research
6. 3. 1	Executive	Read current MFT and other professional literature
6. 3. 2	Executive	Use current MFT and other research to inform clinical practice
6. 3. 3	Executive	Critique professional research and assess the quality of research studies and program evaluation in the literature
6. 3. 4	Executive	Determine the effectiveness of clinical practice and techniques
6. 4. 1	Evaluative	Evaluate knowledge of current clinical literature and its application
6. 5. 1	Professional	Contribute to the development of new knowledge

Note: Printed with permission from the American Association for Marriage and Family Therapy

References

Addis, M. E., Wade, W. A., & Hatgis, C. (1999). Barriers to dissemination of evidence-based practices: Addressing practitioners' concerns about manual-based psychotherapies. *Clinical Psychology: Science and Practice*, 6, 430–441.

Aducci, C. J., & Cole, C. L. (2011). Multiple relationships: Perspectives from training family therapists and clients. *Journal of Systemic Therapies*, 30(4), 48–63.

Aggarwal N. K. (2012). Adapting the cultural formulation for clinical assessments in forensic psychiatry. *Journal of the American Academy of Psychiatry and the Law*, 40, 113–118.

Alderfer, C. (2007). Triangulation—the core of the supervisory process. *Family Therapy Magazine*, 65(5), 32–34.

Almeida, R., Dolan-Del Vecchio, K., & Parker, L. (2007). Foundation concepts for social justice-based therapy: Critical consciousness, accountability, and empowerment. In E. Alarondo (Ed.), *Advancing social justice through clinical practice* (pp. 175–206). Mahwah, NJ: Lawrence Erlbaum.

Amanor-Boadu, Y., & Baptist, J. (2008). Meeting the clinical supervision needs of international student therapists. *Family Therapy Magazine*, 7(6), 46–47.

American Association for Marriage and Family Therapy. (2001). *Code of ethics*. Alexandria, VA: Author.

American Association for Marriage and Family Therapy. (2004). *Marriage and family therapy core competencies*. Retrieved from https://www.coamfte.org/Documents/COAMFTE/Accreditation%20Resources/MFT%20CORE%20Competencies%20(December%202004).pdf.

American Association for Marriage and Family Therapy. (2012). *Code of ethics*. Alexandria, VA: Author.

American Association for Marriage and Family Therapy. (2014). *Approved Supervisor designation: Standards handbook*. Alexandria, VA: Author.

American Association for Marriage and Family Therapy. (2015a). *Code of Ethics*. Alexandria, VA. Retrieved from www.aamft.org/Legal_Ethics/Code_of_Ethics.aspx.

American Association for Marriage and Family Therapy. (2015b). *User's guide to the 2015 AAMFT Code of Ethics*. Alexandria, VA: Author.

American Association for Marriage and Family Therapy. (2020). *The AAMFT blog: Legal & Ethics*. Retrieved from https://blog.aamft.org/ethics/.

American Psychological Association. (2020). *Publication manual of the American Psychological Association* (7th ed.). Washington, DC: Author.

Anderson, S. A., Schlossberg, M., & Rigazio-DiGilio, S. (2000). Family therapy trainees' evaluations of their best and worst supervision experiences. *Journal of Marital and Family Therapy*, 26, 79–91.

Aponte, H. J. (1994). How personal can training get? *Journal of Marital and Family Therapy*, 20, 3–15.

Aponte, H., & Ingram, M. (2018). Person of the therapist supervision: Reflections of a therapist and supervisor on empathic-identification and differentiation. *Journal of Family Psychotherapy*, 29, 43–57.

Aponte, H., & Kissil, K. (Eds.), (2016). *The Person of the Therapist training model: Mastering the use of self.* New York, NY: Routledge.

Aponte, H. J., Powell, F. D., Brooks, S., Watson, M. F., Litzke, C., Lawless, J., & Johnson, E. (2009). Training the person of the therapist in an academic setting. *Journal of Marital and Family Therapy*, 35, 381–394.

Association of Marital and Family Therapy Regulatory Boards. (2016). *Teletherapy guidelines: Telesupervision.* Retrieved from https://amftrb.org/wp-content/uploads/2017/05/Proposed-Teletherapy-Guidelines-DRAFT-as-of-09.12.16.pdf.

Association of Marital and Family Therapy Regulatory Boards. (2019). *2019 AMFTRB marital and family therapy national examination handbook for candidates.* Retrieved from https://ptcny.com/pdf/AMFTRB2020.pdf.

Association of Marital and Family Therapy Regulatory Boards. (2020). *2020 AMFTRB marital and family therapy national examination handbook for candidates.* Retrieved from https://ptcny.com/pdf/AMFTRB.pdf.

Baldwin, K. D. (2018). Faculty and supervisor roles in gatekeeping. In A. M. Homrich & K. L. Hendersons (Eds.), *Gatekeeping in the mental health professions* (pp. 99–125). Alexandria, VA: American Counseling Association.

Barker, P., & Chang, J. (2013). *Basic family therapy* (6th ed.). Hoboken, NJ: Wiley-Blackwell.

Bartle-Haring, S. M., Silverthorne, B. C., Meyer, K., & Toviessi, P. (2009). Does live supervision make a difference?: A multilevel analysis. *Journal of Marital and Family Therapy*, 35, 406–414.

Bateson, G. (1972). *Steps to an ecology of mind.* New York, NY: Ballantine Books.

Baucom, B. R., & Crenshaw, A. O. (2019). Evaluating the efficacy of couple and family therapy. In B. H. Fiese, M. Celano, K. Deater-Deckard, E. N. Jouriles, & M. A. Whisman (Eds.), *APA handbook of contemporary family psychology: Family therapy and training (Vol. 3)*, (pp. 69–86). Washington, DC: American Psychological Association.

Becvar, D. S., & Becvar, R. J., (2012). *Family therapy: A systemic integration* (8th ed.). New York, NY: Pearson.

Becvar, R. J., & Becvar, D. S. (2017). *Systems theory and family therapy: A primer* (3rd ed.). Lanham, MD: Hamilton Books.

Bernard, J. M., & Goodyear, R. K. (2009). *Fundamentals of clinical supervision* (4th ed.). Upper Saddle River, NJ: Pearson.

Bernard, J. M., & Goodyear, R. K. (2019). *Fundamentals of clinical supervision* (6th ed.). New York, NY: Pearson.

Beutler, L. E. (2000). David and Goliath: When empirical and clinical standards of practice meet. *American Psychologist*, 55, 997–1007.

Beutler, L. E., & Harwood, T. M. (2000). *Prescriptive psychotherapy: A practical guide to systematic treatment selection.* New York, NY: Oxford University Press.

Bilot, J., & Peluso, P. (2009). The use of the ethical genogram in supervision. *The Family Journal: Counseling and Therapy for Couples and Families*, 17(2), 175–179.

Bitar, G. W., Bean, R. A., & Bermudez, J. M. (2007). Influences and processes in theoretical orientation development: A grounded theory pilot study. *American Journal of Family Therapy*, 35, 109–121.

Blow, A. J., & Karam, E. A. (2016). The therapist's role in effective marriage and family therapy practice: The case for evidence-based therapists. *Administration and Policy in Mental Health and Mental Health Services Research*, 44, 716–723.

Blow, A. J., & Sprenkle, D. H. (2001). Common factors across theories of marriage and family therapy. *Journal of Marital and Family Therapy*, 27, 385–401.

Blow, A. J., Sprenkle, D. H., & Davis, S. D. (2007). Is who delivers the treatment more important than the treatment itself? The role of the therapist in common factors. *Journal of Marital and Family Therapy*, 33, 298–317.

Blumer, M., Hertlein, K. M., & VandenBosch, M. (2015). Towards the development of educational core competencies for Couple and Family Therapy technology practices. *Contemporary Family Therapy*, 37, 113–121.

Bobele, M., Biever, J. L., Hassan Solorzano, B., & Bluntzer, L. H. (2014). Postmodern approaches to supervision. In T. C. Todd & C. L. Storm (Eds.), *The complete systemic supervisor: Context, philosophy, and pragmatics* (2nd ed., pp. 255–273). Hoboken, NJ: Wiley.

Bordin, E. S. (1979). The generalizability of the psychoanalytic concept of the working alliance. *Psychotherapy: Theory Research, and Practice*, 168, 252–260.

Boston, P. (2010). The three faces of supervision: Individual learning, group learning, and supervisor accountability. In C. Burck & G. Daniel (Eds.), *Mirrors and reflections: Processes of systemic supervision* (pp. 27–48). London, UK: Karnac.

Boszormenyi-Nagy, I., & Spark, G. (1973). *Invisible loyalties: Reciprocity in intergenerational family therapy*. New York, NY: Brunner/Mazel.

Bowen, M. (1978). *Family therapy in clinical practice*. New York, NY: Jason Aronson.

Bowen, M. (1985). *Family therapy in clinical practice*. Northville, NJ: Jason Aronson.

Boyd-Franklin, N. (2003). *Black families in therapy: Understanding the African American experience* (2nd ed.). New York, NY: Guilford.

Briggs, K., Fournier, D. G., & Hendrix, C. C. (1999). Evaluating trainees' skill development: The Family Therapy Skills Checklist. *Contemporary Family therapy*, 21(3), 353–370.

British Association for Counselling and Psychotherapy. (2018). *Ethical framework for the counselling professions*. Retrieved from www.bacp.co.uk/events-and-resources/ethics-and-standards/ethical-framework-for-the-counselling-professions/.

Bronfenbrenner, U. (1979). *The ecology of human development*. Cambridge, MA: Harvard University Press.

Bronfenbrenner, U., & Morris, P. A. (2006). The bioecological model of human development. In R. M. Lerner & W. Damon (Eds.), *Handbook of child psychology* (6th ed., Vol.1, pp. 793–828). Hoboken, NJ: Wiley.

Brown, T. L., Bryant, C. M., Hernández, D. C., Holman, E. G., Mulsow, M., & Shih, K. Y. (2019). *What's your social location? Definitions and illustrations*. National Council on Family Relations. Retrieved from www.ncfr.org/ncfr-report/spring-2019/inclusion-and-diversity-social-location.

Brunelli, L. M. (2019). *Five things to avoid when video conferencing from home*. Retrieved from www.thebalancecareers.com/things-to-avoid-when-video-conferencing-from-home-4150628.

Bubolz, M. M., & Sontag, M. S. (1993). Human ecology theory. In P. G. Boss, W. J. Doherty, R. LaRossa, W. R. Schumm, & S. K. Steinmetz (Eds.), *Sourcebook of family theories and methods: A contextual approach* (pp. 419–447). New York, NY: Plenum.

Busby, D. M., Crane, D. R., Larson, J. H., & Christensen, C. (1995). A revision of the Dyadic Adjustment Scale for use with distressed and nondistressed couples: Construct hierarchy and multidimensional scales. *Journal of Marital and Family Therapy*, 21, 289–308.

Caldwell, B. (2011, Sept/Oct). The dilemma: Can a religious therapist refuse to treat gay and lesbian clients? *Family Therapy Magazine*, 50–52.

Caldwell, B. E., Bischoff, R. J., Derigg-Palumbo, K. A., & Liebert, J. D. (2017). *Best practices in the online practice of couple and family therapy: Report of the online therapy workgroup*. Alexandria, VA: American Association for Marriage and Family Therapy.

Caldwell, K., & Claxton, C. (2010). Teaching family systems theory: A developmental-constructivist perspective. *Contemporary Family Therapy*, 32, 3–21.

Campbell, C. (2018). Educating openness: Umberto Eco's poetics of openness as a pedagogical value. *Signs and Society*, 6, 305–331.

Carpenter, K. M., Cheng, W. Y., Smith, J. L., Brooks, A. C., Amrhein, P. C., Wain, R. M., & Nunes, E. V. (2012). "Old dogs" and new skills: How clinician characteristics relate to motivational interviewing skills before, during, and after training. *Journal of Consulting and Clinical Psychology*, 80, 560–573.

Castronova, M., ChenFeng, J., & Zimmerman, T. S. (2020). Supervision in systemic family therapy. In K. S. Wampler, R. B. Miller, & R. B. Seedall (Eds.), *Handbook of systemic family therapy* (Vol. 1, pp. 577–600). New York, NY: Wiley.

Celano, M. P., Smith, C. O., & Kaslow, N. J. (2010). A competency-based approach to couple and family therapy supervision. *Psychotherapy Theory, Research, Practice, Training*, 47, 35–44.

Chang, J. (2010). The reflecting team: A training method for family counselors. *The Family Journal: Counseling and Therapy for Couples and Families*, 18(1), 36–44.

Chang, J. (2013). A contextual-functional meta-framework for counselling supervision. *International Journal for the Advancement of Counselling*, 35(2), 71–87.

Charlés, L. L., & Nelson, T. S. (2019). Preface. In L. L. Charlés & T. S. Nelson (Eds.), *Family therapy supervision in extraordinary settings: Illustrations of systemic approaches in everyday clinical work* (pp. xv–xvii). New York, NY: Routledge.

Christiansen, A. T., Thomas, V., Kafescioglu, N., Karakurt, G., Lowe, W., Smith, W., & Witatenborn, A. (2011). Multicultural supervision: Lessons learned about an ongoing struggle. *Journal of Marital and Family Therapy*, 37, 109–119. https://doi:10.1111/j.1752-0606.2009.00138.x.

Colapinto, J. (1988). Teaching the structural way. In H. A. Liddle, D. C. Breunlin, & R. C. Schwartz (Eds.), *Handbook of family therapy training and supervision* (pp. 17–37). New York, NY:Guilford.

College of Registered Psychotherapists of Ontario. (2012). *Entry-to-practice competency profile for Registered Psychotherapists*. Toronto, ON: Author.

Collins, S. (Ed.). (2019). Embracing cultural responsivity and social justice: Reshaping professional identity in counselling psychology. *Counselling Concepts*. Retrieved from https://www.researchgate.net/publication/331473611_Embracing_Cultural_Responsivity_and_Social_Justice_Reshaping_Professional_Identity_in_Counselling_Psychology?enrichId=rgreq-4684d21973d9ea16e66ac070063c8646-XXX&enrichSource=Y292ZXJQYWdlOzMzMTQ3MzYxMTtBUzo3MzIxMDY3NzkwMjk1MDRAMTU1MTU1OTI2NjQyNw%3D%3D&el=1_x_2&_esc=publicationCoverPdf.

Commission on Accreditation for Marriage and Family Therapy Education. (2017). *COAMFTE Accreditation Standards Version 12*. Alexandria, VA: Author.

Cook, R. M., Welfare, L. E., & Sharma, J. (2019). Exploring supervisees' in-session experiences of utilizing intentional nondisclosure. *The Clinical Supervisor*, 38, 202–221.

Coren, S., & Farber, B. A. (2019) A qualitative investigation of the nature of "informal supervision" among therapists in training. *Psychotherapy Research*, 29(5), 679–690. https://doi:10.1080/10503307.2017.1408974.

Craighead, W. W., Craighead, L. W., & Miklowitz, D. J. (Eds.) (2008). *Psychopathology: History, diagnosis, and empirical foundations*. New York, NY: Wiley.

Craven, P. A., & Lee, R. E. (2006). Therapeutic interventions with young foster children: A critical review. *Research on Social Work Practice*, 16, 287–304.

Cravens Pickens, J., Morris, N., & Johnson, D. L. (2019). The digital divide: Couple and family therapy programs' integration of teletherapy training and education. *Journal of Marital and Family Therapy*, 46, 186–200.

Cuijpers, P., Reijnders, M., & Huibers, M. J. H. (2019). The role of common factors in psychotherapy outcomes. *Annual Review of Clinical Psychology* 15, 207–231.

D'Aniello, C., & Fife, S. T. (2017). Common factors' role in accredited MFT training programs. *Journal of Marital and Family Therapy*, 43, 591–604.

Daniels, T. G., Rigazio-DiGilio, S. A., & Ivey, A. E. (1997). Microcounseling: A training and supervision paradigm for the helping professions. In C. E. Watkins, Jr. (Ed.), *Handbook of psychotherapy supervision* (pp. 277–295). Hoboken, NJ: Wiley & Sons.

Davis, D., Deblaere, C., Hook, J. N., & Owen, J. (2020). Integrating mindfulness in the real world. In D. Davis, C. Deblaere, J. N. Hook, & J. Owen (Eds.), *Mindfulness-based practices in therapy: A cultural humility approach* (pp. 177–193). Washington, DC: American Psychological Association.

De Jong, P., & Berg, I. K. (2013). *Interviewing for solutions* (4th ed.). Belmont, CA: Brooks/Cole.

de Shazer, S., Dolan, Y., Korman, H., Trepper, T., McCollum, E., & Berg, I. K. (2007). *More than miracles: The state of the art of solution-focused brief therapy*. New York, NY: Haworth.

Deblinger, E., & Heflin, A. H. (1996). *Treating sexually abused children and their nonoffending parents: A cognitive behavioral approach*. Thousand Oaks, CA: Sage.

Degges-Wite, S. E., Colon, B. R., & Borzumato-Gainey, C. (2013). Counseling supervision within a feminist framework: Guidelines for intervention. *The Journal of Humanistic Counseling*, 10, 92–105.

Denton, W. H., Burleson, B. R., Clark, T. E., Rodriguez, C. P., & Hobbs, B. V. (2000). A randomized trial of emotion-focused therapy for couples in a training clinic. *Journal of Marital and Family Therapy*, 26, 65–78.

DeRoma, V. M., Hickey, D. A., & Stanek, K. M. (2007). Methods of supervision in marriage and family therapist training: A brief report. *North American Journal of Psychology*, 9 (3), 415–422.

Di Clemente, C. C. (1999). Motivation for change: Implications for substance abuse treatment. *Psychological Science*, 10(3), 209–213.

Domokos-Cheng Ham, M. (2014, July/August). Social responsibility: A commitment to an effective decision-making process. *Family Therapy Magazine*, 16–20.

Doyle, E., & Gosnell, F. (2019). Performing social justice in family therapy: Exploring the assumptions between the *isms and the *ings. In S. Collins (Ed.), *Embracing cultural responsivity and social justice: Reshaping professional identity in counselling psychology* (pp. 614–638). Victoria, BC: Counselling Concepts.

Drake Wallace, M. J., Wilcoxon, S. A., & Satcher, J. (2010). Productive and nonproductive counselor supervision: Best and worst experiences of supervisees. *Alabama Counseling Association Journal*, 35(2), 4–13.

Duncan, B. L., & Sparks, J. A. (2019). When meta-analysis misleads: A critical case study of a meta-analysis of client feedback. *Psychological Services*, 1–10. https://doi.org/10.1037/ser0000398.

Duncan, B. L., Miller, S. D., & Sparks, J. A. (2004). *The heroic client: A revolutionary way to improve effectiveness through client-directed, outcome-informed therapy* (rev. ed.). San Francisco, CA: Jossey-Bass.

Duncan, B. L., Miller, S. D., Wampold, B. E., & Hubble, M. A. (Eds.) (2010). *The heart and soul of change: What works in therapy* (2nd ed.). Washington, DC: American Psychological Association.

Dwyer, T. F. (1999). "Barging in". In R. E. Lee & S. Emerson (Eds.), *The eclectic trainer* (pp. 133–143). Galena, IL: Geist & Russell.

Emerson, S. (1999). Creating a safe place for growth in supervision. In R. E. Lee & S. Emerson (Eds.), *The eclectic trainer* (pp. 3–12). Galena, IL: Geist & Russell.

Enlow, P. T., McWhorter, L. G., Genuario, K., & Davis, A. (2019). Supervisor–supervisee interactions: The importance of the supervisory working alliance. *Training and Education in Professional Psychology*, 13(3), 206–211.

Esmiol, E. E., Knudson-Martin, C., & Delgado, S. (2012). Developing a contextual consciousness: Learning to address gender, societal power, and culture in clinical practice. *Journal of Marital and Family Therapy*, 38, 573–588.

Falender, C. A., & Shafranske, E. P. (2004). *Clinical supervision: A competency-based approach.* Washington, DC: American Psychological Association.

Falender, C. A., & Shafranske, E. P. (2016). *Supervision essentials for the practice of competency-based supervision: Clinical supervision essentials.* Washington, DC: American Psychological Association.

Falicov, C. J. (1995). Training to think culturally: A multidimensional comparative framework. *Family Process*, 34, 373–388.

Falke, S. I., Lawson, L. Pandit, M. L., & Patrick, E. A. (2015). Participant supervision: Supervisor and supervisee experiences of cotherapy. *Journal of Marital and Family Therapy*, 41, 150–162.

Farber, B. A., & Hazanov, B. (2014). Informal sources of supervision in clinical training. *Journal of Clinical Psychology: In Session*, 60(11), 1062–1072.

Fear, R., & Woolfe, R. (1999). The personal and professional development of the counselor: The relationship between personal philosophy and theoretical orientation. *Counseling Psychology Quarterly*, 12(3), 253–262.

Fife, S. T., D'Anniello, C., Scott, S., & Sullivan, E. (2018). Marriage and family therapy students' experience with common factors training. *Journal of Marital and Family Therapy*, 45, 191–205.

Figley, C. R. (2000). Helping our supervisors in training (SITs) write their philosophy statement. In AAMFT (Ed.), *Readings in family therapy supervision: Selected articles from the AAMFT Supervision Bulletin* (pp. 46–48). Alexandria, VA: AAMFT.

Figley, C. R., & Nelson, T. S. (1989). Basic family therapy skills, I: Conceptualization and initial findings. *Journal of Marital and Family Therapy*, 15, 349–365.

Figley, C. R., & Nelson, T. S. (1990). Basic Family Therapy Skills, II: Structural family therapy. *Journal of Marital and Family Therapy*, 16, 225–239.

Fincham, F. D., Stanley, S. M., & Rhoades, G. K. (2011). Relationship education in emerging adulthood: Problems and prospects. In F. D. Fincham & M. Cui (Eds.), *Romantic relationships in emerging adulthood* (pp. 293–316). Cambridge, UK: Cambridge University Press.

Flemons, D., Green, S. K., & Rambo, A. H. (1996). Evaluating therapists' practices in a postmodern world: A discussion and a scheme. *Family Process*, 35, 43–56.

Fleuridas, C., Nelson, T. S., & Rosenthal, D. M. (1986). The evolution of circular questions: Training family therapists. *Journal of Marital and Family Therapy*, 12, 113–127.

Friedlander, M. L., Escudero, V., & Heatherington, L. (2006). *Therapeutic alliances in couple and family therapy: An empirically informed guide to practice.* Washington, DC: American Psychological Association.

Gehart, D. R. (2010). *Mastering competencies in family therapy*. Belmont, CA: Brooks/Cole.

Gehart, D. R. (2017). *Mastering competencies in family therapy: A practical approach to theory and clinical case documentation* (3rd ed.): Boston, MA: Cengage Learning.

Glenn, E., & Serovich, J. M. (1994). Documentation of family therapy supervision: A rationale and method. *American Journal of Family Therapy*, 22, 345–355.

Goodyear, R. K., Wertheimer, A., Cypers, S., & Rosemond, M. (2003). Refining the map of the counselor development journey: Response to Rønnestad and Skovholt. *Journal of Career Development*, 30(1), 73–80. https://doi.org/10.1177/089484530303000105.

Green, K. (2020). Top 4 HIPAA email disclaimer examples. *The Email Signature Handbook*. Retrieved from www.exclaimer.com/email-signature-handbook/10128-hipaa-email-disclaimer-examples.

Green, M. S., & Dekkers, T. D. (2010). Attending to power and diversity in supervision: An exploration of supervisee learning outcomes and satisfaction with supervision. *Journal of Feminist Family Therapy*, 22(4), 293–312.

Green, S. L. (2011, Nov/Dec). Power or pattern? A brief, relational approach. *Family Therapy Magazine*, 9–11.

Greenwood, L. (2010, July/Aug). Legal concerns regarding impairment. *Family Therapy Magazine*, 50–51.

Haber, R., Carlson, R. G., & Braga, C. (2014). Use of an anecdotal client feedback note in family therapy. *Family Process*, 53, 307–317.

Haberstroh, S., Barney, L., Foster, N., & Duffey, T. (2014). The ethical and legal practice of online counseling and psychotherapy: A review of mental health professions. *Journal of Technology in Human Services*, 32, 149–157.

Hardy, K. V., & Laszloffy, T. A. (1995). The cultural genogram: Key to training culturally competent family therapists. *Journal of Marital and Family Therapy*, 21, 227–237.

Hare-Mustin, R. (1978). A feminist approach to family therapy. *Family Process*, 17, 181–194.

Hargrave, T., & Pfitzer, F. (2011). *Restoration therapy*. New York, NY: Taylor & Francis.

Harris, S. M. (2001). Teaching family therapists about sexual attraction in therapy. *Journal of Marital and Family Therapy*, 27, 123–128.

Harris, S. (2017). Systemic dual-developmental supervision: An approach for psychotherapy practitioners and supervisors. *The Family Journal*, 25, 84–90.

Hartman, A. (1995). Diagrammatic assessment in family relationships. *Families in Society*, 76 (2), 111–122.

Hartwell, E. E., Serovich, J. M., Reed, S. J., Boisvert, D., & Falbo, T. (2017). A systematic review of gay, lesbian, and bisexual research samples in couple and family therapy journals. *Journal of Marital and Family Therapy*, 43, 482–501.

Haug, I. E., & Storm, C. L. (2014). Drawing the line in ethical dilemmas in systemic supervision. In T. C. Todd & C. L. Storm (Eds.), *The complete systemic supervisor: Context, philosophy, and pragmatics* (2nd edition, pp. 19–42. New York, NY: Wiley.

Hays, P. A. (1996). Addressing the complexities of culture and gender in counseling. *Journal of Counseling & Development*, 74, 332–338.

Health Insurance and Portability and Accountability Act (HIPAA). (1996). Washington, DC: US Department of Health and Human Services.

Heinlen, K. T., Welfel, E., Richmond, E. N., & Rak, C. F. (2003). The scope of web counseling: A survey of services and compliance with NBCC Standards for the ethical practice of WebCounseling. *Journal of Counseling & Development*, 81(1), 61–69.

Henggler, S. W., & Schaeffer, C. M. (2010). Treating serious emotional and behavioural problems using multisystemic therapy. *Australian and New Zealand Journal of Family Therapy*, 31(2), 149–164.

Henggler, S. W., & Sheidow, A. J. (2012). Empirically supported family-based treatments for conduct disorder and delinquency in adolescents. *Journal of Marital and Family Therapy*, 38, 30–58.

Henry, W. P., Strupp, H. H., Butler, S. F., Schacht, T. E., & Binder, J. L. (1993). Effects of training in time-limited dynamic psychotherapy: Changes in therapist behavior. *Journal of Consulting and Clinical Psychology*, 61, 434–440.

Hernández, P. (2008). The cultural context model in clinical supervision. *Training and Education in Professional Psychology*, 2(1), 10–17.

Hernández, P., & McDowell, T. (2010). Intersectionality, power, and relational safety in context: Key concepts in clinical supervision. *Training and Education in Professional Psychology*, 4(1), 29–35.

Hernández, P., Bunyi, B., & Townson, R. (2007). Interweaving ethnicity and gender in consultation: A training experience. *Journal of Family Psychotherapy*, 18(1), 57–75.

Hernández, P., Siegel, A., & Almeida, R. (2009). The Cultural Context Model: How does it facilitate couples' therapeutic change? *Journal of Marital and Family Therapy*, 35, 97–110.

Hertlein, K. M., Blumer, M. L., & Mihaloliakos, J. H. (2014). Marriage and family counselors' perceived ethical issues related to online therapy. *The Family Journal*, 23(1), 5–12.

Hicken, A. S. (2008). *Mentoring in marriage and family therapy programs: Graduate perspectives.* [Unpublished thesis] Utah State University.

Hildebrandt, C. (2009). *Marriage and family therapy interns' best and worst supervision experiences.* [Unpublished doctoral dissertation], Alliant International University.

Hill, E. W. (2009). Confronting anxiety in couple and family therapy supervision: A developmental supervisory model based on attachment theory. *Australian and New Zealand Journal of Family Therapy*, 30(1), 1–14.

Holloway, E. (1995). *Clinical supervision: A systems approach.* Thousand Oaks, CA: Sage.

Holloway, E. L. (2016). *Supervision essentials for a systems approach to supervision.* Washington, DC: American Psychological Association.

Hook, J. N., Davis, D. E., Owen, J., Worthington, E. L., Jr., & Utsey, S. O. (2013). Cultural humility: Measuring openness to culturally diverse clients. *Journal of Counseling Psychology*, 60, 353–366.

Huggins, R. (2016a). What's coming and what's here in online therapy. *Free Presentations, Clinician Resources.* Retrieved from https://personcenteredtech.com/2016/05/02/whats-coming-whats-online-therapy/.

Huggins, R. (2016b). *Use Square be HIPAA compliant! Ethics, HIPAA … and what about PayPal?* Retrieved from https://personcenteredtech.com/2016/02/21/square-hipaa-compliant-ethics-hipaa-client-safety-considerations/.

Hughes, R. S. (2000). *Ethics and regulations of cybercounseling.* Greensboro, NC: ERIC Clearinghouse on Counseling and Student Services.

Imber-Black, E. (1988). *Families and larger systems: A family therapist's guide through the labyrinth.* New York, NY: Guilford.

Imel, Z., & Wampold, B. (2008). The importance of treatment and the science of common factors in psychotherapy. In S. D. Brown & R. W. Lent (Eds.), *Handbook of counseling psychology* (pp. 249–262). New York, NY: Wiley.

Inman, A. G. (2006). Supervisor multicultural competence and its relation to supervisory process and outcome. *Journal of Marital and Family Therapy*, 32, 73–85.

Inouye, B., Madsen, J., Palmer-Olsen, L., Faller, G., & Best, M. (2017). Emotionally focused therapy supervision. In J. Fitzgerald (Ed.), *Foundations for couples' therapy: Research for the real world* (pp. 415–425). New York, NY: Routledge.

Jacobs, S., Kissil, K, Scott, D., & Davey, M. (2010). Creating synergy in practice: Promoting complementarity between evidence-based and postmodern approaches. *Journal of Marital and Family Therapy*, 36, 185–196.

Jayarajan, D. (2020). *Secure your meetings with Zoom waiting rooms*. Retrieved from https://blog.zoom.us/secure-your-meetings-zoom-waiting-rooms/.

Jensen Oanes, C., Karlsson, B., & Borg, M. (2017). User involvement in therapy: Couples and family therapists' lived experiences with the inclusion of a feedback procedure in clinical practice. *Australian and New Zealand Journal of Family Therapy*, 38, 451–463.

Jethwa, J., Glorney, E., Adhyaru, J., & Lawson, A. (2019). A grounded theory of multisystemic therapist roles in achieving positive outcomes for young people and families *Journal of Family Therapy, 41*, 1–19.

Johnson, E. A. (2017). *Working together in clinical supervision: A guide for supervisors and supervisees*. New York, NY: Momentum Press.

Johnson, L. N., Wright, D. W., & Ketring, S. A. (2002). The therapeutic alliance in home-based family therapy: Is it predictive of outcome. *Journal of Marital and Family Therapy*, 28, 93–102.

Johnson, S. M. (2003). The revolution in couple therapy: A practitioner-scientist perspective. *Journal of Marital and Family Therapy*, 29, 365–384.

Johnson, S. M. (2008). Emotionally Focused Couples Therapy. In A. S. Gurman (Ed.), *Clinical handbook of couple therapy* (4th ed., pp. 107–137). New York, NY: Guilford.

Johnson, S. M. (2019). *Attachment theory in practice: Emotionally Focused Therapy (EFT) with individuals, couples, and families*. New York, NY: Guilford.

Jordan, K. B. (2000). Live supervision of all therapy sessions: A must for beginning therapists in clinical practica. In AAMFT (Ed.), *Readings in family therapy supervision* (p. 116). Alexandria, VA: AAMFT.

Kaiser, T. L. (1992). The supervisory relationship: An identification of the primary elements in the relationship and an application of two theories of ethical relationships. *Journal of Marital and Family Therapy*, 18, 283–296.

Kaiser, T. L. (1997). *Supervisory relationships: Exploring the human element*. Pacific Grove, CA: Brooks/Cole.

Karam, E. A., Blow, A. J., Sprenkle, D. H., & Davis, S. D. (2015). Strengthening the systemic ties that bind: Integrating common factors into marriage and family therapy curricula. *Journal of Marital and Family Therapy*, 41, 136–149.

Karam, E., & Sprenkle, D. H. (2010). The research-informed clinician: A guide to training the next-generation MFT. *Journal of Marital and Family Therapy*, 36, 307–319.

Kaslow, N. J., Grus, C. L., Campbell, L. F., Fouad, N. A., Hatcher, R. L., & Rodolfa, E. R. (2009). Competency assessment toolkit for professional psychology. *Training and Education in Professional Psychology*, 3(4, Suppl), S27–S45. https://doi.org/10.1037/a0015833.

Kattari, S. K. (2019). The development and validation of the ableist microaggression scale. *Journal of Social Service Research*, 45, 400–417.

Keiley, M. K., Dolbin, M., Hill, J., Karuppaswamy, N., Liu, T., Natrajan, R., Poulson, S., Robbins, N., & Robinson, P. (2002). The cultural genogram: Experiences from within a marriage and family therapy training program. *Journal of Marital and Family Therapy*, 28, 165–178.

Killmer, J. M., & Cook, M. (2014). Providing systems-oriented clinical supervision in agency settings. In T. C. Todd & C. Storm (Eds.), *The complete systemic supervisor: Context* (2nd ed., pp. 108–130). Boston, MA: Wiley.

Kim, J. S., Smock, S., Trepper, T. S., McCollum, E. E., & Franklin, C. F. (2010). Is solution-focused brief therapy evidence-based? *Families in Society: The Journal of Contemporary Human Services*, 91, 300–306.

Kitchener, K. S. (2000). *Foundations of ethical practice, research, and teaching in psychology.* Mahwah, NJ: Lawrence Erlbaum.

Knerr, M., Bartle-Haring, S., McDowell, T., Adkins, K., Delaney, R. O., Gangamma, R., … Meyer, K. (2011). The impact of initial factors on therapeutic alliance in individual and couples therapy. *Journal of Marital and Family Therapy*, 37, 182–199.

Knight, K., Kenny, A., & Endacot, R. (2016). From expert generalists to ambiguity masters: Using ambiguity tolerance theory to redefine the practice of rural nurses. *Journal of Clinical Nursing*, 25, 1757–1765.

Kniskern, D. P., & Gurman, A. S. (1988). Research. In H. A. Liddle, D. C. Breunlin, & R. C. Schwartz (Eds.), *Handbook of family therapy training and supervision* (pp. 368–378). New York, NY: Guilford.

Knobloch-Fedders, L. M., Pinsof, W. M., & Mann, B. J. (2004). The formation of the therapeutic alliance in couple therapy. *Family Process*, 43, 425–442.

Koltz, R. L., Odegard, M. A., Feit, S. S., Provost, K., & Smith, T. (2012). Parallel process and isomorphism: A model for decision making in the supervisory triad. *The Family Journal*, 20, 233–238. https://doi.org/10.1177/1066480712448788.

Korinek, A. W., & Kimball, T. G. (2003). Managing and resolving conflict in the supervisory system. *Contemporary Family Therapy*, 25(3), 295–310.

Kumar, A., Karabenick, S. S., Warnke, J. H., Hany, S., & Seay, N. (2019). Culturally Inclusive and Responsive Curricular Learning Environments (CIRCLEs): An exploratory sequential mixed-methods approach. *Contemporary Educational Psychology*, 57, 87–105.

Laszloffy, T. A., & Habekost, J. (2010). Using experiential tasks to enhance cultural sensitivity among MFT trainees. *Journal of Marital and Family Therapy*, 36, 333–346.

Le Roux, P., Podgorski, C., Rosenberg, T., Watson, W. H., & McDaniel, S. (2011). Developing an outcome-based assessment for family therapy training: The Rochester Objective Structured Clinical Evaluation. *Family Process*, 50, 544–560.

Lebow, J. L. (1987). Developing a personal integration in family therapy: Principles for model construction and practice. *Journal of Marital and Family Therapy*, 13(1), 1–14.

Lebow, J. (1996, November/December). Do-it-yourself research: The practical advantages of studying your own practice. *Family Therapy Networker*, 61–63.

Lebow, J. L. (1997a). The integrative revolution in couple and family therapy. *Family Process*, 36, 1–17.

Lebow, J. L. (1997b). Rejoinder: Why integration is so important in couple and family therapy. *Family Process*, 36, 23–24.

Lebow, J. L. (2006). *Research for the psychotherapist: From science to practice.* New York: Routledge.

Lee, M. M., & Vennum, A. V. (2010). Using critical incident journaling to encourage cultural awareness in doctoral marriage and family therapy students. *Journal of Family Psychotherapy*, 219, 238–252.

Lee, M. Y. (1997). A study of solution-focused brief family therapy: Outcomes and issues. *American Journal of Family Therapy*, 25, 3–17.

Lee, R. E. (1999). Seeing and hearing in therapy and supervision: A clinical example of isomorphism. In R. E. Lee & S. Emerson (Eds.), *The eclectic trainer* (pp. 81–87). Galena, IL: Geist & Russell.

Lee, R. E. (2009). "If you build it, they may not come": Lessons learned from a funded proposal. *Research on Social Work Practice*, 19, 251–260.

Lee, R. E. (2013). *Growing stronger together: A wellness path to increase the resilience in your relationship.* Amazon Books.

Lee, R. E., Emerson, S., & Kochka, P. (1999). Using the Michigan State University Family Therapy Questionnaire for training. In R. E. Lee & S. Emerson (Eds.), *The eclectic trainer* (pp. 107–119). Galena, IL: Geist & Russell.

Lee, R. E., Eppler, C., Kendal, N., & Latta, C. (2001). Critical incidents in the professional lives of first year MFT students. *Contemporary Family Therapy*, 23(1), 51–62.

Lee, R. E., & Everett, C. A. (2004). *The integrative family therapy supervisor*. New York, NY: Brunner-Routledge.

Lee, R. E., & Nelson, T. S. (2014). *The contemporary relational supervisor*. New York, NY: Routledge.

Lee, R. E., & Nichols, W. C. (2010). The doctoral education of professional marriage and family therapists. *Journal of Marital and Family Therapy*, 36, 259–269.

Lee, R. E., Nichols, D. P., Nichols, W. C., & Odom, T. (2004). Trends in family therapy supervision. *Journal of Marital and Family Therapy*, 30, 61–69.

Lee, R. E., & Sturkie, K. (1997). The national marital and family therapy examination program. *Journal of Marital and Family Therapy*, 23(3), 255–269.

Lerner, R. M. (2018). *Concepts and theories of human development* (4th ed.). New York, NY: Routledge.

Lerner, R. M., Agans, J. P., DeSouza, L. M., & Hershberg, R. M. (2014). Developmental science in 2025: A predictive review. *Research in Human Development*, 11, 255–272.

Liddle, H. A. (1988). Systemic supervision: Conceptual overlays and pragmatic guidelines. In H. A. Liddle, D. C. Breunlin, & R. C. Schwartz (Eds.), *Handbook of family therapy training and supervision* (pp. 153–171). New York, NY: Guilford.

Liddle, H. A., Breunlin, D., & Schwartz, R. (Eds.), (1988). *Handbook of family therapy training and supervision*. New York: Guilford.

Lloyd-Hazlett J., & Foster, V.A. (2014). Utilizing interpersonal process recall in clinical supervision to address counselor countertransference. *Vistas Online*. American Counseling Association. Retrieved from https://www.counseling.org/docs/default-source/vistas/article_34.pdf?sfvrsn=40a07c2c_10

Long, J. K., & Bonomo, J. (2006). Revisiting the sexual orientation matrix for supervision: Working with GLBTQ families. *Journal of GLBT Family Studies*, 2, 151–166.

Lorenz, T. (2020, 4/13). A few easy steps to prevent 'Zoombombing.' *New York Times*. B8.

Lowe, R., Hunt, C., & Simmons, P. (2008). Towards multi-positioned live supervision in family therapy: Combining treatment and observation teams with first- and second-order perspectives. *Contemporary Family Therapy*, 30, 3–14.

Machua, R., Johnson, T., & Moro, R. R. (2015). Tablet-assisted live supervision: Eye-bug supervision. *VISTAS Online*. Retrieved from www.counseling.org/docs/default-source/vistas/article_5547f227f16116603abcacff0000bee5e7.pdf?sfvrsn=d9e4472c_4.

Marovic, S., & Snyders, F. (2010). Cybernetics of supervision: A developmental perspective. *The Clinical Supervisor*, 29(1), 35–50.

Marshall, J. P., & Wieling, E. (2003). Marriage and family therapy students' phenomenological experiences of cross-cultural supervision. *Family Therapy*, 30, 167–187.

Marsiglia, F., & Booth, J. M. (2015). Adaptation of interventions in real practice settings. *Research on Social Work Practice*, 25, 423–432.

Martin, D. J, Garske, J. P., & Davis, M. K. (2000). Relation of the therapeutic alliance with outcome and other variables: A meta-analytic review. *Journal of Consulting and Clinical Psychology*, 68, 438–450.

Marziali, E., Mamar, C., & Krupnick, J. (1981). Therapeutic alliance scales: Development and relationship to psychotherapy outcome. *The American Journal of Psychiatry*, 138, 361–364.

Mastoras, S. M., & Andrews, J. J. W. (2012). The supervisee experience of group supervision: Implications for research and practice. *Training and Education in Professional Psychology*, 51(2), 102–111.

Maxwell, M. D., Davis, S. D., Miller, M. M., & Woolley, S. R. (2018). Covenant attachment: A constructivist grounded theory of Christian couples and God. *Journal of Marital and Family Therapy*, 46, 110–123.

McAdoo, H., & Younge, S. N. (2009). Black families. In H. A. Neville, B. M. Tynes, & S. O. Utsey (Eds.), *Handbook of African American psychology* (pp. 103–115). Thousand Oaks, CA: Sage.

McComb, J. L., Diamond, R. M., Breunlin, D. C., Chambers, A. L., & Murray, K. S. F. (2018). Introducing client feedback into marriage and family therapy supervision: A qualitative study examining the transition to empirically informed supervision. *Journal of Family Therapy*, 41, 214–231.

McCollum, E. E., & Wetchler, J. L. (1995). In defense of case consultation: Maybe 'dead' supervision isn't dead after all. *Journal of Marital and Family Therapy*, 21, 155–166.

McDowell, T., Knudson-Martin, C., & Bermudez, J. M. (2018). *Socioculturally attuned family therapy*. New York, NY: Routledge.

McGeorge, C. R., Carlson, T. S., & Toomey, R. B. (2015). Assessing lesbian, gay, and bisexual affirmative training in couple and family therapy: Establishing the validity of the faculty version of the Affirmative Training Inventory. *Journal of Marital and Family therapy*, 41, 57–71.

McGoldrick, M., Anderson, C., & Walsh, F. (Eds.), (1989). *Women in families: A framework for family therapy*. New York, NY: W.W. Norton.

McGoldrick, M., & Giordano, J. (Eds.). (1982). *Ethnicity and family therapy*. New York, NY: Guilford.

McGoldrick, M., Giordano, J., & Garcia-Preto, N. (Eds.). (2005). *Ethnicity and family therapy* (3rd ed.). New York, NY: Guilford.

McGoldrick, M., & Hardy, K. V. (2008). Introduction: Re-visioning family therapy from a multicultural perspective. In M. McGoldrick & K. V. Hardy (Eds.), *Re-visioning family therapy: Race, culture, and gender in clinical practice* (2nd ed., pp. 3–24). New York, NY: Guilford.

McGoldrick, M., & Hardy, K. V. (Eds.). (2019). *Re-visioning family therapy: Addressing diversity in clinical practice* (3rd ed.). New York, NY: Guilford.

McGregor, S. L. T. (2011). Home economics as an integrated, holistic system: revisiting Bubollz and Sontag's 1988 human ecology approach. *International Journal of Consumer Studies*, 35, 26–34.

McLain, D. L., Kefallonitis, E., & Armani, K. (2015). Ambiguity tolerance in organizations: Definitional clarification and perspectives on future research. *Frontiers in Psychology*, 6. Retrieved from https://doi.org/10.3389/fpsyg.2015.00344.

Messer, S. B. (2004). Evidence-based practice: Beyond empirically supported treatments. *Professional Psychology: Research and Practice*, 35, 580–588.

Midori Hanna, S. (2019). *The practice of family therapy: Key elements across models* (5th ed.). New York, NY: Routledge.

Miller, J. K. (2010). Competency-based training: Objective structured clinical exercises (OSCE) in marriage and family therapy. *Journal of Marital and Family Therapy*, 36, 320–332.

Miller, J. K., Linville, D., Todahl, J., & Metcalfe, J. (2009). Using mock trials to teach students forensic core competencies in marriage and family therapy. *Journal of Marital and Family Therapy*, 35, 456–465.

Miller, M. M., & Ivey, D. C. (2006). Spirituality, gender, and supervisory style in supervision. *Contemporary Family Therapy*, 28, 323–337.

Miller, M. M., Korinek, A., & Ivey, D. C. (2004). Spirituality in MFT training: Development of the Spiritual Issues in Supervision Scale. *Contemporary Family Therapy*, 26, 71–81.

Miller, S. D., Duncan, B. L., Brown, J., Sparks, J., & Claud, D. (2003). The Outcome Rating Scale: A preliminary study of the reliability, validity, and feasibility of a brief visual analog measure. *Journal of Brief Therapy*, 2, 91–100.

Mindell, A. (2001). *Metaskills: The spiritual art of therapy* (2nd ed.). Portland, OR: Lao Tse Press.

Minuchin, S. (1974). *Families and family therapy*. Cambridge, MA: Harvard University Press.

Minuchin, S., & Fishman, H. C. (1981). *Family therapy techniques*. Cambridge, MA: Harvard University Press.

Mittal, M., & Wieling, E. (2006). Training experiences of international doctoral students in marriage and family therapy. *Journal of Marital and Family Therapy*, 32, 369–383.

Morgan, M. M., & Sprenkle, D. H. (2007). Toward a common factors approach to supervision. *Journal of Marital and Family Therapy*, 33, 1–17.

Mowery, R. L. (2009a, Sept/Oct). Expanding from ethical compliance to ethical empowerment: Supervisors are key. *Family Therapy Magazine*, 48–51.

Mowery, R. L. (2009b, Nov/Dec). Expanding from ethical compliance to ethical empowerment: Supervisors are key (part 2). *Family Therapy Magazine*, 32–33.

Muran, J. C., & Barber, J. P. (2010). *The therapeutic alliance: An evidence-based guide to practice*. New York, NY: Guilford.

Murphy, M. J., & Wright, D. (2005). Supervisees' perspectives of power use in supervision. *Journal of Marital and Family Therapy*, 31, 283–295.

Mutchler, M., & Anderson, S. (2010). Therapist personal agency: A model for examining the training context. *Journal of Marital and Family Therapy*, 36, 511–525.

National Board for Certified Counselors (NBCC). (2016). *Policy regarding the provision of distance professional services*. Retrieved from https://EthicsNBCCPolicyRegardingPracticeofDistanceCounselingBoard.pdf.

Nelson, M. L., & Friedlander, M. L. (2001). A close look at conflictual supervisory relationships. *Journal of Counseling Psychology*, 48, 384–395.

Nelson, T. S. (1991). Gender in family therapy supervision. *Contemporary Family Therapy*, 13 (4), 357–369.

Nelson, T. S. (2010). *Doing something different: Solution-focused brief therapy practices*. New York, NY: Taylor & Francis.

Nelson, T. S. (Ed.). (2014). *Education and training in solution-focused brief therapy*. New York, NY: Routledge.

Nelson, T. S. (2019). *Solution-focused brief therapy with families*. New York, NY: Routledge.

Nelson, T. S., Chenail, R. J., Alexander, J. F., Crane, D. R., Johnson, S. M., & Schwallie, L. (2007). The development of core competencies for the practice of marriage and family therapy. *Journal of Marital and Family Therapy*, 33(4), 417–438. https://doi.org/10.1111/j.1752-0606.2007.00042.x.

Nelson, T. S., & Figley, C. R. (1990). Basic Family Therapy Skills, III: Brief and strategic schools of family therapy. *Journal of Family Psychology*, 4(1), 49–62.

Nelson, T. S., & Graves, T. (2011). Core competencies in advanced training: What supervisors say about graduate training. *Journal of Marital and Family Therapy*, 37, 429–451.

Nelson, T. S., Heilbrun, G., & Figley, C. R. (1993). Basic skills in family therapy, IV: Transgenerational theories of family therapy. *Journal of Marital and Family Therapy*, 19, 253–266.

Nelson, T. S., & Johnson, L. N. (1999). The basic skills evaluation device. *Journal of Marital and Family Therapy*, 25, 15–30.

Nelson, T. S., & Prior, D. D. (2003). Theory of change projects in marriage and family therapy programs. *Contemporary Family Therapy*, 25, 133–151.

Nelson, T. S., & Smock, S. S. (2005). Challenges of an outcome-based perspective for marriage and family therapy education. *Family Process*, 44, 355–362.

Nichols, M. (2019). Supervision of therapists working with transgender client. In J. C. Wadley & R. Siegel (Eds.), *The art of sex therapy supervision* (pp. 202–221): New York, NY: Routledge.

Nichols, W. C. (1975). *Training and supervision* [Cassette recording 123]. Claremont, CA: AAMFT.

Nichols, W. C. (1988). An integrative psychodynamic and systems approach. In H. A. Liddle, D. C. Breunlin, & R. C. Schwartz (Eds.), *Handbook of family therapy training and supervision* (pp. 110–127). New York, NY: Guilford.

Nichols, W. C., & Everett, C. A. (1986). *Systemic family therapy*. New York, NY: Guilford.

Nichols, W. C., & Lee, R. E. (1999). Mirrors, cameras, and blackboards: Modalities of supervision. In R. E. Lee & S. Emerson (Eds.), *The eclectic trainer* (pp. 45–61). Galena, IL: Geist & Russell.

Niño, A., Kissil, K, & Apolinar Claudio, F. L. (2015). Perceived professional gains of master's level students following a person-of-the-therapist training program: A retrospective content analysis. *Journal of Marital and Family Therapy*, 41, 163–176.

Niño, A., Kissil, K., Cooke, L. (2016). Training for connection: Students' perceptions of the effects of the person-of-the-therapist training on their therapeutic relationships. *Journal of Marital and Family Therapy*, 42, 599–614.

Norcross, J. C., & Wampold, B. E. (2011). Evidence-based therapy relationships: Research conclusions and clinical practices. In J. Norcross (Ed.), *Psychotherapy relationships that work: Evidence-based responsiveness* (2nd ed., pp. 420–445). New York, NY: Oxford University Press.

Northey, W. F., & Gehart, D. R. (2019). The condensed MFT core competencies: A streamlined approach for measuring student and supervisee learning using the MFT core competencies. *Journal of Marital and Family Therapy*, 46, 42–61. https://doi.org/10.1111/jmft.12386.

O'Brian, N., & Rigazio-DiGilio, S. A. (2016). Lesbian, gay, and bisexual supervisees' experiences of LGB-affirmative and non-affirmative supervision in COAMFTE-accredited training programs. *Journal of Feminist Family Therapy*, 28, 115–135.

Okafor, E., Stevenson Wojciak, A., & Helfrich, C. M. (2014). Unheard voices: The experiences of supervisors in training. *Contemporary Family Therapy*, 36, 369–379.

Ormont, L. R. (2001). Cultivating the observing ego in the group setting. In L. R. Ormont (Ed.), *The technique of group treatment: The collected papers of Louis R. Ormont* (pp. 337–354). Madison, CT: Psychosocial Press.

Ostergard, O. K., Randa, H., & Hougaard, E. (2020). The effect of using the Partners for Change Outcome Management Systems feedback tool in psychotherapy: A systematic review and meta-analysis. *Psychotherapy Research*, 30, 195–212.

Overton, W. F., & Molenaar, P. C. M. (2015). Concepts, theory, and methods in development science: A view of the issues. In W. F. Overton & P. C. M. Molenaar (Eds.), *Handbook of child psychology and developmental science, theory and method* (7th ed., Vol. 1, pp 1–8). Hoboken, NJ: Wiley.

Owen, J. (2012). Systemic alliance in individual therapy: Factor analysis of the ITAS-SF and the relationship with therapy outcomes and termination status. *Journal of Marital and Family Therapy*, 38, 320–331.

Palmer-Olsen, L., Gold, L. L., & Woolley, S. R. (2011). Supervising emotionally focused therapists: A systematic research-based model. *Journal of Marital and Family Therapy*, 37, 411–426.

Peluso, P. R. (2003). The ethical genogram: A tool for helping therapists understand their ethical decision-making styles. *The Family Journal: Counseling and Therapy for Couples and Families*, 11(3), 286–291.

Peluso, P. R. (2006). Expanding the use of the ethical genogram: Incorporating the ethical principles to help clarify counselors' ethical decision-making styles. *The Family Journal: Counseling and Therapy for Couples and Families*, 14(2), 158–163.

Penn, P. (1982). Circular questioning. *Family Process*, 219, 267–280.

Pergamit, M., Gelatt, J., Stratford, B., Beckwith, S., & Martin, M. C. (2016). *Family interventions for youth experiencing or at risk for homelessness: Research report*. Washington, DC: Urban Institute. Retrieved from https://aspe.hhs.gov/system/files/pdf/205401/FamilyInterventions.pdf.

Perosa, L. M., & Perosa, S. L. (2010). Assessing competencies in couples and family therapy counseling: A call to the profession. *Journal of Marital and Family Therapy*, 36, 126–143.

Pierce, C. M., Carew, J. V., Pierce-Gonzales, D., & Wills, D. (1977). An experiment in racism: TV commercials. *Education and Urban Society*, 10(1), 61–87.

Piercy, F. P., Earl, R. M., Aldrich, R. K., Nguyen, H. N., Steelman, S. M., Haugen, E., Riger, D., Tsokodayi, R. T., West, J., Keskin, Y., & Gary, E. (2016). Most and least meaningful learning experiences in marriage and family therapy education. *Journal of Marital and Family Therapy*, 42, 584–598.

Piercy, F. P., & Sprenkle, D. H. (1986). Family therapy theory building: An integrative training approach. In F. P. Piercy (Ed.), *Family therapy education and supervision* (pp. 5–14). New York, NY: Haworth.

Piercy, F. P., & Sprenkle, D. H. (1988). Family therapy theory-building questions. *Journal of Marital and Family Therapy*, 14(3), 307–309.

Pinsof, W. M. (1983). Integrative problem-centered therapy: Toward the synthesis of family and individual psychotherapies. *Journal of Marital and Family Therapy*, 19, 19–35.

Pinsof, W. M. (1994). An integrative systems perspective on the therapeutic alliance: Theoretical, clinical, and research implications. In A. O. Horvath & L. S. Greenberg (Eds.), *The Working alliance: Theory, research, and practice* (pp. 173–195). New York, NY: Wiley.

Pinsof, W. (1995). *Integrative problem-centered therapy: A synthesis of biological, individual, and family therapy*. New York, NY: Basic Books.

Pinsof, W. M., Breunlin, D. C., Russell, W. P., Lebow, J. L., Rampage, C., & Chambers, A. L. (2018). *Integrative systemic therapy: Metaframeworks for problem solving with individuals, couples, and families*. Washington, DC: American Psychological Association.

Pinsof, W., & Chambers, A. L. (2009). Empirically informed systemic psychotherapy: Tracking client change and therapist behavior during therapy. In J. H. Bray & M. Stanton (Eds.), *The Wiley-Blackwell handbook of family psychology* (pp. 431–446). New York, NY: Wiley-Blackwell.

Podsakoff, P. M., MacKenzie, S. B., Lee, J-Y., & Podsakoff, N. P. (2003). Common method biases in behavioral research: A critical review of the literature and recommended remedies. *Journal of Applied Psychology*, 88, 879–903.

Pratt, K. J., Palmer, E., Cravens, J. D., Ferriby, M., Balk, E., & Cai, Y. (2016). Marriage and family therapy trainees' reports of explicit weight bias. *Journal of Marital and Family Therapy*, 42, 288–298.

Probst, T., Jakob, M., Kaufmann, Y. M., Müller-Neng, J. M. B., Bohus, M., & Weck, F. (2018). Patients' and therapists' experiences of general change mechanisms during bug-in-the-eye and delayed video-based supervised cognitive-behavioral therapy. A randomized controlled trial. *Journal of Clinical Psychology*, 74, 509–522.

Proctor, B. (2000). *Group supervision: A guide to creative practice*. Thousand Oaks, CA: Sage.

Protinsky, H. (1997). Dismounting the tiger: Using tape in supervision. In T. C. Todd & C. L. Storm (Eds.), *The complete systemic supervisor: Context, philosophy, and pragmatics* (pp. 298–307). Boston, MA: Allyn & Bacon.

Prouty, A. M., Thomas, V., Johnson, S., & Long, J. K. (2007). Methods of feminist family therapy supervision. *Journal of Marital and Family Therapy*, 27, 85–97.

Purtilo, R., Doherty, R., & Haddad, A. (2019). *Health professional and patient Interaction* (9th ed.). New York, NY: Elsevier.

Quinn, W. H. (1996). The client speaks out: Three domains of meaning. *Journal of Psychotherapy*, 7(2), 71–83.

Quinn, W. H., Nagirreddy, C., Lawless, J., & Bagley, R. (2000). Utilizing clients' voices in clinical supervision. In AAMFT (Ed.), *Readings in family therapy supervision* (pp. 98–100). Alexandria, VA: AAMFT.

Ratliff, D. A. (2000). Theoretical consistency: Cut flowers or living plants. In AAMFT (Ed.), *Readings in family therapy supervision: Selected articles from the AAMFT Supervision Bulletin* (pp. 39–42). Alexandria, VA. (Out of print. Used copies available at www.amazon.com).

Reed, G. M., Kihlstrom, J, F., & Messer, S. B. (2006). *What qualifies as evidence of effective practice? In J. C. Norcross, L. E. Beutler, & R. F. Levant (Eds.),* Evidence-based practices in mental health: Debate and dialogue on the fundamental questions (pp.13–55). Washington, DC: American Psychological Association.

Reinhardt, R. (2019). *Tame your practice.* Retrieved from www.tameyourpractice.com/blog/cloud-practice-management-system-table-contents/.

Rigazio-Digilio S. A. (2016). MFT supervision: An overview. In K. Jordan (Ed.), *Couple, marriage, and family therapy supervision* (pp. 25–49). New York, NY: Springer.

Riva, M. T., & Cornish, J. A. (2008). Group supervision practices at psychology predoctoral internship programs: 15 years later. *Training and Education in Professional Psychology*, 23, 18–25.

Rober, P. (2010). The interacting-reflecting training exercise: Addressing the therapist's inner conversation in family therapy training. *Journal of Marital and Family Therapy*, 36(2), 158–170.

Rober, P. (2017). Addressing the person of the therapist in supervision: The therapist's inner conversation method. *Family Process*, 56, 487–500.

Robyak, J. E., Goodyear, R. K., & Prange, M. (1987, June). Effects of supervisors' sex, focus, and experience on preferences for interpersonal power. *Counselor Education and Supervision*, 26, 299–309.

Rogers, C. (2003). *Client-centered therapy: Its current practice, implications, and theory.* London, UK: Constable & Robinson.

Romans, J. S. C., Boswell, D. L., Carlozzi, A. F., & Ferguson, D. B. (1995). Training and supervision practices in clinical, counseling, and school psychology programs. *Professional Psychology: Research and Practice*, 26, 407–412.

Rønnestad, M. H., & Skovholt, T. M. (2003). The journey of the counselor and therapist: Research findings and perspectives on professional development. *Journal of Career Development*, 30(1), 5–44. https://doi.org/10.1177/089484530303000102.

Rosenberg, T., & Pace, M. (2010, July/Aug). When a bad day is more than just a bad day: Guidelines for burnout for early career therapists and supervisors. *Family Therapy Magazine*, 44–48.

Rothwell, J. D. (2010). *In the company of others: An introduction to communication.* New York, NY: Oxford University Press.

Rousmaniere, T., Goodyear, R., Miller, S. D., & Wampold, B. E. (Eds.) (2017). *The cycle of excellence: Using deliberate practice to improve supervision and training*. T. Rousmaniere, R. K. Goodyear, S. D. Miller, & B. Wampold (Eds., pp. 267–275). New York, NY: Wiley.

Routon, M. (2018). *A phenomenological inquiry into counseling trainees' experiences of reviewing video-recorded psychotherapy sessions in supervision.* [Unpublished doctoral dissertation] Fielding Graduate University.

Rubin, A., & Parrish, D. (2007). Challenges to the future of evidence-based practice in social work education. *Journal of Social Work Education*, 43, 405–428.

Ruscio, A. M., & Holohan, D. R. (2006). Applying empirically supported treatments to complex cases: Ethical, empirical, and practical considerations. *Clinical Psychology: Science and Practice*, 13, 146–162.

Russell, C. S., DuPree, W. J., Beggs, M. A., Peterson, C. M., & Anderson, M. P. (2007). Responding to remediation and gatekeeping challenges in supervision. *Journal of Marital and Family Therapy*, 33, 227–244.

Safran, J. D., Muran, J C., Demario, A., Boutwell, C., Eubanks-Carter, C., & Winston, A. (2014). Investigating the impact of alliance focused training on interpersonal process and therapists' capacity for experiential reflection. *Psychotherapy Research*, 24, 269–285.

Sager, C. J. (1994). *Marriage contracts and couple therapy: Hidden forces in intimate relationships.* Lanham, MD: Rowman & Littlefield.

Sahebi, B. (2020). Clinical supervision of couple and family therapy during COVID-19. *Family Process.* Retrieved from https://onlinelibrary.wiley.com/doi/full/10.1111/famp.12591.

Sapyta, J., Riemer, M., & Bickman, L. (2005). Feedback to clinicians: Theory, research, and practice. *Journal of Clinical Psychology*, 61, 145–153.

Saunders, B. E., Berliner, L., & Hanson, R. F. (Eds.) (2004). *Child physical and sexual abuse: Guidelines for treatment* (revised report, April 26, 2004). Charleston, SC: National Crime Victims Research and Treatment Center.

Schanche, E., Hjeltnes, A., Nielsen, G. H., Stige, S. H., & Stiegler, J. R. (2019). "Nothing is just smooth or perfect": What can students learn from intensively reviewing psychotherapy conducted by experienced therapists whilst being focused on emotional processes? *Counselling and Psychotherapy Research*, 19, 366–376.

Schiavone, C. D., & Jessell, J. C. (1988). Influence of attributed expertness and gender in counselor supervision. *Counselor Education and Supervision*, 28, 29–43.

Schomburg, A. M., & Prieto, L. R. (2011). Trainee multicultural case conceptualization ability and couples therapy. *Journal of Marital and Family Therapy*, 37, 223–235.

Schur, T. J. (2002). Supervision as a disciplined focus on self and not the other: A different systems model. *Contemporary Family Therapy*, 24(3), 389–422.

Segal, E. A. (2018). *Social empathy: The art of understanding others.* New York, NY: Columbia University Press.

Selicoff, H. (2006). Looking for good supervision: A fit between collaborative and hierarchical methods. *Journal of Systemic Therapies*, 25(1), 37–51.

Selvini Palazzoli, M., Boscolo, L., Cecchin, G., & Prata, G. (1980). Hypothesizing, circularity, and neutrality revisited: An invitation to curiosity. *Family Process*, 195, 3–12.

Sexton, T. L. (2009). Functional Family Therapy: Traditional theory to evidence-based practice. In J. H. Bray & M. Stanton (Eds.), *The Wiley-Blackwell handbook of family therapy* (pp. 327–340). Hoboken, NJ: Wiley-Blackwell.

Sexton, T., Gordon, K. C., Gurman, A., Lebow, J., Holtzworth-Munroe, A., & Johnson, S. (2011). Guidelines for classifying evidence-based treatments in couple and family therapy. *Family Process*, 50, 377–392.

Shajani, Z., & Snell, D. (2019). *Wright and Leahey's nurses and families: A guide to family assessment and intervention*. Philadelphia, PA: F. A. Davis.

Sharpless, B. A., & Barber, J. P. (2012). Corrective emotional experiences from a psychodynamic perspective. In L. G. Castonguay & C. E. Hill (Eds.), *Transformations in psychotherapy: Corrective experiences across cognitive behavioral, humanistic, and psychodynamic approaches* (pp. 31–49). Washington, DC: American Psychological Association.

Shelef, K., & Diamond, G. (2008). Short form of the revised Vanderbilt Therapeutic Alliance Scale: Development, reliability, and validity. *Psychotherapy Research*, 18(4), 433–443.

Shipman, D., & Martin, T. (2017). Clinical and supervisory considerations for transgender therapists: Implications for working with clients. *Journal of Marital and Family Therapy*, 45, 92–105. https://doi:10.1111/jmft.12300.

Skovholt, T. M., & Rønnestad, M. H. (1995). *The evolving professional self: Stages and themes in therapist and counselor development*. New York, NY: Wiley.

Smith, R., Cornish, J., & Riva, M. (2014). Contracting for group supervision. *Training and Education in Professional Psychology*, 8, 236–240.

Smith, R. D., Riva, M. T., & Cornish, J. A. (2012). The ethical practice of group supervision: A national survey. *Training and Education in Professional Psychology*, 6(4), 238–248.

Snyder, D. K., & Aikman, G. G. (1999). Marital satisfaction inventory-revised. In M. E. Maruish (Ed.), *The use of psychological testing for treatment planning and outcomes assessment* (2nd ed., pp. 1173–1210). Mahweh, NJ: Erlbaum.

Soloski, K. L., & Deitz, S. L. (2016). Managing emotional responses in therapy: An adapted EFT supervision approach. *Contemporary Family Therapy: An international Journal*, 38, 361–372.

Sparks, J. A., & Duncan, B. L. (2018). The Partners for Change Outcome Management System: A both/and system for collaborative practice. *Family Process*, 57, 800–816.

Sparks, J. A., Kisler, T. S., Adams, J. F., & Blumen, D. G. (2011). Teaching accountability: Using client feedback to train effective family therapists. *Journal of Marital and Family Therapy*, 37, 452–467.

Sperber, E. (2015). *The architecture of psychotherapy*. Retrieved from https://opinionator.blogs.nytimes.com/2015/06/09/the-architecture-of-psychotherapy/.

Sprenkle, D. H. (2005). *What is responsible for therapeutic change: The common factors alternative*. Invited address presented at the AAMFT, Kansas City, MO.

Sprenkle, D. H., & Blow, A. (2004). Common factors are not islands—they work through models: A response to Sexton, Ridley, & Kleiner. *Journal of Marital and Family Therapy*, 30, 151–157.

Sprenkle, D. H., & Blow, A. (2007). The role of the therapist as the bridge between common factors and therapeutic change: More complex than congruency with a worldview. *Journal of Family Therapy*, 29, 109–113.

Sprenkle, D. H., Davis, S. D., & Lebow, J. L. (2009). *Common factors in couple and family therapy: The overlooked foundation for effective practice*. New York, NY: Guilford.

Spring, B., Pagoto, S., Kaufmann, P. G., Whitlock, E. P., Glasgow, R. E., Smith, T. W., Trudeau, M. A., & Davidson, K. W. (2005). Invitation to a dialogue between researchers and clinicians about evidence-based behavioral medicine. *Annals of Behavioral Medicine*, 30, 125–137.

St. Louis County. (2014). *Treating each other in good ways: Respect in the workplace.* Retrieved from www.greenleaf.org/wp-content/uploads/2014/09/Respect-in-the-Workplace-for-Greenleaf-conference.pdf.

Stanton, M. (1981). An integrated structural/strategic approach to family therapy. *Journal of Marital and Family Therapy*, 7, 427–439.

State of Florida. (2018). Board of clinical social work, marriage and family therapy, and mental health counseling. Title XXXII, Chapter 491, Section 004.

Sterner, W. R. (2009). Influence of the supervisory working alliance on supervisee work satisfaction and work-related stress. *Journal of Mental Health Counseling*, 3(3), 249–263.

Stoltenberg, C. D., & McNeill, B. W. (2010). *IDM supervision: An integrative developmental model for supervising counselors and therapists* (3rd ed.). New York, NY: Routledge.

Stone Fish, L., & Busby, D. M. (2005). The Delphi method. In D. S. Sprenkle & F. P. Piercy (Eds.), *Research methods in family therapy* (2nd ed., pp. 238–253). New York, NY: Guilford.

Storm, C. L. (2000a). Greasing your pen: Showing you know the literature. In AAMFT (Ed.), *Readings in family therapy supervision: Selected articles from the AAMFT Supervision Bulletin* (pp. 43–45). Alexandria, VA: AAMFT. (Out of print. Used copies available 07/2020 at www.amazon.com).

Storm, C. L. (2000b). Live supervision as a window: An interview with Braulio Montalvo. In AAMFT (Ed.), *Readings in family therapy supervision* (pp. 238–248). Alexandria, VA: AAMFT. (Out of print. Used copies available 07/2020 at www.amazon.com).

Storm, C. L. (2007). What is unique about supervising couple therapists? A beginning answer. *Journal of Couple and Relationship Therapy*, 6(1/2), 219–230.

Sturkie, K., & Paff Bergen, L. (2000). *Professional regulation in marital and family therapy.* Boston, MA: Allyn & Bacon.

Sude, M. E., & Gambrel, L. E. (2017). A contextual therapy framework for MFT educators: Facilitating trustworthy asymmetrical training relationships. *Journal of Marital and Family Therapy*, 43, 617–630.

Sue, D. W. (2010/2020). *Microaggressions in everyday life: Race, gender, and sexual orientation.* Reissued as Kindle ebook (2020). Hoboken, NJ: Wiley.

Sung, S. Y., Antefelt, A., & Choi, J. N. (2017). Dual effects of job complexity on proactive and responsive creativity: Moderating role of employee ambiguity tolerance. *Group & Organization Management*, 42, 388–418.

Szapocznik, J., & Hervis. O. (2020). *Brief strategic family therapy*. Washington, DC: American Psychological Association.

Tanner, M., Gray, J. L., & Haaga, D. A. F. (2012). Association of cotherapy supervision with client outcomes, attrition, and trainee effectiveness in a psychotherapy training clinic. *Journal of Clinical Psychology*, 68, 1241–1252.

Taylor, B. A., Hernández, P., Deri, A., & Rankin, P. R., IV, & Siegel, A. (2006). Integrating diversity dimensions in supervision: Perspectives of ethnic minority AAMFT Approved Supervisors. *The Clinical Supervisor*, 25(1/2), 3–21.

Taylor, S. E., Peplau, L. A., & Sears, D. O. (2006). *Social psychology* (12th ed.). Upper Saddle River, NJ: Pearson Education.

Tervalon, M., & Murray-Garcia, J. (1998). Cultural humility versus cultural competence: A critical distinction in defining physician training outcomes in multicultural education. *Journal of Health Care for the Poor and Underserved*, 9(*2*), 117–165.

Thomas, F. N. (1994). Solution-oriented supervision: The coaxing of expertise. *The Family Journal*, 2, 11.

Thomas, F. N. (2010). Impaired, or compromised? Plan for the worst, hope for the best. *Family Therapy Magazine*, 7, 32–36.

Thomas, F. N. (2013). *Solution-focused supervision: A resource-oriented approach to developing clinical expertise*. New York, NY: Springer Science.

Thomas, J. T. (2007). Informed consent through contracting for supervision: Minimizing risks, enhancing benefits. *Professional Psychology: Research and Practice*, 38(3), 221–231.

Thomas, J. T. (2010). Mandated supervision: Ethical challenges for supervisors and supervisees. In J. T. Thomas (Ed.), *The ethics of supervision and consultation* (pp. 183–210). Washington, DC: American Psychological Association.

Thurber, S. L. (2005). *The effects of direct supervision on therapist behavior: An initial functional analysis*. [Unpublished doctoral dissertation]. ProQuest Information & Learning. AA13161356.

Tilden, T., Wampold, B.E., Ulvenes, P., Zahl-Olsen, R., Hoffart, A., Barstad B., Olsen, I. A., Gude, T., Pinsof, W. M., Zinbarg, R. E., Nilssen, H. H., & Håland, A. T. (2021). Feedback in couple and family therapy: A randomized clinical trial. *Family Process*, 59, 36–51.

Todd, T. C. (1997). Problems in supervision: Lessons from supervisees. In T. C. Todd & C. L. Storm (Eds.), *The complete systemic supervisor: Context, philosophy, and pragmatics* (pp. 241–252). Boston, MA: Allyn & Bacon.

Todd, T., & Storm, C. (Eds.). (2014). *The complete systemic supervisor: Context philosophy, and pragmatics* (2nd ed). Chichester, UK: Wiley.

Tomm, K. (1984). One perspective on the Milan systemic approach: Part II. Description of session format, interviewing style, and interventions. *Journal of Marital and Family Therapy*, 10, 253–271.

Tomm, K. M., & Wright, L. M. (1979). Training in family therapy: Perceptual, conceptual, and executive skills. *Family Process*, 18, 227–250. http://dx.doi.org/10.11575/PRISM/34892.

Totsuka, Y. (2014) 'Which aspects of social GGRRAAACCEEESSS grab you most?' The social GGRRAAACCEEESSS exercise for a supervision group to promote therapists' self-reflexivity. *Journal of Family Therapy*, 36, 86–106.

Tremblay, N., Wright, J., Mamodhoussen, S., McDuff, P., & Sabourin, S. (2008). Refining therapeutic mandates in couple therapy outcome research: A feasibility study. *American Journal of Family Therapy*, 36, 137–148.

Trepal, H., Haberstroh, S., Duffey, T., & Evans, M. (2007). Considerations and strategies for teaching online counseling skills: Establishing relationships in cyberspace. *Counselor Education and Supervision*, 46(4), 266–279.

Tromski-Klingshirn, D. (2006). Should the clinical supervisor be the administrative supervisor? *The Clinical Supervisor*, 25(1), 53–67.

Truax, C. B., Shapiro, J. G., & Wargo, D. G. (1968). The effects of alternate sessions and vicarious therapy pretraining on group psychotherapy. *International Journal of Group Psychotherapy*, 18(2), 186–198.

Tsai, M., Callaghan, M., Kohlenberg, R. J., Follette, W. C., & Darrow, S. M. (2009). *A guide to functional analytic psychotherapy: Awareness, courage, love, and behaviorism*. New York, NY: Springer Science.

Uman, L. S. (2011). Systematic reviews and meta-analyses. *Journal of the Canadian Academy of Child and Adolescent Psychiatry*, 20, 56–59.

Ungar, M. (2006). Practicing as a postmodern supervisor. *Journal of Marital and Family Therapy*, 32, 59–71.

Ungar, M., & Costanzo, L. (2007). Supervision challenges when supervisors are outside supervisees' agencies. *Journal of Systemic Therapies*, 26(2), 68–83.

US Department of Health and Human Services. (1996). *Understanding health information privacy*. Retrieved from www.hhs.gov/ocr/privacy/under-standing/index.html.

US Department of Health and Human Services (2017). *HIPAA for Professionals.* Retrieved from www.hhs.gov/hipaa/for-professionals/index.html.

VMware Workstation 3.2. (2020). *Host only networking.* Retrieved from www.vmware.com/support/ws3/doc/ws32_network6.html.

von Bertalanffy, L. (1968). *General system theory: Foundations, development, applications.* New York, NY: Norton.

Vygotsky, L. S. (1986). *Thought and language* (rev. ed.). Cambridge, MA: MIT Press.

Walsh, F. (2012), Clinical views of family normality, health, and dysfunction: From deficit to strengths perspective. In F. Walsh (Ed.), *Normal family processes* (4th ed., pp. 27–54). New York, NY: Guilford Press.

Walsh, F. (2016). *Strengthening family resilience* (3rd ed.). New York, NY: Guilford.

Wampold, B. E. (2010). The research evidence for common factors models. In B. L. Duncan, S. D. Miller, B. E. Wampold, & M. A. Hubble (Eds.), *The heart and soul of change: Delivering what works in therapy* (2nd ed., pp. 49–81). Washington, DC: American Psychological Association.

Wampold, B. E., Ollendick, T. H., & King, N. J. (2006). Do therapies designated as empirically supported treatments for specific disorders produce outcomes superior to non-empirically supported treatment therapies? In J. C. Norcross, L. E. Beutler, & R. F. Levant (Eds.), *Evidence-based practices in mental health: Debate and dialogue on the fundamental questions* (pp. 299–328). Washington, DC: American Psychological Association.

Wark, L. (2000). Research: Trainees talk about effective live supervision. In AAMFT (Ed.), *Readings in family therapy supervision* (p. 119). Alexandria, VA: AAMFT.

Watkins, C. E. (2018). Educationally corrective experiences as a common factor in psychotherapy supervision. *Journal of Psychotherapy Integration*, 28, 242–252.

Watzlawick, P., Bavelas, J. B., & Jackson, D. J. (1967). *Pragmatics of human communication.* New York, NY: W. W. Norton.

Watzlawick, P., Weakland, J., & Fisch, R. (1974). *Change: Principles of problem formation and problem resolution.* New York, NY: W. W. Norton.

Watts Jones, T. D. (2016). Location of self in training and supervision. In K. V. Hardy & T. Bobes (Eds.), *Culturally sensitive supervision and training: Diverse perspectives and practical applications* (16–24). New York: Routledge.

Wedge, M. (1996). *In the therapist's mirror: Reality in the making.* New York, NY: W. W. Norton.

Westen, D., Novotny, C. M., & Thompson-Brenner, H. (2004). The empirical status of empirically supported psychotherapies: Assumptions, findings, and reporting in controlled clinical trials. *Psychological Bulletin*, 130, 631–663.

Wetchler, J. L., & McCollum, E. E. (1999). Case consultation: The cornerstone of supervision. In R. E. Lee & S. Emerson (Eds.), *The eclectic trainer* (pp. 62–75). Galena, IL: Geist & Russell.

Whipple, J. L, Lambert, M. J., Vermeersch, D. A., Smart, D. W., Nielsen, S. L., & Hawkins, E. J. (2003). Improving the effects of psychotherapy: The use of early identification of treatment failure and problem-solving strategies in outcome. *Journal of Counseling Psychology*, 50, 59–68.

White, M., & Russell, C. (1995). The essential elements of supervisory systems: A modified Delphi study. *Journal of Marital and Family Therapy*, 21, 33–54.

White, M. B., & Russell, C. S. (1997). Examining the multifaceted notion of isomorphism in marriage and family therapy supervision: A quest for conceptual clarity. *Journal of Marital and Family Therapy*, 23, 315–333.

Whitman, S. M., & Jacobs, E. G. (1998). Responsibilities of the psychotherapy supervisor. *American Journal of Psychotherapy*, 52, 166–175.

Wiebe, S. A., & Johnson, S. M. (2016). A review of the research in Emotionally Focused Therapy for couples. *Family Process*, 55, 390–407.

Williams, L. (1994). A tool for training supervisors: Using the supervision feedback form (SFF). *Journal of Marital and Family Therapy*, 20, 311–315.

Willie, C. V., & Reddick, R. J. (2010). *A new look at Black families* (6th ed.). Lanham, MD: Rowan & Littlefield.

Winston, E. J., & Piercy, F. P. (2010). Gender and diversity topics taught in Commission on Accreditation for Marriage and Family Therapy Education programs. *Journal of Marital and Family Therapy*, 36, 446–471.

Withers, M. C., & Nelson, T. S. (2015). A method for creating individualized practice-based evidence. *Journal of Family Psychotherapy*, 26, 210–225.

Wood, A. (2004). *Therapists who do not seek therapy: An examination of marriage and family therapists in three western states* [Unpublished master's thesis]. Utah State University.

Woodside, D. B. (2000). Reverse live supervision: Leveling the supervisory playing field. In AAMFT (Ed.), *Readings in family therapy supervision* (pp. 113–114). Alexandria, VA: AAMFT.

Wrape, E. R., & McGinn, M. M. (2019). Clinical and ethical considerations for delivering couple and family therapy via telehealth. *Journal of Marital and Family Therapy*, 45, 296–308.

Wright, L. M., & Leahey, M. (2009). *Nurses and families: A guide to family assessment and intervention* (5th ed.). Philadelphia, PA: F. A. Davis.

Yalom, I. D. (2005). *Theory and practice of group psychotherapy* (5th ed.). New York, NY: Basic Books.

Yingling, L. C. (2000). What is a systemic orientation—really? In AAMFT (Ed.), *Readings in family therapy supervision: Selected articles from the AAMFT Supervision Bulletin* (pp. 36–38). Alexandria, VA: AAMFT.

York, C. D. (1997). Selecting and constructing supervision structures: Individuals, dyads, co-therapists, groups, and teams. In T. C. Todd & C. L. Storm (Eds.), *The complete systemic supervisor: Context, philosophy, and pragmatics* (pp. 320–333). Boston, MA: Allyn & Bacon.

Zimmerman, T., Castronova, M., & ChenFeng, J. (2016). Diversity and social justice in supervision. In K. Jordan (Ed.), *Couple, marriage, and family supervision* (pp. 121–150). New York, NY: Springer.

Zinbarg, R. E., & Goldsmith, J. (2017). *Report on the Systemic Therapy Inventory of Change (STIC) feedback system.* Evanston, IL: The Family Institute at Northwestern University.

Zür, O. (2007, July/August). The ethical eye: Don't let "risk management" undermine your professional approach. *Psychotherapy Networker*, 48–55.

Zür, O. (Ed.). (2017). *Multiple relationships in psychotherapy and counseling: Unavoidable, common, and mandatory dual relations in therapy.* New York, NY: Routledge.

Zygmond, M. J., & Boorhem, H. (1989). Ethical decision making in family therapy. *Family Process*, 28, 269–280.

Subject Index

Author Index

9780367568962